TOP 170 UNUSUAL THINGS TO SEE IN ONTARIO

RON BROWN

A Boston Mills Press Book

Published by Boston Mills Press, 2022
Copyright © 2022 Boston Mills Press
Text copyright © Ron Brown 2022
Photographs © 2022 Ron Brown, except as listed on this page

First printing

Library and Archives Canada Cataloguing in Publication
Title: Top 170 unusual things to see in Ontario / Ron Brown.
Other titles: Top one hundred seventy unusual things to see
    in Ontario
Names: Brown, Ron, 1945- author.
Description: Includes index. | Previously published under title:
    Top 160 unusual things to see in Ontario.
Identifiers: Canadiana 20220175608 |
    ISBN 9781990140020 (softcover)
Subjects: LCSH: Ontario–Guidebooks. |
    LCSH: Curiosities and wonders–Ontario–Guidebooks. |
    LCGFT: Guidebooks.
Classification: LCC FC3057 .B78 2022 |
    DDC 917.1304/5–dc23

Distributed by Firefly Books Ltd.
50 Staples Avenue, Unit 1
Richmond Hill, Ontario L4B 0A7

P.O. Box 1338, Ellicott Station
Buffalo, New York 14205

Cover design: Stacey Cho
Interior design: Noor Majeed

Printed in China

PHOTO CREDITS

Bebe S. Brown: back cover (bottom)

Jaffer, Naeem: 319

Moffett, Susan: 337

Ontario Ministry of Natural Resources: 337

Pagiamtzis, Kostas: 303

Shutterstock
Adwo: 38
Alexander Sviridov: 243
Curioso: 220-21
Derek R. Audette: 23
Elijah Lovkoff: 255
emkaplin: 234
Horst Petzold: 250
JFunk: front cover
mikecphoto: 29, 230-31
Norman Pogson: 25
Paul Backewich: 54
Roxana Gonzalez: 132-33
Spiroview Inc: 211

Seeman, Corey: 122

CONTENTS

Thomas Foster modelled his memorial to his wife after India's Taj Mahal. *See page 188.*

INTRODUCTION

ONTARIO IS FULL of hidden treasures. Down village streets, in city lanes and along quiet country roads lie its most unusual sights — houses that seem to float, a river that disappears, log cabins in the centre of a major city. All await the curious explorer. Monuments to murders, massacres and mysterious spy camps bring to life the lesser-known aspects of Ontario's hidden heritage.

This book features my pick of Ontario's top 170 unusual things to see. Most of the listings are easy to find and are open to the public.

In this edition, the places are grouped into four geographic regions. Maps pinpoint each location within the region.

So head out and discover whichever treasure appeals at the moment. Temples, towers and quirks of nature offer insight into an Ontario that few even know exists. And that's what looking for treasure is all about.

The Teaching Rocks in Petroglyph Provincial Park tell the story of Indigenous life. **See pages 76-77.**

The dunes form the backbone of Sandbanks Provincial Park and will eventually move further into the lake they lie on. **See pages 54-55.**

EASTERN ONTARIO

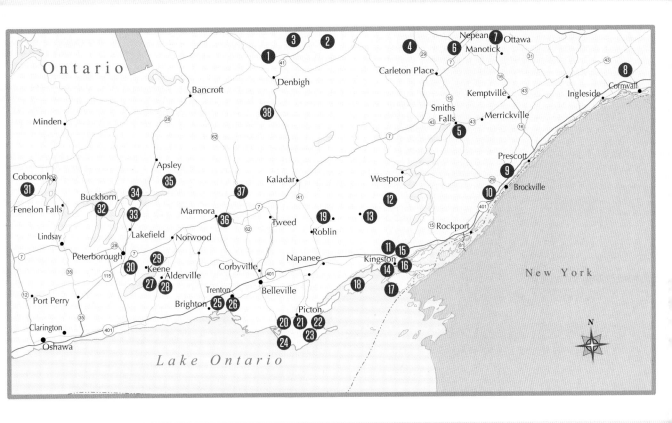

① NEWFOUNDOUT
The Lost Farming Settlement

THE BLACK DONALD Hills of eastern Ontario are among the highest mountains in the province. Views from their lofty and windswept summits extend across the wide sweep of the Ottawa Valley to the far Laurentian Mountains in Quebec. Atop this plateau, rugged hills and monstrous boulders were an unpleasant greeting to settlers who, in the 1860s, had trudged up the Opeongo Colonization Road to seek their prized farm lots.

At various intervals, sideroads crept up the steep hillsides from the busy settlement road. Near Plaunts Mountain, another sideroad led to yet another tract of land. Here more than a dozen farm families hauled their worldly goods up the narrowing trail and began to carve out their farms. They named their isolated little world Newfoundout.

The settlers built their crude shanties and barns out of the plentiful logs. Apple trees were planted, and sheep and chickens wandered the yards. Cattle grazed in the rocky pastures. Any hopes of growing crops, however, were quickly dashed by the stony soil and numerous boulders, many the size of a small house.

Amenities were few. While some farmers sawed logs or performed blacksmithing, there were no stores, schools or churches. But the distance and the hardship and the sterility of the farmland gradually took their toll, and one by one the families packed their belongings and went back down the mountain. By 1950, Newfoundout was completely abandoned. It had become a lost settlement.

The narrow trail still winds through the trees and up the steep mountainside, but above the slope, empty barns and roofless cabins abound. Rusting cars and shattered farm equipment litter the overgrown pastures. More distant farmers often log the area or graze their cattle, but Newfoundout has no human inhabitants. It does, however, have a spiritual one.

Sometime around the turn of the twentieth century, one Sylvester Briggs was urging his team up the steep and narrow roads of Plaunts Mountain. Suddenly a tree crashed into his horses, sending his wagon careening back down the mountain. As it plunged over the side, the wagon crushed Briggs' leg, leaving the unfortunate teamster — unable to walk or drag himself home — to starve to death. His body was found two years later. Even today, local residents will gladly regale the listener with accounts of Briggs still calling out on that lonely, dark mountain for help that never came.

Newfoundout extends along Newfoundout Road, south of Opeongo Road and west of Highway 41.

A plateau atop in the Black Donald Hills, which hide the ruins of Newfoundout.

2 BONNECHERE CAVES

A Maze of Eroded Limestone

IN 1953, NEAR Eganville, Ontario, Tom Woodward lowered himself into a dark and brooding sinkhole beside the rushing Bonnechere River. Armed only with a flashlight, he moved deeper into a twisting watery cavern. Narrow openings with little headroom led to even narrower side tunnels. As he made his way through the cave Woodward's hand brushed against a soft and furry wall, for the cave was home to thousands of bats.

The caves near Eganville are fracture caves, created when giant chunks of limestone break away from a cliff face and then collapse against it. What Woodward was seeing, dimly, was a solution cave. Twenty thousand years ago, the region lay beneath a massive ice sheet. As the glacier melted, torrents of melt water found fissures in the ancient limestone and began to erode them creating today's caves.

Two years after his first exploration, Woodward drained the cave and opened it to tourists. Today visitors from near and far jam the parking lot waiting for their one-hour tour which begin every 20 or 40 minutes depending upon the number of visitors.

Guides explain their origins along with a geological time line at the start of the tour. The group of amateur cavers then descends into the narrow twisting tunnel with its levelled floor and lighting.

The cave is at times narrow and low; at other points it opens into a large cavern, one so vast that weddings have occasionally occurred in it. While the bats have largely gone, stalactites hang from the walls and ceiling and other-worldly formations line the walls. At one point the guide turns off the lights to show what the cave is like in complete darkness and what must have confronted Woodward when his light went out so many years ago.

When the tourist season is ended, the cave is allowed to once again fill with water to maintain its natural balance. The caves lie about 9 kilometres east of Eganville.

Although the Bonnechere caves are only 10,000 years old, stalactites have already begun to form on the cave walls.

3 LITTLE CHURCH ON THE HILL

The Rockingham Church

ROCKINGHAM BEGAN LIFE as a mill town deep in the Ottawa Valley. To entice the new settlers into the area, the government offered them land for free. One of those settlers was one John Watson who immigrated to Canada in 1858. Along the Peterson Road he found a little valley with a rushing stream. He erected a sawmill. And Rockingham, as the little village was called, soon acquired a store, hotel, blacksmith and various little industries.

In 1875, St. Leonard's Anglican Church was built on a hill overlooking the valley. Its board and batten walls contained high rounded windows and its steeple stretched skyward. Worshippers arrived by horse or on foot and made their way up the steep slope to the church.

By 1900 the population was more than 100 but soon the timber was depleted, and the arrival of the Booth Line Railway took traffic away from the pioneer roads. As the population of the village shrank, the church was closed. In 1967 it was slated for removal.

The heritage-minded community, however, was one of those which prized its pioneer roots and convinced the parish to hold off on plans for demolition of the building. In the 1970s they began much needed repairs to the walls and roof. In 1995, the community formed the Friends of the Rockingham Church and continued the repairs. Meetings and events, which conclude with the ringing of the bell, take place regularly today.

Today the much-photographed church, its boards glowing orange in the sun, and with its historic cemetery, retains its lofty perch high on the hill. Inside are the original pews and pump organ. With no electricity or other modern amenities, it remains as the pioneers would remember. Even the steep grassy climb up the hill remains unaltered by steps or walkways.

The little church on the hill in Rockingham still stands thanks to the dedication of heritage-minded local community.

With its five stone arches, the Pakenham Bridge is the only one of its kind in North America.

Right: In addition to its stone arch bridge, Pakenham's main street contains numerous historic structures.

4 PAKENHAM'S STONE ARCH BRIDGE

North America's Longest

AMONG ONTARIO'S HERITAGE features, bridges are the least appreciated; yet Ontario boasts many distinctive bridges. For example, West Montrose, near Kitchener, is the only remaining covered bridge in Ontario; and a railway swing bridge provides the only road access to Manitoulin, the world's largest freshwater island. One of the most beautiful of Ontario's bridges is Pakenham's bridge, the only five-span stone arch bridge in North America.

Built in 1901, it replaced a rickety wooden structure. The old bridge was so unsafe that it was illegal to cross "at a faster pace than a walk." Designed by the firm of O'Toole and Keating, the new 85-metre bridge is made up of five 25-metre stone arches on piers that are 3 metres thick. The huge stones for the bridge were dragged from a nearby quarry. The largest stone is 3 metres long by nearly a metre square, and weighs 5 tonnes.

In 1984, Ontario's Ministry of Transportation, along with the Ontario Heritage Foundation and Ottawa's National Capital Commission, restored the bridge, inserting reinforced concrete into the deck and parapet walls in the stonework. Framed by its wooded limestone shoreline, the bridge is a popular subject for photographers and artists.

Pakenham village itself is also worth a visit. Despite its location, well inland from Ontario's first towns and villages, Pakenham got off to an early start. By 1831 it had become the site of a sawmill, store and post office, and was named Little Falls. In 1840, Andrew Dickson sold the first village lots, and just twenty years later the village claimed a population of eight hundred. Despite getting the railway in the 1880s, Pakenham failed to grow, and the population is about the same today, which has helped preserve its rich heritage.

Take time to enjoy the main street and its many historic buildings. The wooden Old Crowe Creek shop sits next to the Pakenham General Store located in an historic 1830s stone building. It is said to be the oldest general store still operating in Ontario. A bit further along the street is the Centennial Restaurant occupying a two-storey brick structure. Opposite the restaurant, also in a two-storey stone building, is a grocery and cannabis store and the Remedy's RX Pharmacy, all housed in the town's ancient structures. Meanwhile back at the bridge, you can relax in a pair of parks which have been created on both approaches to the historic structures.

Pakenham is on Highway 15 about halfway between Almonte and Arnprior, and about 60 kilometres west of downtown Ottawa. Caution should be used if crossing the bridge on foot; there is no sidewalk, the roadway is narrow and County Road 20 can be busy.

⑤ HIGH-RISE PRIVY

Smiths Falls' Two-Storey Outhouse

FEW OF TODAY'S generation know much of that grand Canadian institution, the outhouse. Yet, for many generations of Canadians, that early-morning trek to the frigid wooden seat was as much a part of everyday life as a warm morning shower is today.

Privies are rare nowadays. But even when they were standard equipment, a two-storey outhouse was almost unheard of, unless you lived in Smiths Falls, Ontario.

In the 1850s, Joshua Bates, a Smiths Falls miller, chose a site next to his Rideau River grist mill to build a house. No ordinary house, it had some unusual features — an indoor brick bake oven, mirror-image facades and an outhouse that was two storeys high.

The logistics of how a two-storey outhouse might function without unpleasant consequences for the lower occupant are not readily apparent. A closer look, however, solves the riddle. Unlike most, this privy is connected to the house itself. The structure is wide enough that the upper facility need not be located directly above the lower one. In fact, a vertical partition separates the upper facility on one side from the lower facility on the other. While the door to the lower chamber leads directly off the downstairs porch, that to the upper room leads from an upstairs hallway. A simple but effective arrangement, when you think about it.

In 1977 the town purchased the outhouse and the house attached to it and created a museum, restoring it to an 1867 appearance. Now known as the Heritage House Museum, it is located at 11 Old Sly's Road, in the southeast part of Smiths Falls.

While you are in town, check out the Railway Museum of Eastern Ontario with its preserved Canadian Northern station and a collection of railway equipment. It is located on William Street West. Back on Beckwith Street, be sure to stop at the Rideau Canal Visitor Centre to learn about this UNESCO World Heritage site. The visitor centre is located in a former mill. On the south side of the bridge which crosses the canal, La Boat is found in the former lockmasters' home. From this point you can follow the Smith's Falls Heritage Trail along the bank of the canal.

At first glance, this two-storey outhouse in Smiths Falls defies logic.

A rare converted log blacksmith shop stands in the Village of Golden Lake.

Right: This former stage coach stop is part of the Ottawa Valley's log legacy.

❻ WOODEN COMMUNITIES
The Log Heritage of the Ottawa Valley

FOR THOUSANDS OF years, Ontario's First Nations inhabitants used nature for their shelter. Tipis were made from animal skins and longhouses from tree bark. When the first Europeans began to arrive, they too turned to what was around them for their basic needs.

Hastily built log shanties offered a crude shelter until replaced with a more solid log home. But after a few years in that drafty dwelling, the time would come for a frame house, perhaps even with a bit of insulation comprised of sawdust. As farming became more prosperous, stone and brick became the construction material of choice, often incorporating central heating.

Today's farmscape largely reflects that evolution, but few areas have managed to retain parts of that pioneer log legacy like the Ottawa Valley. This rolling, often mountainous region extends westward from Ottawa into the Black Donald Mountains and on to Barry's Bay. The area's many back roads reveal numerous log barns. The "string" barn is a distinctive local barn style, where a series of log or wood additions, sometime built to enclose the barnyard itself, are attached to the original structure.

While many of the original log homes are now gone, a few unusual log structures still linger. In Golden Lake, on Highway 60, a two-storey log blacksmith shop now houses a coffee and gift shop with its cylinder gas pump standing outside. On Highway 17, a few kilometres west of Petawawa, lies Ferguson's Stopping Place, a once popular and award-winning B & B situated in a former stagecoach stop and constructed of log, just like eight other structures on the property.

The Waba Cottage Museum and Gardens near White Lake preserves a log school from the community of Lochwinnoch, as well as a log church from Sand Point within a garden setting. The cottage is a replica of Archibald McNab's two-storey stone summer home. The grounds are set on the shore of White Lake and have a landscaped park and picnic area. Even Ottawa itself displays a pair of early log homes mere steps from the Byward Market.

Good examples of log barns stand along the Ferguslea Road, the Homestead Road south of Latchford Bridge and along the Schutt Road. The Opeongo Line is also noted for it many log barns.

7 THE DIEFENBUNKER
Canada's Cold War Capital

DURING THE 1950s the entire world was on edge. Tensions between the Soviet Union and the western world were rising and the threat of nuclear annihilation was on every one's mind. Bomb drills and siren testing were almost universal, as families created fallout shelters in their basements.

In 1959, Canada's then prime minister John Diefenbaker commissioned the construction of a fallout shelter that would house key government officials who would keep the government running what remained of the country in the event of nuclear war.

The site selected was a hillside near Carp, Ontario, where the soil and the terrain provided maximum protection from a five-megaton nuclear blast. Completed in just 18 months the Diefenbunker, as the Central Government Emergency Headquarters was fondly called, descended four levels beneath the ground and covered 100,000 square feet, It contained 350 rooms and enough supplies to feed 500 people for 30 days.

The upper level was accessed through a long tunnel and contained a medical and decontamination centre and emergency radio room. The second level contained government offices, a war room, emergency communications room, a radio room for the CBC emergency broadcasting centre as well as sleeping quarters and the prime minister's office and apartment.

On the third level the staff could relax in the recreation hall and dining room. The lowest level contained a Bank of Canada vault, machine room and the morgue.

With the easing of Cold War tensions in the 1990s, the Diefenbunker was decommissioned and turned over to the local municipality. It soon became a National Historic Site. In 1998 it opened as a museum, and attendance grew steadily, with a record 88,000 visitors in 2017. Today those visitors can follow a self-guided tour and see the original facilities and try to imagine the genuine fear that prompted the excavation of this Cold War capital.

The entrance to the Diefenbunker is through a long bomb-proof tunnel.

8 A FARMLAND CATHEDRAL
The Ruins of St. Raphael

RUINS, ROMANTIC AND picturesque, are associated more with Europe than with North America. Here, ruins tend to be of factories and mills, harsh forms that reflect our obsession with industry rather than beauty. But the ruins of the magnificent St. Raphael Cathedral on County Road 18, 40 kilometres northeast of Cornwall, contain a history, romance and grace that one would more closely identify with Greece or Rome.

In 1783, the revolutionary war in the United States was over, and in return for their loyalty and courage, those who fought for England were rewarded with land grants in what would become Ontario. After trooping wearily behind their commander, Sir John Johnson, the officers and men of the 1st Battalion, King's Royal Regiment of New York (most of Highland Scots origin), finally arrived on the banks of the Raisin River. Here, in eastern Ontario's Charlottenburg Township, their land grants awaited them.

Two years later, five hundred more Scots arrived direct from the Highlands, led by their parish priest, Alexander Macdonnell. The parish grew and prospered. The first Father Macdonnell died in 1803 and was replaced by another priest of the same name. The second Father Macdonnell succeeded in making his parish, which he called St. Raphael, the administrative centre of the Catholic Church in Upper Canada.

In 1815 he ordered the building of a large stone church on a hilltop overlooking the farms of his flock. In 1821 the church was consecrated, and when the priest was appointed bishop, the church became a cathedral. It was the largest church in Upper Canada. Five years later he added the Iona Seminary.

For a century and a half, the cathedral dominated the rolling farmlands from its hilltop perch. Then, in 1970, fire roared through the structure. Flames lashed out through the windows, as the roof collapsed in a whirl of sparks. But again the tenacity of their roots came to the fore, bolstered now by the infusion of French-Canadian Catholics, and the parishioners decided the ruins should be neither demolished nor replaced, but rather remain a ruin.

In 1992, a falling stone temporarily closed the site. In 1999 St. Raphael became a National Historic Site, and Friends of St. Raphael Ruins raised $670,000 to stabilize the walls. Once again, visitors may walk through the gates (although weddings are not permitted).

The picturesque ruins of St. Raphael Cathedral.

9 THE BATTLE OF THE WINDMILL

A Piece of Prescott's History

TRADITIONAL WINDMILLS HAVE long since vanished from the landscape of Ontario. Indeed there were few to begin with and those that did exist to power grist mills were replaced with other forms of power. Despite the disappearance of the windmills, there is one that still survives in eastern Ontario.

It was built using local fieldstone in 1832 at a lofty point of land on the St. Lawrence River by Thomas Hughes, a merchant newly arrived from the West Indies. Just 16 years later, it became the site of one of Ontario's more unusual battles.

A rebellious mood was festering in both Upper and Lower Canada (Ontario and Quebec) in the 1830s. Despite a few local uprisings, the rebellion was largely futile and many of the rebels fled to the United States to try an attack from there. In 1838 a small band of rebels, which included American sympathizers, captured the British ship *Sir Robert Peel* on Lake Ontario and started out for Windmill Point with its strategic advantage atop a 15-metre embankment, where they occupied the mill.

Their occupation was short-lived, however, as the British, under Sir John Colborne, sent in 2,000 troops to surround the structure. On the night of November 16th, the British attacked, killing and capturing many of the invaders.

In 1872, the federal government purchased the 20-metre windmill and converted it into a lighthouse. Although declared a National Historic Site as early as 1920, it remained in use as a lighthouse until it was decommissioned in 1978, designated a heritage building in 1996 and a heritage lighthouse in 2013.

Following repairs in 2002 due to a minor earthquake, it was opened to the public. It is located about 2.5 kilometres east of Prescott on Windmill Road and open during the summer only. Tied in with the history of the windmill is Fort Wellington, a restored fort a short distance to the west.

Now an historic attraction, the windmill near Prescott oversaw a key battle and served for over a century as a lighthouse on the St. Lawrence River.

Trains once rumbled under the town of Brockville.

⑩ RAILS UNDER BROCKVILLE
Canada's Oldest Railway Tunnel

THEY SAID, "EVERY railway has to have a tunnel," so the builders of Ontario's earliest railway, the Brockville and Ottawa (B and O), built one.

Until the 1850s, the colonies that would become Canada had relied on muddy pioneer roads and perilous water routes to move people and products. Railways had been operating for two decades in the United States and Britain, and in the mid-1850s Canadians decided that it was their turn. Although the Grand Trunk and the Great Western Railway both began operating in Ontario in the 1850s, neither at that time had a tunnel. The B and O Railway was designed to link the St. Lawrence River route with Ottawa and to tap the forests and farms between. And because the town of Brockville was built on a ledge of limestone that cut off the waterfront, the railway engineers decided to blast a tunnel.

Begun in 1854, the tunnel would stretch nearly a kilometre through the limestone mesa. On December 31, 1860, the first wood-burning steam locomotive puffed its way through the darkness, the dim glow from its kerosene headlamp barely illuminating the way. It was Canada's first railway tunnel and the envy of a soon-to-be nation on the verge of the railway era.

But the engineering miracle that was the old Brockville tunnel was later forgotten when, in 1889, the Grand Trunk began digging its 1,800-metre tunnel beneath the St. Clair River to link Sarnia, Ontario, with Port Huron, Michigan. It marked the first time that tunnel builders used compressed air, and the event was featured in newspapers and engineering journals around the world.

Meanwhile, back in Brockville, the engines of the B and O, and later those of the CPR, continued to rumble through the darkness of the old tunnel until use of the passage was discontinued in 1954. A separate spur continued to access the waterfront until 1970.

Visitors can now wander through the damp tunnel viewing stalactites and experiencing a stunning sound and light show worthy of the colourful Fremont Street experience in Las Vegas.

11 WATERWAY FROM THE PAST

The Rideau Canal

IN 1826, THE Duke of Wellington's mind looked to Upper Canada, where memories of the 1812 war with the Americans were still fresh. Wary that the major transportation corridor, the St. Lawrence River, lay on the U.S. border, Wellington proposed a canal that would link Kingston, on Lake Ontario, with Wright's Town (now Gatineau), then a small sawmill village on the north side of the Ottawa River, a remote location.

To carry out the difficult job he coaxed Colonel John By out of retirement. For five years, two thousand men sweated in malarial swamplands, hacking bush, trenching channels and hauling huge limestone blocks for the fifty dams and forty-seven locks. The estimated death rate from malaria was more than 50 percent.

In 1832, By's 200-kilometre waterway opened for traffic, a remarkable feat given the remoteness and total lack of mechanical assistance. A small sawmill town sprang up at the canal's eastern terminus and was named Bytown, after the canal's builder. But By did not return home a hero. Instead, he was recalled to England for allowing his £577,000 budget to swell to more than £870,000.

The canal would provide a key commercial link for the many little mill towns along its path. Then, with the arrival of the railway, its use faded, not rising again until the 1950s and '60s, when the popularity of recreational boating boomed. In 1932, the federal government proposed closing the historic waterway. It was saved only by its role as a vital water-control system.

The canal is famed not just for its pleasure-boating but for the fact that it remains historically intact, right down to the hand operation of its locks and swing bridges. In fact, in a rare gesture of heritage preservation, the federal government placed the canal's operation in the hands of Parks Canada and has identified the route as a historical monument. In June 2007, UNESCO added the Rideau Canal to its list of World Heritage Sites, one of the first such waterways to be so named.

By's military blockhouses still stand at Kingston Mills, Newboro and Merrickville. At Jones Falls are a triple set of locks, a one-time powder magazine and the world's highest stone dam of its day. The Scottish stonemasons who toiled to construct the stone walls and locks have also left a lasting legacy in the beautiful stone stores and homes of Perth, Merrickville and Kingston. Colonel By may have died a broken man, but even he would have been astonished at the durability of his legacy.

UNESCO has declared the canal and Kingston's fortifications a World Heritage Site.

⑫ THE RATSNAKE
Don't Look Up

THAT LARGE BLACK snake dangling lazily from a tree overhead is not a creature from the dark forests of the Amazon; it is Canada's largest snake, the grey ratsnake. Canada is not noted for its proliferation of snakes, with small harmless examples being the norm. In Ontario, only the endangered Massasauga rattlesnake carries any venom but it is of insufficient strength to cause death.

Found mainly in the rocks and meadows of eastern Ontario, the ratsnake can grow to more than two and a half metres in length. Local legend tells of a farmer who once killed a specimen that measured five metres. While its treetop perch is not unusual, for birds make up part of its diet, it may more commonly be found slithering though grasslands or languishing in the open to enjoy the heat of a summer's day.

Sadly, the species is on the endangered list. Habitat destruction has reduced its range to a small area north and east of Kingston.

Ratsnakes hibernate in groups. Female grey ratsnakes generally lay their eggs during the summer and the offspring, which may number up to 23, require seven years to mature.

A slim species with white throat and checkerboard pattern on their black backs, they prefer open meadows but may also lurk in rock crevices, or in trees. Sadly, efforts by the province of Ontario to list the creature on its Species at Risk list have encountered protest from local landowners and municipal councils fearing that protecting the snake's habitat may inhibit their freedom to permit future development in the area.

The easiest way to locate one would be to follow the trails in Murphys Point or Frontenac Provincial Parks in eastern Ontario where they are protected, and the road signs plead "Please brake for snakes."

But it is their habit of dangling from tree branches that presents the most disconcerting image for the casual stroller whether they are seeking out this large critter or not.

The grey ratsnake will often climb trees in search of bird eggs to eat.

⑬ IT CAME FROM OUTER SPACE

The Holleford Meteor Crater

MOST OF US have at one time or another gazed in amazement at the night sky and watched streaks of light. On rare occasions we can hear the crackle as a "close one" burns up in the atmosphere. These are true visitors from outer space — meteors.

About twice a day, somewhere in Canada, a meteor thuds to the Earth. Most are only about 100 grams in weight and make little impact; but a few have struck with a tremendous explosion, ripping apart the ground and leaving telltale circular craters or altered minerals.

To date, scientists have recorded about two dozen meteor craters in Canada. The 95-kilometre-wide strike in Sudbury is Canada's largest. The impact of what must have been an enormous meteor was so broad and deep that it completely altered the mineralization of the bedrock and created Canada's greatest nickel deposit.

Of the five meteor craters in Ontario (others are near Brent in Algonquin Park, at Wanapitei Lake west of Sudbury, and at the Slate Islands in Lake Superior), that at Holleford, north of Kingston, is the most readily visible from the ground. It was first discovered in 1955 by a team of scientists at the Dominion

Observatory in Ottawa by poring over aerial photographs. Later research concluded that the extraterrestrial interloper must have arrived around 550 million years ago and measured 90 metres across. Exploding into the ground at an estimated 55,000 kilometres an hour, it left a crater 2.35 kilometres deep and 25 metres wide. Over time, sediment raised the depth to its present 30 metres.

To reach it, drive to Hartington on Highway 38, about 25 kilometres north of Exit 611 on Highway 401. From the centre of the village take the Holleford Road east for about 3 kilometres and follow the road as it bends to the north (left). Another 1.5 kilometres brings you to a T intersection, where you turn right. Then, after another 1.6 kilometres, the road descends a slope. This is the southwest wall of the crater. The road continues east along the slope of the crater for another kilometre to the Crater Farm and the one-time hamlet of Holleford, where a plaque stands by the fence on the north side of the road.

As with most meteor craters in Canada, erosion has softened its features and vegetation covers much of its slope. Yet it is hard not to stand and wonder at how the ground must have shaken when this visitor from outer space thundered to Earth.

This crater in the ground occurred when a meteor exploded into the Earth's crust.

Tours of the Kingston Penitentiary have become one of Kingston's largest tourist attractions.

⑭ THE BIG HOUSE
Inside the Kingston "Pen"

OPENED IN 1835, Kingston Penitentiary is one of Canada's oldest and most historic lock-ups. The prison's cells measured a metre wide and just over two metres deep. Bunks rested on hinges and could be raised during the day. Four wings of cell blocks, five levels high, radiated out from a central tower from which guards could keep watch.

Under the direction of its first warden, Henry Smith, hardships and punishments were so severe that in 1847 a commission set up to investigate conditions inside the prison recommended Smith's removal. Punishments such as flogging and waterboarding continued until the 1970s. Hangings did not occur here as they were the responsibility of the county jails. Boys as young as eight and girls as young as nine were sentenced to prison, in one case for up to seven years for stealing biscuits, tea and a lady's hat.

Extensive additions began following Smith's removal including a hospital, new walls and corner guard towers and workshops. More recent innovations include more spacious segregation units and housing for family visitations. In later years, an area of the prison yard was set aside for First Nations prisoners to conduct their ceremonies. Among the oldest sections are the workshops where prisoners made canvas bags for Canada's postal service.

While escapes were few and unsuccessful, one that was successful was committed by Norman "Red" Ryan and four other inmates in 1923. They set a fire in the stables and amid the smoke and confusion escaped over the wall. Ryan made it as far as Minneapolis where he was recaptured. One of Canada's worst prison riots occurred in the Pen in 1971 when two people were killed when rioters took both guards and inmates hostage.

Former prison guards lead tours sharing their first-hand accounts of life in the Big House. Completed in 1873, the former warden's residence across the street is now the Kingston Penitentiary Museum. The contents are often a gruesome reminder of the living conditions that inmates suffered.

Kingston's domed City Hall was once destined to be Canada's seat of government.

⑮ THE DOMES OF KINGSTON

Ontario's Grandest City Hall

DESPITE APPARENT DISINTEREST in their built heritage by successive city councils, Kingston has managed to retain some of Ontario's most historic buildings and streetscapes. The domed Kingston City Hall tops the list of the city's most stunning structures.

There was a time when this edifice almost became home to Canada's new government. With the creation of the United Provinces of Canada in 1841, the British selected Kingston to be the colony's capital. A devastating fire in 1840 had destroyed much of the old market area, clearing the ground for new buildings and a grand new parliament building was slated to be built there.

During its brief time in the new capital city, the colony's legislature met first in a converted hospital and then in a grand waterfront mansion known as Alwington House (which burned in 1958). The legislature then moved into another grand mansion called Summerhill, which was built in 1839. Following the government's departure from there, Summerhill became the first building to house the new Queen's University and today it remains the residence of the president of the university.

Excited by his city's possible new status as the capital of the United Provinces, the then-mayor John Counter and his council commissioned the construction of a fine new building suitable for the legislature. George Browne of Toronto was hired as the architect and he designed one of Ontario's finest municipal structures. But the British government ultimately chose Montreal over Kingston as the new capital city and the legislative building became the new city hall. To help recover building costs, the city council rented parts of the building out to a succession of private interests, including saloons, shops, churches, private associations, a bank and a small theatre, all the while carrying on as the city's municipal centre.

The city hall provided two large meeting halls, offices and meeting space for city officials, as well as quarters for the custom house, post office, police station and jail. These latter functions have since ceased to exist, although the police station is now a museum.

After fires in 1865 and 1908, and renovations (the latest in 2002), the grand domed building has remained a city hall. It has become one of Kingston's major tourist attractions. A seasonal farmers' market continues its traditional role behind the building. In 1985, the National Historic Sites and Monuments Board of Canada declared the building a National Historic Site.

Guided and self-guided tours lead visitors through the elaborate council chambers, meeting halls and the staircase that leads to the dome with its windows, clocks and copper roof.

Kingston's Martello Towers provided a flexible
but short-lived line of defence against the Americans.

⑯ MARTELLO TOWERS
Kingston's Little Round Forts

FOR ONTARIO'S HISTORY lovers, Kingston is as good as it gets. With its beautiful stone houses and institutional buildings (some dating from the 1790s), its historic forts and the houses where Canada's first prime minister, Sir John A. Macdonald, slept, the city can keep a history buff occupied for weeks. But the structures that cause the most quizzical looks are the little round forts that seem to be almost everywhere.

Named Martello Towers after their role in repelling an attack at Cape Mortella on Corsica in 1796, these were the last word in defence. Their small size meant that they could be placed in defensive locations otherwise too small for a normal-sized fort. Their circular shape deflected cannon balls, and their high, small windows made them almost impossible to enter. They permitted a flexible line of defence and were almost impregnable.

Of the dozen or so built in Canada (Britain built about two hundred worldwide in the defence of the Empire) half are in Kingston.

The oldest were the towers built in Halifax between 1796 and 1798; those in Kingston were added during the 1840s when the Oregon Crisis between Canada and the United States once again raised the spectre of American invasion. But the military usefulness of the forts in Kingston was relatively short-lived, as by 1860, newly introduced naval guns had the capacity to demolish the sturdy bastions with a single shot.

Of Canada's surviving Martello Towers, those in Kingston, with their distinctive roofs and their neat stonework, are considered the most appealing architecturally. All are readily visible. While two are connected to the museum fortress of Fort Henry, two others, the Murney Tower near Macdonald Park and Fort Frederick Tower, are both museums. The one at Fort Frederick was the only tower to be three storeys high, and is part of the Royal Military College. The third pair, those known as Shoal Tower and Cedar Island Tower, lie offshore.

The Simcoe Island ferry is Ontario's smallest and one of its least-known ferry services.

17 SIMCOE ISLAND FERRY

Ontario's Smallest Ferry

AS ONTARIANS HURL their cars along the expressways and toll roads, few pause to consider the more leisurely pace of a ferry ride. Many have tried the popular MS *Chi-Cheemaun*, which swallows 115 cars at a time and glides them across Georgian Bay to and from Manitoulin Island. Few, however, realize that Ontario claims no fewer than sixteen car ferry services, nearly all of them free. Three car ferries cross each of the Ottawa and St. Clair rivers, a pair are for island First Nations reserves, while Canada's southernmost ferry links mainland Ontario with Pelee Island, Canada's most southerly occupied island. But the greatest concentration of ferries lies near Kingston.

Here, at the entrance to the St. Lawrence River, a handful of large, flat islands attracted early pioneer settlers. Although the populations have subsequently declined, the islands remain occupied, the ferries their lifeline to the mainland.

The largest of the five, the *Wolfe Islander III*, carries more than fifty cars and trucks to busy Wolfe Island. While others link Howe Island and Amherst Island to the mainland, the smallest of them all is the three-car ferry to Simcoe Island. Announced only by a small sign, the landing is nothing more than a beach. Here, the little ferry grinds against the sand and unceremoniously plunks down its gangway. Because it links Simcoe Island only to Wolfe Island, and not to the mainland, the ferry coincides its schedule with that of the *Wolfe Islander III*, or runs as required.

Once home to more than a dozen farm families, Simcoe Island is now more popular for cottaging, and only a pair of farms survive. At the far western end of the limestone island stands the historic Nine-Mile Point Lighthouse. Now automated, the 15-metre tower dates from 1833 and is popular with lighthouse enthusiasts, although it is surrounded by privately owned land. Although it is only one of many public and private vehicle ferries that ply Ontario's waters, the Simcoe Island ferry is the smallest of the car ferries, and takes you on an unusual excursion to a place where cars are an anomaly rather than the norm.

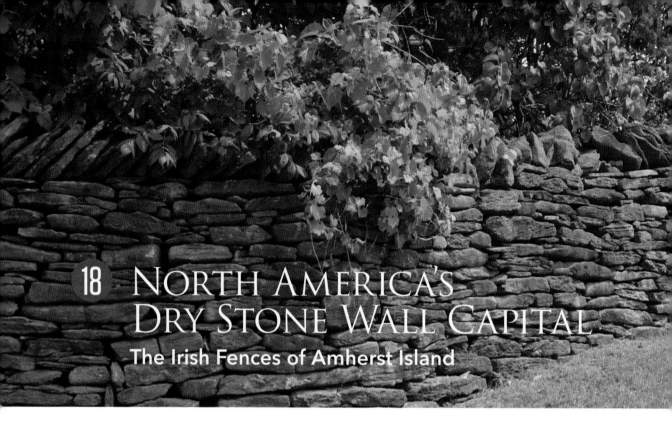

18 NORTH AMERICA'S DRY STONE WALL CAPITAL
The Irish Fences of Amherst Island

ANYONE WHO DRIVES, cycles or hikes along the roads of Ontario's dwindling farm country can't help but notice the many styles of fences which line them. Among the more modern are electric and barbed wire fences. In the more distant and traditional farm country, it is still possible to find rail and stump fences and a few made of boulders extracted from the nearby fields.

However, along the rural routes of Amherst Island the traveller will find something entirely different: fences known as "dry stone walls." Largely found in Ireland and Scotland, the neat, flat limestone slabs crowned with vertical pieces that line the roads of Amherst Island originated with early Irish settlers. Their beauty and longevity have earned the island the title of the "dry stone wall capital of North America."

Arriving mostly from Ards County in Ireland, the settlers brought with them distinctive wall building techniques. The stone slabs come in various sizes or small flat pieces, much of it from quarries around Kingston, as well as from the fields of the island itself. When the slabs are assembled, they produce a formidable fence guaranteed to keep livestock under control and any damage is easily repaired. The walls are also stunningly attractive and greatly cherished by island residents and visitors alike. They are among Ontario's more unusual rural heritage features.

Many of these walls have weathered changes to farming methods and the harsh winter climate. Experts suggest that the abrasive surface of the stones and the shallow depth of the soil covering the bedrock have provided them with a good foundation and helped to ensure their longevity; that, and the care they have received over time. Current owners, including descendants of the original wall builders, many of whom still own the farms today,

North America's "Dry Stone Wall Capital" of Amherst Island reflects the Island's Irish heritage.

have carefully preserved this unusual piece of island history and participate in regular workshops on the repair and maintenance of the walls. A few owners have even made a pilgrimage to Ireland to learn more about the building techniques. Every year on the island, they participate in the Dry Stone Wall Festival, which, in 2018, earned a segment on the CBC's *Rick Mercer Report*. It was in that year that a facsimile of the famous Feidin Wall in Ireland was constructed on the island to celebrate the heritage of the walls. It stands on Front Road a short distance west of Stella, the town's main village and its ferry landing.

A journey around the small island reveals the more prominent of the dozen remaining walls. East of Stella, a long and lovingly maintained wall lines the road at the front of the Poplar Dell farm vacation property; the oldest portion of this historic home dates to 1822. A short distance further east, another well maintained stone wall encloses the Pentland Cemetery. While many other stone walls line the roads, the most striking runs along the Hitchins Farm at the intersection of the Second Concession and Emerald Road. This fence curves around the corner of the two roads and is highlighted by a stone gateway.

Canadian MP, and former astronaut, Marc Garneau has declared that "All efforts should be made to preserve these walls and protect Amherst Island's cultural heritage for all Canadians." Meantime, to help make that happen, the Dry Stone Wall Association of Canada has proposed that the walls of Amherst Island become a National Historic Site. That is a solid idea.

The Amherst Island ferry terminal on the mainland lies on Highway 33 in the community of Millhaven.

43

19 THE HELL HOLES OF EASTERN ONTARIO

Napanee's Strange Topography

A WALK THROUGH THE forest can sometimes be a dangerous thing, not necessarily from wolves or bears or even deer hunters, but from a careless step into a hole, especially when the hole leads to Hell.

The limestone ridge along the Salmon River north of Napanee contains some of the area's most unusual natural features. There are caves, crevices and odd-looking rock columns. But the strangest of the oddities are what locals call the "Hell Holes."

To early settlers unfamiliar with geology, these holes in the forest floor seemed to have no end. While most are little larger than foxholes, a few are large enough to allow a human to squeeze through. Those who braved the descent found caverns that stretched in many directions.

Geologists refer to these phenomena as "karst" features. Karst topography occurs when soft limestone layers beneath a hard upper layer dissolve in water. This weathering causes caves and caverns, and the Hell Holes. Similar to caves, the holes in the forest floor can open into large, pitch-black rooms, one of which was once large enough to hold twenty people (it later collapsed). While there are other locations in Ontario with similar features, the ridge by the Salmon River, near the village of Roblindale, offers the greatest concentration of these cavities.

Most are located in the privately run Hell Holes Park. Here, a self-guided trail, a little over 3 kilometres long, leads not only to the strange holes but also over natural rock bridges, through eerie canyons lined with layered cliffs and columns, and then to the Devil's Horse Stable hole, 7.5 metres deep and 2.5 by 3.5 metres square. A ladder leads to those depths.

Hell Holes Park is located on Centreville Road about 5.5 kilometres east of Highway 41, and 10.7 kilometres north of Highway 401 (Exit 579). Snacks, gifts and, of course, flashlights are available in the log cabin shop. It is said that one visitor even took his wedding vows in the Hell Holes. The duration of this marriage is not known.

Early pioneers thought that these bottomless pits led straight to Hell.

Ontario's "Goat Pastures," or alvars, are unusual areas of thin or nonexistent soil cover that support rare plant and animal ecosystems.

20 ONTARIO'S GOAT PASTURES

The Alvar Communities

THEY MAY BE hard to identify at first, and they certainly do not count among Ontario's more spectacular landscapes, but they are one of our most unusual natural features. Indeed, Ontario's alvars are among the most important in North America.

Scientists define alvars as open areas of thin soil over flat limestone or marble rock with little in the way of vegetation. They are, in other words, rock deserts or, as frustrated early farmers derisively called them, "goat pastures."

The Ontario government has moved to protect these unusual areas, as they frequently contain endangered and rare species of plants and animals. They also attract hordes of birdwatchers to witness such species as loggerhead shrikes, upland sandpipers or grasshopper and clay-coloured sparrows.

In Ontario, alvars are found in areas where the limestone bedrock creeps close to the surface — on Manitoulin Island, in eastern Ontario and on the fringes of cottage country east of Lake Simcoe.

Alvars can vary in their appearances. They can look like grasslands, shrublands and even bare limestone.

Unsuspecting pioneer settlers found the unforgiving soils a shock and a disappointment. While the level plains looked promising, the hard limestone beds just a few centimetres beneath the surface broke many a shovel and plough, as well as spirit. Most such farmers would simply take off what lumber they could and move on, leaving stumps sitting on top of the rock. Many logged alvars can still be seen today. In other areas, these farms were gathered into larger units to create shrubby cattle ranches.

In Ontario, alvar landscapes are most striking in an area known as the Carden Plain, located east of Lake Simcoe. Farm roads originally surveyed for the settlers have disappeared or become mere rutted tracks. The Ontario Ministry of Natural Resources has designated the Carden Plain and other alvars as areas of natural and scientific interest (ANSI) and are working with private landowners to preserve these strange habitats. The Carden Plain lies between Kawartha Roads 6 and 36, near Dalrymple.

Other alvars can be found around Napanee, throughout Prince Edward County and on Manitoulin Island.

21 THE LAKE ON THE MOUNTAIN

A Mystery in Prince Edward County

AT FIRST IT looks natural enough — a little lake sparkling in the sun, surrounded by willow trees. But look behind you, and 100 metres below, at the foot of a limestone cliff, spreads Lake Ontario's Bay of Quinte. Then it begins to sink in. The little lake beside you is sitting on the brink of a cliff, with no visible outlet and no visible source.

Located in Prince Edward County, 7 kilometres from the town of Picton, the lake has long puzzled geologists. How did it get there? Why has it stayed there? Until just a few years ago no one even knew how deep it was. Then, as they explored its depths, geologists determined that it was spring fed and about 60 metres deep.

But just as they were solving these puzzles, the scientists uncovered another, even more intriguing mystery. The fluctuations in the water level of the lake seemed to coincide with those occurring in Lake Erie, more than 300 kilometres away and with no direct connection.

Its origins, too, have defied explanation. While most theories involving glacial whirlpools, meteors and volcanoes have been dismissed, the one most commonly accepted involves the collapse of a massive limestone cave beneath the surface. The early First Nations believed it was the lake of the gods, and called it Onokenoga.

The attractions around the lake are numerous and don't have a lot to do with its mysteries. A 103-hectare provincial park beside the lake provides picnicking and hiking, while across the road a lofty viewpoint offers vistas of the Bay of Quinte, the mainland shore, and the free Glenora ferries that shuttle back and forth carrying Highway 33 traffic.

Adjacent to the park, Van Alstine's store, built in 1796, now houses the Lake on the Mountain Resort, part of which is also located in the House Across the Road, better known as the Wilson-Frizell house, which dates from 1896. At the foot of the cliff the several buildings that comprise the Glenora mill complex are among the oldest stone mill buildings in the province. But all attention focuses upon the Lake on the Mountain. It has been a mystery since it was discovered, and it will likely remain a mystery for some time to come.

Picton's mysterious Lake on the Mountain lurks near the lip of the cliff that overlooks the Glenora mill.

㉒ WARTIME GHOSTS

Camp Picton

A VISIT TO THE top of the cliff that overlooks the attractive lakeside town of Picton reveals more than just a stunning view of the town below. It also unveils an intact collection of abandoned air base buildings — hangars, barracks and officers' apartments. Unlike most remaining Second World War military buildings, these are all covered with wood-shingle siding. The 28-hectare base was known as Camp Picton.

The base was established in 1939 and became an air-training facility in 1941, when most of the buildings were constructed. At its peak, the base housed forty-five officers and eight hundred rank and file. From the seven hangars, planes took off to practise on the nearby bombing ranges while gunnery practice took place to the south of the camp.

In late 1944, the gunnery and bombing training ended, and the camp was turned over to the RCAF, which operated it as an equipment-maintenance facility.

At the beginning, relations with the population of Picton were rocky, and complaints of drunkenness, rowdyism and venereal disease flooded the commander's office.

After the war ended, the base became a training centre with new facilities that included a post office, skeet range and theatre,

as well as sporting facilities for badminton, basketball, floor hockey and archery.

In 1960, the base changed roles once again, becoming and remaining an operational base until 1969, when all military operations there ceased, and the base was abandoned.

Now privately owned and known as Loch-Sloy Business Park, the few buildings in use house small industries and a fire department, while air cadets and a flying club use a number of the hangars.

But the overall appearance remains that of a massive ghost town. Rows of wood-shingled barracks stand along weed-strewn roads, playing fields lie overgrown and the two-storey officers' apartments look out on shrubby lawns. So authentic does the facility feel that in 1993, the CBC used it as a location in its made-for-TV movie *Dieppe*. The current owners are working to preserve what is the last Second World War base of its kind in the world. Surprisingly, this remarkable piece of Canada's wartime history lacks any kind of heritage designation, federal, provincial or local, and as of 2021 was sold to a private company which promises to respect the site's heritage.

To reach this ghostly sight, follow Church Street south from the centre of Picton.

Rows of barracks line the weedy street in the abandoned air base overlooking Picton.

23 A City for the Birds

Picton's Birdhouse City

In the shadow of a cliff near Picton, Ontario, there lies a city that is strictly for the birds. Started in 1980 by the Prince Edward Region Conservation Authority, Birdhouse City is a collection of more than 100 birdhouses. Not just any birdhouses, they have been designed to copy many of the area's actual buildings. The city is the legacy of former authority superintendent Doug Harnes, whose skill in woodworking led to the creation of this bird city's first structures.

The first to be built was a re-creation of the Massasauga Park Hotel. Measuring more than 1.5 metres square, it was supported by two poles and boasted three thousand miniature shingles. Pretty soon everyone got into the act, and birdhouses of all descriptions began to show up. Participants in Experience '80 contributed a paddle wheeler, a police car and a "fly-in" theatre, while the local McDonald's donated, naturally, a McDonald's "fly-through."

Visitors arrive, often by the busload, to see a Greek temple, a Pennsylvania Dutch barn and Picton's historic Crystal Palace, while the "departed" can find comfort in the "Nest In Peace" Funeral Home.

Nor was city planning overlooked. The architectural drafting class of Prince Edward Collegiate planned the city with streets like Finch Avenue and Swallow Drive. The Lake Ontario Cement Company donated labour and material for a central fountain. This unusual display consists of more than 100 distinctive birdhouses built to entice purple martins, wrens, bluebirds, chickadees and tree swallows. Eagles need not apply.

Sadly, due to financial constraints, many of the structures have seen maintenance slip, and several need repair and repainting. Still, birds love it. The purple martins, the wrens and the bluebirds flit from cottage to carousel to the Thrush Bank. When winter comes, however, most of the residents become "snow birds."

Birdhouse City is in the Macaulay Mountain Conservation Area on County Road 8.

"Empty nesters" in Picton's Birdhouse City.

Dunes at West Lake.

24 THE DUNE THAT ATE A TOWN

Sandbanks Provincial Park

ALTHOUGH IT DIDN'T exactly "eat" a town, a giant wall of sand did move across Prince Edward County between 1890 and 1920 to consume a sizeable settlement. And it was all due to beer.

When the U.S. government slapped a surtax on whiskey during the Civil War, American consumers switched to beer. And the best barley for beer was considered to be Canadian. Canadian farmers hurriedly turned all available fields to barley production. But Prince Edward County, with its mild climate and close proximity to U.S. ports just across Lake Ontario, became Ontario's major barley exporter. Cattle were hustled off their pastures and onto the most marginal lands in the county, the dunes.

Following the retreat of the last glaciers, the Prince Edward Peninsula built up a long beach of sand. Over the centuries the prevailing winds whipped the sand into a ridge of dunes that measured 8 kilometres long, 2 kilometres wide and 50 metres high. Over time, a mat of grasses and shrubs had stabilized the dunes. But once the cattle started to roam them, eating the fragile cover, the dunes grew restless and started once more to move.

Slowly at first, then with increasing determination, the dunes moved inland. Fields, fences and then outbuildings and barns soon disappeared under the moving yellow wall. The West Bay Road had to be realigned a number of times to avoid being consumed. The advancing dunes spared nothing. A brick factory stood stubbornly in the way of the dunes until wind-whipped sand finally forced the owners to dismantle the plant and flee.

Desperate, the farmers planted willows on the dunes, but those had little effect. Finally, after the First World War had ended, a reluctant Ontario government established a tree nursery on them. As roots and branches grabbed the blowing sand the dunes' advances slowed, but they haven't stopped.

Today, on the south shore of West Lake, both in and near the popular Sandbanks Provincial Park, you can see the advancing dunes. Cedar trees, once buried and now exposed, show double sets of roots, while relics of the pioneer brick factory still litter its ill-fated site. Although the dunes no longer advance across the countryside, the winds continue to whip the sand into West Lake. Eventually, the dunes that ate a sizeable settlement will claim the lake and turn it into little more than a pond. Their appetite is insatiable.

The dunes form the backbone of Sandbanks Provincial Park and lie on County Road 12, about 10 kilometres southwest of the village of Bloomfield.

25 THE GLEN MILLER ERRATIC

Trenton's Big Boulder

WHILE CLAWING BOULDER after boulder from their fields, many farmers curse the last ice age, claiming bitterly that all they harvested was a new crop of rocks. And they aren't far wrong. For in fields infested with boulders, the freezing and thawing of the ground in the spring in fact squeezes a fresh crop of boulders from beneath the surface.

Most such rocks were deposited during the last ice age, which some scientists claim covered Ontario to a depth of more than a kilometre. As the ice sheets cracked and began to melt about twenty thousand years ago, the torrents of meltwater spewed sand, gravel and rocks into the gaping crevasses. In central Ontario, the ice sheet melted in a long line where the glacial debris formed a ridge of rocky and sandy hills, a bouldery line that stretches from Orangeville in the west to Trenton in east. The deposit is widely known today as the Oak Ridges Moraine.

But it was at Trenton that the ice disgorged its biggest boulder, one the size of a house. Geologists call it the Glen Miller Erratic, their name for boulders that the ice sheets carried far from their parent bedrock. In Glen Miller, the Trenton suburb where it sits, residents simply call it the Bleasdell Boulder.

Its veins of quartz and granite suggest that it has travelled a long distance from its origin in the Canadian Shield far to the north, a testament to the power of the great glaciers. And despite the young forest now surrounding it, the huge stone towers well above the humbled viewer. In fact it contains its own cave, large enough for a person to stand upright. Known now as the Bleasdell Boulder, it is Ontario's largest erratic, measuring 8 metres wide and 7 metres high. Thanks to the efforts of Paul and Maria Heissler, the geologic oddity lies within a conservation area on Highway 33 north of Highway 401.

Trenton's Big Boulder testifies to the awesome power of the glaciers that covered Ontario during the last ice age.

26 TRENTON'S AD ASTRA STONES

National Air Force Museum of Canada

"PER ARDUA AD astra" means "Through adversity to the stars" and it is the worthy motto of the Royal Canadian Air Force. Today, Ad Astra is the name on 12,000 brick-shaped stones lying in the yard of the National Air Force Museum of Canada in Trenton.

The idea began as a fundraiser in 1996 for the museum itself. A hundred stones would have been considered a success; however more than 600 were sold in the first year alone, and by 2021, more than 12,000 stones lay in the ground in the museum's yard.

Although the first stones were sold in honour of WWII veterans, the memorials came to include veterans of other wars and those who served in peacetime and the thousands of women who served as well. Although the stones show no rank, they do indicate the hometown of the member, as well as their dates of birth and death. In addition, the stones display the air force roundel with the words "Ad Astra." Many of the stones are grouped around cairns dedicated to the battalions in which they served. The granite bricks are made by Campbell Monuments of Belleville.

The museum, according to its website, "is dedicated to preserving and telling the history of Canadian military aviation. From its first flight on a frozen lake in Nova Scotia through to today's humanitarian relief missions, the Museum captures the spirit, the daring and the courage of the men and women of the RCAF."

More than 36 aircraft are on display in the airpark where the stones lie. The museum itself houses a vast collection of vintage aircraft, including a WWII Halifax NA337 Bomber dredged from the bottom of Lake Mjosa in Norway in the 1990s and restored over a period of 10 years. It is the sole surviving example of this aircraft.

Among the many displays and tributes is a full-scale mock-up of the tunnel used in the 1944 "great escape" from the Stalag Luft III air force POW camp. Of the 79 who made it through the tunnel, only six remained free.

The ad astra stones in Trenton's National Air Force Museum of Canada pay tribute to those who served in Canada's air force.

The historic carousel in Roseneath is Canada's oldest country carousel.

27 'ROUND AND 'ROUND WE GO

The Roseneath Carousel

A SMALL FAIRGROUND IN a tiny Ontario village is probably the least likely place to find one of Ontario's most historic amusement rides, and that is the hundred-year-old carousel in the village of Roseneath located just east of Rice Lake.

Hidden within a large, circular, orange-coloured shed, the carousel was built in Abilene, Kansas, in 1906 — a time before TVs and computer games, when amusement parks and fairgrounds were common sources of recreation.

By 1932, the carousel with its forty basswood horses and two wooden boats had made their way to Mohawk Park beside a tram line in Brantford, Ontario, where it languished. In that year, the rail line closed and the ride was placed in storage. The head of the Roseneath Agricultural Society heard about the hidden treasure, and for $675 purchased it and moved it to the Roseneath fairgrounds. To protect the find from the elements, the society erected a sixteen-sided wooden shed. By 1986, with the carousel in dire need of refurbishing, a fundraising campaign was launched.

Horses had to be painstakingly repainted in the same colours as the originals, while some parts were re-carved. Much of this exacting labour was done by master carver Konstantin von Waldburg.

Unfortunately, the sixteen screen panels in the centre of the carousel had become so fragile they could not be restored. New panels commemorating local scenes now rest in their places, most of them the work of local artist Ron Bolt.

Thanks to $400,000 in donations and much volunteer labour, the historic merry-go-round was back in business by 1995.

Although the "gold rings" have long since vanished, music plays from a genuine 1934 Wurlitzer pipe organ with actual paper scrolls. The tunes today are likely to be "Rock Around the Clock" or "Locomotion."

Ontario does possess another heritage carousel, that in Port Dalhousie. Although the latter is considered to be a Coney Island-style ride, the one in Roseneath falls into the country fair category and is said to be the only such structure in Canada.

28 THE SYMBOLIC CENOTAPH
Alderville First Nation

MOST ONTARIO COMMUNITIES contain memorials to honour members who have served and died defending Canada in time of war. Most date from the end of the First World War and are usually simple plaques, while others offer more elaborate statuary. But the cenotaph that rises above the First Nations community of Alderville near Rice Lake seems at first to be a puzzling agglomeration of cubes, orbs, pillars and chains.

As with much in First Nations cultures, the Alderville Cenotaph is highly symbolic. The large cube that surmounts the 18-metre-high white structure represents the four corners of the Earth. The three globes symbolize the Holy Trinity, and the three pillars the three holy virtues of faith, hope and charity.

All are mounted on a square base, its sides representing the four freedoms for which those remembered fought: freedom of speech, freedom of religion, freedom of the press and freedom from fear.

Nine smaller cubes are for those Alderville First Nations persons who perished in the First World War, and the thirty-five links honour those who served. The concrete structure rises 18 metres and was the first in Canada to commemorate the contribution and sacrifice of First Nations peoples in Canada during the First World War. Subsequent plaques commemorate those who served in the Second World War and the Korean War.

The cenotaph was designed in 1927 by Alf and Clarence McKeel and constructed by local volunteers.

The 300 residents of the community are of the Ojibwa First Nations, relocated here from the Bay of Quinte around 1830. An additional thousand band members live off the reserve.

The band also administers the nearby rare Black Oak savannah, a remnant landscape of tall grass prairie and scattered black oak. It was designated by the band council in 2000 as a Natural Heritage Site.

The First Nations cenotaph at Alderville was the first in Canada to honour First Nations' service in the First World War.

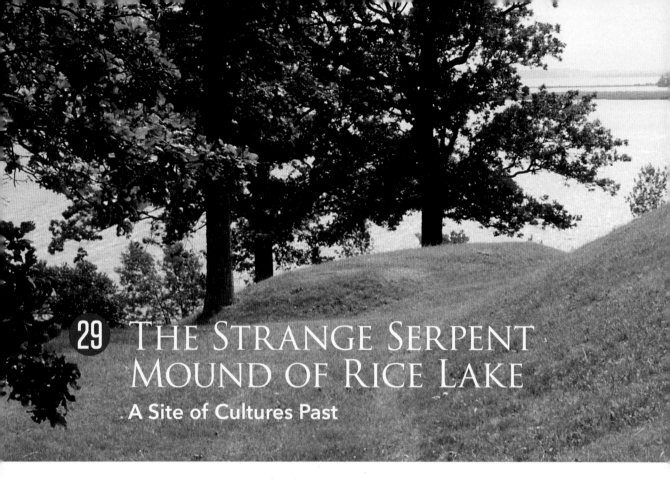

29 THE STRANGE SERPENT MOUND OF RICE LAKE
A Site of Cultures Past

IRONICALLY, THE STRONGEST visual evidence of Ontario's Indigenous heritage deals not with life, but with death. Usually, places where early peoples in Ontario lived are seldom discernible to any but the trained archaeologist. Yet where they died can leave prominent physical features.

Take, for example, Rice Lake's unusual serpent mound. Although no other such mounds exist elsewhere in Canada, burial mounds in the shape of giant snakes are common in the Ohio Valley of the United States.

The mound on the north shore of Rice Lake is 2 metres high, 8 metres wide and a twisting 60 metres long. Several other burial mounds, in the more common oval shapes, surround it. An example of the latter also exists at Taber Hill Park in Scarborough, uncovered

when the site was being prepared for housing. Archaeologists can't decide whether the serpent mound was intended to resemble a snake, since it lacks a "head," or was an ordinary burial mound that was somehow extended.

Following the retreat of the glaciers around twelve thousand years ago, the Arctic-like area abounded in caribou, bison and possibly even mammoths. The first inhabitants were nomadic. As the climate warmed, forests covered the tundra, bringing smaller game like deer and rabbits. Berries and root crops became part of the staple diet. The time of the nomads was about to end.

Around 1000 BC, the mound-building culture entered the area. Originating in the Ohio Valley, it gradually made its way into Ontario, culminating in the collection of mounds on Rice Lake. There is no evidence that this was a

The Rice Lake area offers Canada's greatest concentration of tear-shaped glacial hills known as "drumlins." The Serpent Mounds (closed at this writing) were built amid the drumlin field. (Thanks to Elmhirst's Resort on Rice Lake for kind research assistance on that scenic area.)

village site. The absence of bones from winter game indicates that it was, rather, a summer gathering place for trading, rice harvesting and burials.

Around AD 500 a revolutionary new way of life arrived. Corn and squash replaced hunting and gathering. Permanent villages were built, with longhouses surrounded by palisades. Pits, instead of mounds, were used for burials. The presence of burial pits just north of the mounds, and a habitation area west of them, confirms the existence of the new lifestyle. Consecutive harvests eventually leached the soil, and the inhabitants moved to more fertile grounds.

The arrival of the Europeans in the late eighteenth and early nineteenth centuries ended that way of life, as First Nations peoples were moved onto reserves. A logging dam near the outlet to Rice Lake flooded the rice beds, and a way of life ended forever. Today, the mounds are part of Serpent Mounds Park, where a long-vanished culture and custom can be interpreted by a modern world.

Lying at the end of Serpent Mounds Road south of Keene, the park and campground are administered by the Hiawatha First Nation. At present, the tribe has closed off access while they undertake work on the grounds.

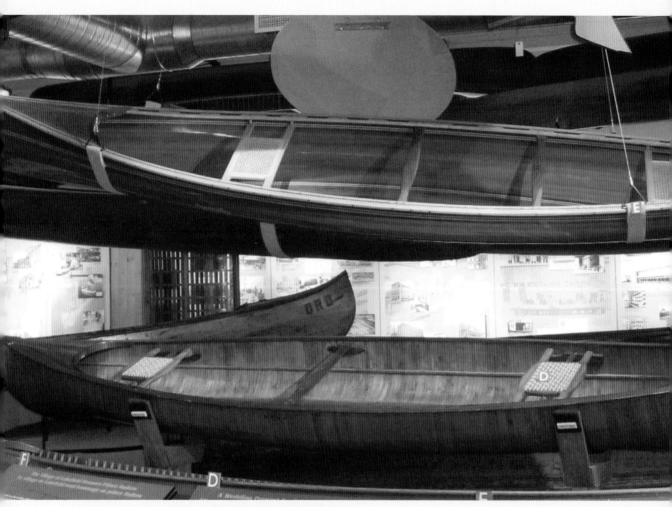

The Royal Canoes in the Canadian Canoe Museum
in Peterborough never had a royal paddler.

③⓪ A History of Paddling
Peterborough's Canadian Canoe Museum

W HAT COULD BE more Canadian than canoes? And what kind of museum is more "Canadian" than a museum that shows them.

The Peterborough Canoe Museum collection began modestly enough in the 1950s as a private collection assembled by Professor Kirk Wipper at Camp Kandalore, near Minden. As the collection grew, a proper place to store it became necessary, and so appeared the Kanawa Canoe Museum.

But the fleet kept expanding and, by the 1990s, a still larger facility was needed. In 1996, the canoes moved into today's Canadian Canoe Museum in Peterborough. Now housing Canada's largest canoe collection, the museum contains more than six hundred canoes and kayaks.

The museum, currently on Monaghan Road, is laid out as a walk through time. The self-guiding tour leads past examples of dugout canoes, some of them several metres long, and dozens of kayaks that hang from the walls. There's also the freighter canoe, which the fur trade era ushered in, with room for twelve voyageurs and their enormous bundles of fur that could weigh as much as 80 kilograms.

Although it is highly unlikely that royalty ever paddled a canoe (that is, until Prince William and his bride, Catherine, did so on their 2011 visit to Canada), three Royal canoes on display include those given to Queen Elizabeth and Prince Philip and to Prince Charles and Princess Diana, both as wedding gifts. A third Royal canoe was given to Prince Andrew by Lakefield College School as a memento of his school days at that institution. Andrew is now the museum's Royal patron.

But perhaps the most intriguing canoe in the collection is a real silver canoe. This was a gift given in the 1840s to Governor George Simpson by a soldier of the Coldstream Guards out of sheer respect for Simpson's inspirational leadership. Crafted by Garrard's of London, it was acquired by the museum from descendants of Simpson's family.

Visitors to the museum are also likely to see artisans at work carving canoe paddles or making blankets and boots or even building a genuine birch bark canoe itself. And don't forget to check out the leather fringed jacket worn by Pierre Trudeau during his carefree paddles in his own canoe.

A new enlarged museum is planned adjacent to the liftlock.

③ BOATS IN THE AIR
The Kirkfield Lift Lock

SNAKING THROUGH THE middle of Ontario is a 368-kilometre water highway, a chain of lakes linked by short streams that connect Lake Ontario on the east and Georgian Bay on the west. Its name is familiar to most Ontarians as the Trent-Severn Waterway. To Ontario's early pioneers it was their lifeline — their only highway. Along its lakes, especially the Kawarthas, they floated out their logs, took their wheat to the mill and travelled for their food.

Although the isolated settlers cried for canals to link the lakes and rivers as early as the 1820s, governments did not act until 1833, when the first lock was constructed at Bobcaygeon. By 1892 a system of locks and canals was nearly complete. But at Peterborough and Kirkfield the level of the water fell so sharply that four costly and water-consuming locks would be required at each location. For a solution, the engineers at Montreal's Dominion Bridge Company, contractor for the canal, looked to an insignificant village in England named Weaver Creek.

There, the locks on the canal were operated by an unusual system known as hydraulic lift locks. Two watertight boxes, each big enough to hold a boat, were balanced hydraulically side by side. As the upper box filled, it became heavier than the lower box and descended, forcing the lower box to the upper level as the lower box opened to release the cargo. This in turn made the lower container lighter and the positions changed. Savings over traditional locks both in time and construction costs, and especially in water usage, were enormous.

Built between 1896 and 1907, two such lift locks groaned into operation at Peterborough and Kirkfield, as Ontario watched in awe. The larger of the two, at Peterborough, looms 20 metres in the air, while that at Kirkfield measures about 17 metres. Each lock contains 1,500 tonnes of water. The two remain the largest in the world, and are the only examples of their kind in North America.

But they were too late to help the settlers. By then the countless little railway companies had created a dense network of railway lines that made water transportation obsolete.

Today, recreation remains the sole function of the Trent Canal and its lift locks. To reflect this emphasis, the whole Trent Canal system is run by the federal department responsible for recreation, Parks Canada. Even for landlubbers the sight of a bucket of boats high in the air has become a tourist attraction in its own right. The lock at Kirkfield is accessible by following signs north from Highway 48 in that village, while that in Peterborough is found by following signs from Highway 28.

"There's a boat over your head." The great lift locks at Peterborough and Kirkfield are the only pair of their kind in North America.

The "Adam and Eve" boulders in Buckhorn have become a local attraction.

32 BUCKHORN

Ontario's Boulder City

UNLIKE ITS MORE famous American cousins (Boulder City, Colorado; Boulder City, Nevada), Buckhorn is an attractive canal-side hamlet scenically situated where the waters of Pigeon Lake flow through the lock of the Trent Canal into those of Buckhorn Lake. It is one of cottage country's more scenic locations, where the brilliant pink rock outcrops of the Canadian Shield seemingly glow in the bright sunshine.

But Buckhorn also offers one of the area's most extensive fields of pink boulders. Most of these globes range in size from a grapefruit to a beach ball. There are a few, however, that stand out for their unusual size; these are the "Adam and Eve" rocks and the "Teetering" rock.

Geologists call rocks such as these "erratics" and have labelled Buckhorn Ontario's "erratic capital." Some twenty thousand years ago, the vast ice sheets that crept across the province wrenched these stones from the surface and carried them perhaps several kilometres, or even just a few metres.

Looming more than 5 metres above a granite floor, the "Adam and Eve" boulders stand like twins in a forest opening on a ridge above the aptly named "Adam and Eve Road." Sitting on a parcel of land donated to the municipality in 1963 by the Charles Jones family and maintained by Buckhorn Sand and Gravel, they have become a minor local attraction. From a small roadside parking area, steps lead to a commemorative plaque that helps visitors appreciate this unusual geological feature.

On the south side of the Buckhorn lock, visible beside Highway 23, stands the "Teetering" rock — so named because the 5-metre-high erratic rests on a base so narrow that it appears ready to tip over at the touch of a hand. The woods and yards throughout the vicinity display fields of smaller boulders.

The disappearing Indian River.

33 THE DISAPPEARING INDIAN RIVER
Warsaw Caves Conservation Area

NOW YOU SEE it; now you don't. After flowing wide and swift through the farmland of Peterborough County, the Indian River simply disappears. From its source in Dummer Lake, just south of Stoney Lake, the river meanders southward until, near the village of Warsaw, it enters an area of limestone and vanishes.

Limestone is noted for its solubility in water. Water not only erodes limestone but can also dissolve it, creating spectacular caves and potholes, known as kettles. But water is also able to seep between the porous layers of limestone and seemingly disappear, and that's just what the Indian River does.

Normally, rivers can flow through an area of limestone and stay in view. The Niagara River does. However, in the vicinity of Warsaw, a large outcrop of porous limestone blocks the flow of the river, and rather than go over or around the rock, the river has found enough cracks to simply flow through it.

From the parking lot in the Warsaw Caves Conservation Area, a path leads past kettles and caves to the river. As you cross the rock fall that blocks the river, you will notice something peculiar — the expanse of fast-flowing water swirls straight toward you and then disappears into the rock beneath your feet. You can hear the strange echoing gurgle of the water as the river makes its way underground. Beyond that point lies the now-dry former river bed, then about a half-kilometre downstream the water bubbles back up to the surface to continue its course to Rice Lake. The trail also leads to a large pothole, a phenomenon created by erosion of the bank when the river was larger.

A popular spot for picnickers, the park also offers a small beach, 15 kilometres of trails, campgrounds and a network of caves for the cautious explorer. But it is the disappearing river that will provide you with the most vivid memory of this peculiar place.

The Warsaw Caves Conservation Area lies north of Warsaw on County Road 4.

The picturesque church, St. Peter's on-the-Rock in Stoney Lake
northeast of Peterborough, is accessible only by boat.

34 THE CHURCH ON THE ROCK

St. Peter's of Stoney Lake

IN 1914, SETTLEMENT around Stoney Lake was still evolving. Settlers had been arriving since the opening of the Buckhorn Road in the 1860s, but it was not until after the turn of the twentieth century that railways and steam ships began bringing vacationers to its rocky shores.

Unlike the other lakes in the Kawartha chain, Stoney Lake lies mostly within the Canadian Shield. Here the granite outcrops create hundreds of islands that are criss-crossed by a maze of channels, crowned by pine trees and laden with hidden shoals. The other lakes in the chain, such as Pigeon Lake and Sturgeon Lake, were created by installing dams in order to facilitate the shipment of logs from the forests to the mills.

While these water bodies are overrun with shoreline cottages, condos and permanent homes, Stoney Lake retains its true northern ambience (although mega-homes are starting to appear on road-accessible shorelines).

But since those early days of self-sustained cottaging, when kerosene lamps and wood stoves were primary fixtures, one church has stood firm. Unlike any other church in

Ontario, St. Peter's on-the-Rock dominates a small rock outcrop in the middle of the lake, accessible only by boat and somewhat ironically situated at the convergence of two channels named Hell's Gate and Devil's Elbow.

Construction of the simple wooden church, which can hold 225 worshippers (and often does), started following a fundraising effort in 1913. From 1896 until then, worshippers had been using various locations around the lake when they finally decided that they needed a permanent place of worship. A local lumberman, F.W. Lillicrap offered one of his islands for the church, while local farmer John Cassidy and his brother undertook the job of building the 24 metre by 45 metre structure.

The first wedding occurred in 1919 and the first funeral in 1931. In 1971, an unusually heavy snow load collapsed the roof, but in short order $3,000 was raised to build a new one. This single-storey white wooden church still perches on its tiny island and still remains accessible by boat only. Highway 28 leads to Stoney Lake northeast from Peterborough. Tours of the lake are available from the dock at the Viamede Resort in Mount Julian.

35 THE TEACHING ROCKS
Peterborough's Petroglyphs

THE HOLLOW ECHO of water gurgling beneath the rocks at their feet made the two young geologists uneasy. There, in the stillness of the forest north of Stoney Lake, they felt as though they had entered a hallowed place. As they swept away the moss from the white crystalline rocks, something caught their eye. Something odd. The surface of the rock was not smooth, as it should have been. Rather, it contained strange etchings, more than nine hundred of them. Although they did not know it on that day in May 1954, the two men had uncovered one of North America's largest and most mysterious Indigenous petroglyphs, the Teaching Rocks, carved as long ago as AD 900.

Like the Christian Bible, the Teaching Rocks tell an Indigenous story of life. As each young male entered adolescence, the elders of the tribe would lead him to the site, guided by the sound of waterfalls and special guide rocks. One lesson at a time, the elders taught the youngsters the meaning of life, as the Ojibway understood it and as the Teaching Rocks revealed it. The medicine wheel told them that life began as the sunrise in the east. Midday represented midlife, and the west meant old age, while the north referred to the afterlife. The spirits portrayed in the carvings taught that man must coexist with nature.

After each lesson finished, the elders would cover the stones with moss to preserve the carvings from erosion. In 1976, the site, sacred to the First Nations, became a provincial park under the cooperative stewardship of the Curve Lake First Nation. A decade later, to protect the surface from the elements, a glass enclosure was added.

The site is located 55 kilometres northeast of Peterborough, near Highway 28. Here, you wonder at the strange shapes and possibly apply your own interpretations. Then you can watch the Ministry of Natural Resources' award-winning 20-minute film, *The Teaching Rocks*. Prepared by Lloyd Walton, the film reveals the mysteries as told and narrated by the Ojibway themselves. As you walk back to your car through the woods, you look around you and see nature through different eyes, those of its original stewards.

The mysteries of the Indigenous etchings in Petroglyphs Provincial Park have been solved in an award-winning movie, *The Teaching Rocks*, produced by Ontario's Ministry of Natural Resources.

This mammoth open pit at Marmora is gradually filling with water.

36 ONTARIO'S BIGGEST POOL
The Big Hole of Marmora

THE HUGE PIT may ultimately become Ontario's biggest pool. For as each year passes the gaping cavity left by the Marmoraton Iron Mine fills with a little more water. Though nobody will be swimming in it any day soon, it makes for one of Ontario's most unusual mining sights.

Mining days in Marmora date back to 1820. An iron magnate named Charles Hayes hacked a trail through the dark forests of central Hastings, hundreds of kilometres from the nearest city of any size. Here he began the construction of a mine, mill and smelter for the production of iron. The community of Marmora quickly grew to a population of two hundred.

For a time, Marmora and its neighbour, Blairton, now a ghost town, were the leading iron producers in the country. Difficulty in transporting the iron out, however, proved their undoing. When canals were completed along the St. Lawrence River, cheaper iron could be imported, and Marmora's iron-mining days were over. Almost.

In 1948 an aeromagnetic survey revealed strange magnetic anomalies east of the town.

Drilling quickly followed, revealing an immense body of ore, 700 metres long and 150 metres deep. The only problem was the 45 metres of limestone that lay on top of it.

In 1951, Bethlehem Steel Company began to haul away the intervening rock, and was soon removing a million tonnes of magnetic ore every year. Canadian National Railway trains carried it to the company's plant in Lackawanna, New York, where it was concentrated and pelletized. By the late 1970s the ore supply was exhausted, leaving a massive circular pit a third of a kilometre across and fully 200 metres deep.

During the mine's operation, a viewing area was provided so that the public could watch the monster trucks grind up out of the gaping hole, loaded with ore. Although the mine no longer operates, the viewing area reveals the emerging lake. The road to the viewing area leads south of Highway 7, just 1.4 kilometres east of the traffic lights in Marmora. Marmora's original iron smelter site is now marked by a plaque in a small park near the downtown area.

37 GHOSTS OF THE GOLD FIELDS

Ontario's Eldorado

THE WORDS "GOLD rush" conjure images of Barkerville, B.C., or the Klondike, with their boom-town buildings and barroom brawls. They scarcely evoke thoughts of southern Ontario, in particular the rugged hills north of Belleville.

Yet that is exactly where Ontario's first gold rush took place. It all began in 1866 when court clerk and part-time prospector Marcus Powell discovered a gold-laden cave on the farm of John Richardson. One nugget, he boasted, was the size of a butternut.

Once word got out, the rush was on. Grizzled gold seekers streamed in from as far away as the Cariboo Goldfields in British Columbia. And in the centre of the gold field, the boom town of Eldorado suddenly appeared. A shanty town of eighty buildings on muddy streets, it was as rough and tumble as any of its western counterparts. When sceptical prospectors, led by the notorious Cariboo Cameron, threatened to tear apart some of the mine buildings, twenty-five mounted police were quickly dispatched to keep order.

But they didn't need to stay long, for the gold rush was short-lived. Because the gold was chemically fixed to the parent rock, and impossible to mill using existing techniques, the only profit was through fraud. Disillusioned investors salted the claims with imported gold specimens and sold them to unsuspecting greenhorns.

Finally, about the turn of the century, a new milling process allowed extraction to begin and the overgrown mines sprang back to life. A few mills were erected, and the Central Ontario Railway added a simple wooden station. But even their second life was short, for the gold deposits were smaller than was first thought. After a few years of sputtering activity, the mines fell silent and Eldorado became a ghost town.

Hotels, former stores and even a few of the tiny miners' cabins dot the once-busy network of streets. Of the eighty or so original buildings, only two dozen survive, many with a decidedly boom-town air about them. The structures straddle a 1-kilometre section of Highway 62, a dozen kilometres north of Madoc. Here, a blue historic plaque commemorates Ontario's earliest golden boom town. But high up in the hills above the town, the roofless ruins of the early mills still lie, overgrown and uncelebrated.

Eldorado was the site of Ontario's first gold rush.

38 CANADA'S GIBRALTAR

Bon Echo Rock

GLOWING GOLD AND red in the rays of the evening sunset, and framed by pine and birch trees, Bon Echo Rock is a ready-made subject for a painting or a photograph. Rising from a geological fault line for 1.6 kilometres along Mazinaw Lake, this 91-metre cliff has acquired the nickname "Canada's Gibraltar."

Its appeal dates back a long time. For centuries, Indigenous canoeists paused at the foot of the sheer rock face and, using ochre and bear grease, painted their impression of the life they lived and the creatures they revered. These birds, mammals and even human figures are still portrayed in what is considered Ontario's largest-known collection of pictographs.

The place also appealed to Flora MacDonald Denison. In 1910, Denison, one of Ontario's earliest women's-rights advocates, bought the Bon Echo Inn. She transformed the resort into a retreat for Canadian artists and formed the Walt Whitman Club of Bon Echo. For many years the haven drew such artists as Group of Seven painter Frank Johnston, who sketched the cover of Denison's literary magazine, the *Sunset of Bon Echo*.

In 1919, Flora Denison added what has become the rock's most unusual feature — a tribute to poet Walt Whitman carved into the rock face. In letters a foot high are the words from his poem "Leaves of Grass."

My foothold is tendon'd and mortised in granite
I laugh at what you call dissolution,
and I know amplitude of time.

The tribute is visible only from the water and is just north of the narrows that divide Upper and Lower Mazinaw Lake.

Bon Echo Provincial Park was created in 1959 after Flora Denison's son Merrill, English Canada's first important twentieth-century playwright, turned the site over to the Ontario government. It is eastern Ontario's largest provincial park.

Casual campers can drive to one of the more than five hundred campsites, while those seeking seclusion can canoe or hike to more remote locations. While rock climbers scale or rappel the sheer granite face, the more passive among us are content to simply stand at the narrows and paint, take photographs or just try out the echo of Canada's Gibraltar.

The park lies on Highway 41, about 40 kilometres north of Highway 7 at Kaladar.

The remarkable Bon Echo Rock has been dubbed "Canada's Gibraltar."

Near Collingwood, one of the castles of the cuesta lies in ruin. **See pages 88–89.**

SOUTHWESTERN ONTARIO

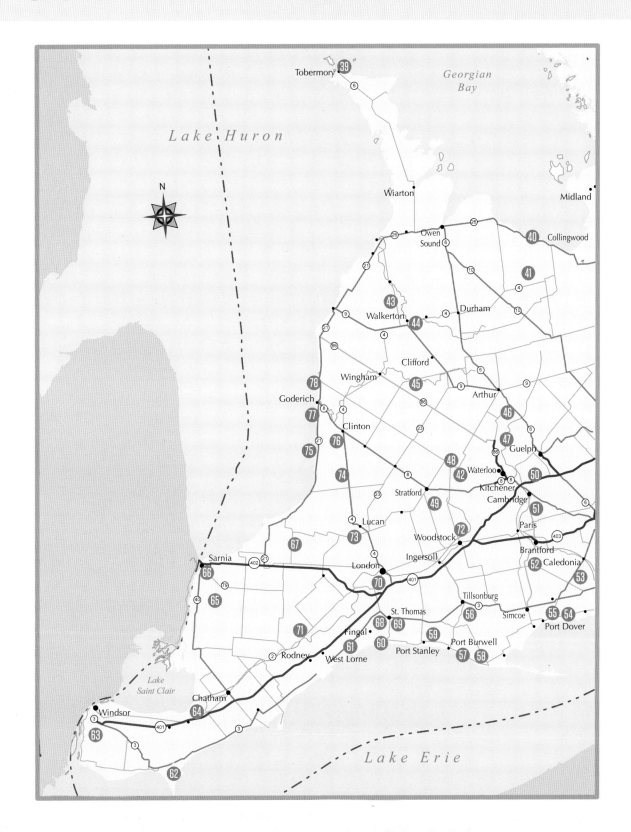

39 THE MAGICAL CYPRUS LAKE GROTTO

Bruce Peninsula

THE TIMELESS AND irresistible forces of nature sometimes create magical landscapes. Few people enter a cave to go diving. Yet within the boundaries of one of Ontario's newest national parks, the Bruce Peninsula National Park, cave swimmers can dive into waters 12 metres deep. The grotto, at 20 metres long, ranges in width from 9 to 12 metres and looks out onto a small cove surrounded by rugged grey cliffs and a beach of broken boulders. Its isolation, its rugged beauty and the tranquility of a turquoise blue lagoon, make the setting almost magical.

For tens of thousands of years, the waves of Georgian Bay relentlessly pounded away at the limestone cliffs of the Bruce Peninsula. Deep inside, rainwater crept through cracks in the limestone to dissolve the rock from within. The result is a shoreline of cliffs, caves, the unusual rock pillars known as "flowerpots" and the Cyprus Lake Grotto. This outstanding assembly of unusual natural features, along with many rare species of flora and fauna, has long made the peninsula a popular destination for hikers and nature lovers. Overseeing the wide bay at the village of Lion's Head lurks just that, the profile of a lion's head protruding from the face of the escarpment across the bay. Over the years, erosion has altered its rocky face.

Over the years, however, the lack of public land has hindered access for most. To remedy this, Parks Canada created a new national park to allow Canadians to experience one of their nation's great natural wonders. Local politics and hostility, however, prevented the park from taking in the entire northern peninsula. As a result, Bruce Peninsula National Park consists of three unconnected segments. The Fathom Five segment is set aside for divers to explore the underwater caves and shipwrecks. Flowerpot Island contains the best examples of these towering limestone pillars, while the Cypress Lake segment contains the grotto and shoreline.

Beside the grotto, trails lead to overhanging cliffs, underground passages and natural caves. The park is located on Highway 6 between Wiarton and Tobermory.

Limestone pillars known as "flowerpots" in Bruce Peninsula National Park.

40 CASTLES OF THE CUESTA
From Mansions to Ruins

Running from Queenston in the Niagara Peninsula to Tobermory some 400 kilometres to the north, the mighty Niagara Escarpment has been made a UNESCO world biosphere reserve. The escarpment's craggy cliffs are home to an assortment of rare flora and fauna as well as countless waterfalls and stunning views. Many of its water power sites grew into bustling mill towns like Belfountain and Cataract. Its splendid heights attracted wealthy homeowners who built grand castles.

Sitting atop Spirit Rock, overlooking the Georgian Bay port of Wiarton, is the Corran. This grand stone mansion was built by Alexander McNeill in 1881. The seventeen-room castle was decorated with oriental carvings, old weaponry and tapestries. Gardens, lawns and orchards covered its grounds. McNeill named the mansion after his childhood home in Ireland. Corran means "point of land running into the sea."

After McNeill's death the home fell to his son Malcolm, who showed little interest in keeping the property up and sold it in 1960 to a seasonal occupant. Ripe for vandalism, the Corran was set on fire and gutted. Today the haunting stone shell is protected by the local conservation authority.

And if "haunted" is what you are looking for, there is also the sprawling ruin of the Hermitage tucked into the escarpment's Dundas Valley near historic Ancaster. This stone mansion was built in 1830 by the Reverend George Sheed. After changing hands several times, the Hermitage became a hotel in the 1880s. However, fires in 1910 and again in 1934 left the fine buildings a ruined skeleton. Like the Corran, the Hermitage is protected by a conservation authority. The ghost of a jilted lover who hanged himself in the nearby gatehouse is said to haunt the place. The conservation area lies on Mineral Springs Road, west of Hamilton.

A castle that no one protects and that continues to crumble is Osler Castle, high in the Blue Mountains near the town of Collingwood. Built in 1893 by Britton Bath Osler, the castle was intended as a retreat for Osler's wife who, in the smoky city, suffered from asthma. She died shortly after the castle opened to great fanfare, and Osler himself soon followed her. Over the last century, the castle has stood — a lost and forgotten ruin. Its stone walls still stretch above the overgrown meadow around it. The castle can be reached by a side trail running from the Bruce Trail, north of Simcoe County Road 19.

Above: The Corran ruin overlooks the Niagara Escarpment near Wiarton.

Top: The Hermitage, a ruin near Ancaster, is said to be haunted by a jilted lover.

Left: Osler Castle is a lost ruin high in the Blue Mountains near Collingwood.

89

41 THE HOLE IN THE HILL

The Strange Story of the Eugenia Arches

DRY MOST OF the year, and unknown to most Ontario travellers, Eugenia Falls in the Beaver Valley has been the site of some strange activities. In the 1850s, a case of mistaken identity led to a short-lived gold rush. Mistaking the shiny lustre of iron pyrite for gold, a pair of hunters sparked a flurry of digging and panning until the shine proved to be only fool's gold.

The next venture was more practical. In the 1870s, William Hogg from Hogg's Hollow, just north of Toronto, bought land adjacent to the falls and built a small electric plant to provide power to a few local communities. Buoyed by his success, Hogg went back to Toronto to try to sell city officials his power for their expanding streetcar system; however, the Adam Beck plant at Niagara Falls was closer and more reliable, so Toronto's politicians sent a dejected Hogg back to Eugenia.

In 1903 a group of Toronto businessmen formed the Georgian Bay Power Company and tried once again to capitalize on the questionable power potential of the falls. To maximize the drop, they excavated a tunnel through the hill beside the falls to the bottom of the valley far below. They began digging the tunnel in 1906, but unexpected problems with quicksand pushed the cost to over $1 million. Still, by 1907 the tunnel

was finished. At 264 metres long, 2.7 metres high and 2.6 metres wide, it was big enough to drive a buggy through. And someone did just that.

Perhaps it was pride of workmanship, but the distinguishing features of the tunnel were the beautiful stone arches at either end, described by some as Roman in appearance. The plant never did operate, and the tunnel remained dry. Instead, a dam was built at Eugenia Lake itself, from which an even greater and more reliable fall of water could supply a larger plant built further down the Beaver Valley. For many years the wooden flumes remained a landmark in the Beaver Valley, but they have since been removed.

Although the tunnels themselves have long collapsed, the arches have withstood weathering and erosion. They are located in the Eugenia Falls Conservation Area, in the village of Eugenia, which lies on Grey County Road 13. The larger and more complete of the two arches stands near the brink of the falls on the opposite side of the river from the path and parking lot. (For safety reasons, the park authority discourages visitors from crossing the river above the falls.) The second arch, near the base of the hill, has collapsed and can be found only after a long and steep hike and a bit of luck.

The entrance to the long-lost tunnel at Eugenia.

42 SILENT VALLEY

A Gentle Gorge with Secrets to Share

ONTARIO'S NIAGARA ESCARPMENT is composed of spectacular valleys and gorges. Most are well known, but then there is Silent Valley which leads cavers deep into darkened tunnels and caverns.

Far from any travelled road, this gentle gully, located 15 kilometres southeast of Owen Sound, has many secrets to share for those fortunate enough to visit. Along its 6-plus kilometres of trails, hikers will discover rare fossils and rock formations, caves and caverns, the remains of an early pioneer homestead and the remains of a mysterious plane crash.

It was sometime after 1860 that John Wilson and his family took up land in the valley, built a cabin and a large barn. They excavated a deep well and lined it with stones. At 7 metres deep, the well leaves one in awe of the industrious and inventive skills that Ontario's early pioneers used to conquer the hardships of the day.

The oddest secret of the woods, however, is the wreckage of a plane which disappeared on September 26, 1970. Pilot John Lassen boarded the Cessna 205 aircraft with his wife and two other passengers and took off from Toronto for a trip to Griffen Island near Owen Sound. At 3:30 a severe thunderstorm moved into the area and by 3:40 Lassen radioed that he was trouble. Minutes later he went silent. It was not until 2014 that the scattered remnants of his doomed flight were located in the woods of Silent Valley. Investigators have concluded that the storm was so violent that it tore his aircraft apart in mid-flight. The sad remnants are still visible, now roughly re-assembled close to where the doomed flyers plunged to the ground.

Silent Valley and its mysteries lie along side trails that run from the main Bruce Trail. There are also trails from the end of Concession Road 2, a short drive north of County Road 18 and about 8 kilometres east of Highway 10/6 just south of Owen Sound.

The book *Silent Valley* by Ron Savage provides an excellent guide.

Aircraft Disaster

On September. 26, 1970 the pilot and passengers of this Cessna 205 were en route from Toronto Pearson International Airport to Griffith Island. At about 3:30 pm that day they ran into a violent thunderstorm. The storm was so severe that the plane began to disintegrate in mid air. The plane crashed at this site resulting in the tragic deaths of all four occupants of the plane.

This property was purchased on June 3, 2013 with donations from BTC supporters

The Bruce Trail Needs Your Support
Become a Member • Volunteer • Donate

The remains of the doomed Cessna 205 lie in the underbrush of Silent Valley.

A lookout point on Schmidt Lake in
the massive Greenock Swamp.

Right: Few roads penetrate the dense
and historic Greenock Swamp.

43 OF LOGGING AND MOONSHINE

Secrets of the Greenock Swamp

THE GREENOCK SWAMP is Ontario's last great wetland. This 8,000-hectare area of impenetrable maples, ferns and muck was once more than seven times its present size and represented the last tract of unsurveyed land in pioneer Ontario.

Although they are now gone, tall, straight white pines grew thick across the swamp, the very species the British navy so zealously sought after. But the swamp would not make life easy for the loggers. During winter — the only time the swamp could be entered — the loggers lived in three camps. To solve the problem of getting the logs out, Henry Cargill, a local lumberman, cut several canals through the dense undergrowth, along which the logs were floated to his busy mills in the nearby town of Cargill. Following the elder Cargill's death in 1903, his son W.D. took over and built a miniature rail line to haul out the remaining pine.

By the 1920s, the logging was finished, but the Prohibition era was in full swing. What better place to establish illicit moonshine stills than the dark interior of a vast, dense swamp. That era has come back with a guided swamp tour called Bootlegging Lore of the Great Swamp.

Considered one of the largest wetlands in Ontario, the Greenock Swamp consists of vast tracts of cedar, stands of silver maple, thickets, fens and bogs. The oval-shaped marsh includes ten lakes and a few "islands."

More than half the swamp is owned by the Saugeen Valley Conservation Authority, which is laying out a boardwalk and trails. These will allow visitors and scientists to finally get a close look at a stunning example of one of Ontario's vanishing natural heritage landscapes — its great swamps.

The Conservation Authority has already laid out 5.5 km of trails through a portion of the swamp and provides a small parking area beside Schmidt Lake Road. A short, 0.3-km walk from the parking area leads to a small viewing deck overlooking the lake.

Start your visit in Cargill at the Greenock Swamp Visitor Centre Museum and Bookstore in Henry Cargill's home village. Displays include historic photos and stories of Cargill and his logging enterprise. The museum is also the place to inquire about swamp tours.

From Cargill, proceed south to Concession 8 and then turn west. The road becomes Schmidt Lake Road and leads to the parking area and lookout.

Cargill lies 14.5 km north of Walkerton, and west of County Road 3.

The Greenock Swamp lies north of Highway 9, about 20 kilometres west of Walkerton. It is accessed by Concession Road 6 between County Roads 1 and 23.

And you shall be
like a watered garden,
like a spring of water
whose waters fail not.
Isaiah 58:11

DEDICATED TO THE INDOMITABLE SPIRIT
OF THE PEOPLE OF WALKERTON.
TO ALL WHO SUFFERED
AND THOSE WHO DIED.

Unveiled by Her Excellency
the Rt. Hon. Adrienne Clarkson C.C., C.M.M., C.D.
Governor General of Canada
June 16, 2001

Walkerton's memorial fountain recalls the tragedy of the tainted water that killed seven residents and hospitalized much of the farming town's population.

44 DEATH FROM THE TAP
Walkerton's Memorial of Tragedy

MAY 12, 2000, was a torrential spring day. Heavy rains poured down on the cattle farms that surround the Bruce County town of Walkerton. As the raindrops joined into trickles and then into streams, the water washed over the cow droppings and plunged into the town's water wells. Normally, the treatment applied to drinking water would render the polluted water harmless.

Five days later, town residents began to suffer wrenching cramps, fever and bloody diarrhea. Within a week they began to die. Two weeks after the deluge, more than 150 people were in hospital and another 500 were sick. By the time the epidemic was over, seven people had died and 2,300 taken ill.

Taking much of the blame for the disaster was the controversial government of Premier Mike Harris, whose policy had been to cut or privatize many services, including the regulation of municipal water quality and the enforcement of safe-water guidelines. But the main culprits were the town's own water-management staff, who had failed to use the proper doses of chlorine and routinely neglected to monitor the quality of the water pouring from the town's taps.

The tragedy sparked an extensive commission of inquiry headed by Justice Dennis O'Connor, a book, a CBC news special and construction of a memorial.

When the epidemic struck, the town was in the process of creating a heritage garden dedicated to the community's history. Following the deaths, Harry Jongerden, head gardener for the popular Stratford Festival, expanded the design to incorporate a water memorial dedicated to the victims. Donations poured in until $140,000 had been raised; volunteers from the town and several surrounding communities offered their labour. Seven heritage plaques now line a path that winds past the gardens and leads to a commemorative fountain with a memorial plaque that reads, "Dedicated to the indomitable spirit of the people of Walkerton, to all who suffered and those who died."

On June 16, 2001, a year after the deadly outbreak, Canada's then governor general, Adrienne Clarkson, stepped before a crowd of more than one thousand people and praised the community "for putting on a brave face in the throes of heartache and pain" and for their determination to look to the future.

The memorial garden lies at the south end of Walkerton near the corner of First Street and Yonge.

45 WROXETER

A "Former Ghost Town" Brought Back to Life

IN WHAT MUST be Ontario's most unusual village entrance sign, that at Wroxeter announces that you are about to enter a "former ghost town."

That unusual distinction arose from an entry in a much earlier book by this author, entitled *Ghost Towns of Ontario*. The inclusion related to the main street of this leafy riverside village, where fifteen of the eighteen business establishments were at that time boarded up.

In an era when main streets grew around the water power of a nearby stream and when transportation between such communities was slow and muddy, shops catering to every need abounded. Hotels, general stores, harness makers, butchers and bakers all operated out of separate establishments. Wroxeter was no exception and, by 1874, twenty businesses flourished along the main street. Industries included four mills and a furniture factory. An influx of seasonal workers briefly gave the settlement the population it needed to become an incorporated village.

But thanks to the water power supplied by the Maitland River, other villages began to grow as well — places like Fordwich, Gorrie and, especially, Wingham, all enjoying a location on the Toronto, Grey & Bruce Railway. Then, with the shift of grain-growing to western Canada and the closing of the rail lines, many villages declined. The auto age and improved roads shifted business to Wingham, and the stores and businesses on Wroxeter's main streets closed one by one, until by the 1980s nearly all were shuttered.

But Wroxeter, despite the spectral appearance of the commercial core, was no ghost town — as the three hundred or so residents can attest. The dubious exposure provided the impetus to greatly improve not just the main street, but the river area as well. And to celebrate its revitalized heritage, the community inaugurated a "ghost town" hoedown.

Wroxeter is still pretty quiet, and most residents still go to Wingham to shop. But today, the community is true to its roadside sign, which proudly declares that it is truly now a *former* ghost town.

After being included in a book about ghost towns, the residents of this western Ontario town reclaimed their community, proclaiming it a "former" ghost town.

46 THE SUDDEN SPLENDOUR OF THE ELORA GORGE

A Canyon in Farmland

SUDDENLY AND UNEXPECTEDLY, in the flat farmlands northwest of Guelph, there appears a crack. No ordinary crack, the Elora Gorge is a canyon 2 kilometres long and more than 20 metres deep — a wonderland of hanging gardens, caves, caverns, dry valleys and odd-looking rock formations.

The gorge represents the outcropping of a dolostone formation known by geologists as the Guelph Formation, rich in fossils and reefs, and four hundred million years old. When the glaciers left the area about twenty thousand years ago, the waters began to wear down the rock until a long gorge took shape. The remnant of that post-glacial torrent is today's Grand River.

The various shapes and formations found in the gorge have fanciful names. Dividing the river into a foaming waterfall, the Tooth of Time is formed by the remains of an eroded ledge. Close by, the Lovers' Leap promontory juts into the fork formed by Irwin Creek and the Grand River. Farther downstream, the waters of a long-vanished river that plunged over the edge of the cliff carved a series of rock columns that resemble castle ramparts. An extinct waterfall has carved out a 40-metre-wide amphitheatre known as the Devil's Punch Bowl.

The Cascade is the filmy plunge of a small creek into the gully. Across from it the Hanging Garden shows off various mosses and ferns drooping from an overhanging cliff. Several caves along the riverbank make unusual swimming holes, and the Hole in the Wall provides passage for a trail right through the rock itself.

But hidden under the nearby farmlands there also lies an earlier, pre-glacial gorge, which parallels today's defile. While the existence of this mystery gorge is revealed only through the drilling of local wells, it can be seen near Fergus where the route of the earlier gorge crosses that of the newer one, causing the rocky wall of today's gorge to vanish at that point.

The strange beauty and the appeal of the rushing river have turned the gorge into a popular park. Trails follow both riverbanks and wind along the bottom of the gorge. Inner tubes are rented to those who wish to cool off on a hot summer day by floating downstream and viewing the gorge in its entirety and without obstruction.

The Elora Gorge Conservation Area, which also has campgrounds, is a short distance southwest of the popular village of Elora.

This unexpected crack in flat farmland contains many unusual rock formations.

47 WEST MONTROSE
The Last Covered Bridge

THE CLATTER OF hoofbeats and the groaning of a wagon wheel echo among the wooden rafters of the old covered bridge. A scene for a western movie? No, an everyday event at West Montrose, 15 kilometres north of Waterloo, just off Regional Road 22.

The area is heavily populated by the Old Order, "horse-and-buggy" Mennonites, and these black-garbed traditionalists frequently guide their horse-drawn wagons or buggies through what is Ontario's last covered bridge.

In an era when wood was less expensive and commonly used for bridge construction, walls and roofs were often added to prevent the deterioration caused by rain and heavy snow. Despite the utility and popularity of this style in eastern Canada, Ontario's British army road builders steered clear of it, and fewer than a dozen such bridges were built in this province. The one at West Montrose is the only survivor.

Built in 1881 by a Mennonite barn builder named John Baer, it remained the Grand River's only crossing in the area until 1960, when a new concrete structure was completed less than a kilometre away. The bridge measures 60 metres long, and was illuminated by

Of Ontario's historic covered bridges, the one at West Montrose
on the Grand River is the only survivor.

twenty shuttered windows and coal-oil lanterns, later replaced by electric lights. A feature rarely found on other covered bridges is the 1.8-metre overhang above each entrance.

To allow continued use of the historic structure, truss reinforcements have been added to the inside, the roof has been re-shingled and the substructure replaced. To complement this postcard scene, the village of West Montrose, huddled around the western approach to the bridge, has retained many of its simple nineteenth-century buildings. A part of pioneer Ontario can be both seen and heard at the West Montrose covered bridge.

The Grand River boasts many heritage bridges along its 300-kilometre course. In fact, the river contains Ontario's greatest concentration of historic bowstring bridges, with graceful arches above the road. The longest is the eight-arch bridge in Caledonia, while six-arch structures span the river in Freeport and Bridgeport.

48 THE CRYPTIC GRAVESTONE

Rushes Cemetery

VISITORS TO THE Rushes pioneer cemetery, west of Kitchener, have long scratched their heads in puzzlement at the mass of letters that cover the strange grave marker. While the size of the stone and the graphic etched on it are not unlike those found on thousands of other nineteenth-century grave markers, the message definitely is not. For covering the entire face of the gravestone is a mass of 225 letters and numbers with no apparent order or sense. Yet the message is in there, if you can figure it out.

Rushes Cemetery is an ordinary-looking pioneer cemetery. Situated atop a hill, the cemetery is neatly trimmed and surrounded by rolling farmland. Cars rush past on the busy road, while an occasional Mennonite buggy creaks by at a more leisurely pace. But it is in the far corner of Rushes cemetery that the now famous "Bean marker," with its cryptic inscription, attracts the most attention.

Samuel Bean was born in 1838 in Wilmot Township, and became an Evangelist minister as well as a medical doctor. Local legend claims he also read the entire Bible sixty-five times. In 1865 he married Henrietta Furry, who died only seven months later. His second marriage, to Susanna Clegg, didn't last much longer. To commemorate their passing, Bean devised what may be one of Ontario's most mystifying and most-visited grave markers, with what at first glance is a nonsensical and random arrangement of letters that totally cover the front of the marker.

While the dedication may appear impossible to decipher, by determining where to start the message and the order in which the words are spelled, the message is suddenly and plainly revealed. The original grave marker had deteriorated to the point where the letters became unreadable. But to help keep alive this interesting piece of local lore, heritage proponents in 1982 erected a duplicate stone beside the original.

The grave marker itself is illustrated here, and the reader is invited to try and solve the puzzle. Clue: don't start at either the top or the bottom. Rather, begin at the seventh column from the left, and at the seventh letter from the top. The answer is at the back of this book.

Rushes cemetery is located 3 kilometres north of the attractive country village of Wellesley, on Waterloo Regional Road 5.

Can you solve the message on this odd grave marker? *See page 360 for the answer.*

GONE HOME

BEAN

HENRIETTA   SUSANNA

S V W E T B S A 15 S T M O R E
E I R T E 2 Y D & H N S 10 H E
M I A D 17 & S H T N O A R M T
N A Y D H D N E F S M Y E H E
E N S O W M A B E O 2 D 26 T T
E V & E I R O M I F S G E E E
H R S 27 D I I E T W R 7 A O M
D A U H T A N M I S A 86 B. T
H T S E S M E R E T E L I E S.
Y E A I P H N I T A Y R I P M
E W N 8 6 5 A G E D 23 A P E L
E R N H S N W F W O I D T D H
I G A I 2 D I E H D E 27 H G O
T F R M O B T R N W N E V N A
F S O G D U A E O I H A E M Y

READER MEET US IN HEAVEN

49 3-D-CEPTION

The Trompe l'Oeil Murals of Castle Kilbride

LIKE MOST NINETEENTH-CENTURY mansions, Castle Kilbride is a monument to the excesses of the Industrial Age. Born to a Scottish weaver, James Livingston arrived in Canada in 1854 at the age of sixteen, where he worked first on a farm, then in a flax mill. In 1864, along with his brother, he rented a flax mill in the village of Wellesley. Within just three years the pair had built their own flax mill in Baden, adding a linseed-oil mill to their operation. Linseed oil was a key ingredient in paint and soap, and in high demand in Ontario's booming cities.

In 1877, Livingston, known as the "Flax and Oil King of Canada," decided to build his "castle." Set back from the road, surrounded by a wrought-iron fence and topped with an Italianate belvedere, Castle Kilbride quickly became a local landmark.

The elegance was evident on the exterior, but it was the inside that drew the most attention. Created by a local artist who signed his name as "Schasstein," three-dimensional murals, known by the French term trompe l'oeil, were painted on the mansion's walls and many of its ceilings. In the main hall, Schasstein created columns, statues and vases, all seemingly three-dimensional. More await in the library, where 3-D tassels surround the ceiling, framing cornices, mouldings and more murals.

In 1988, the castle and its grounds were sold to a developer and its contents auctioned. But as so often happens in small communities, the local residents were not about to let their most prominent building disappear. In 1993, the Township of Wilmot bought the property and began restoration. By holding a celebrity auction, they were able to recover many of the original contents, including an old toy collection. New municipal offices were added to the back of the building, and the interior was brought up to museum standards. A gift shop and washrooms were also added (although the original two-hole brick outhouse still stands outside).

Thanks largely to the remarkable murals, Parks Canada has declared the building a National Historic Site.

The castle is located on Regional Road 1. Baden lies on Regional Road 1, 18 kilometres west of Kitchener.

Castle Kilbride is a Baden landmark.

50 KITCHENER'S PIONEER TOWER
Cultural Cooperation

THE KITCHENER AREA is Ontario's capital of unusual towers. Besides the rustic sheave tower near Blair, Kitchener has the stone pioneer tower.

Dominating the Grand River Valley from one of its loftiest banks, the tower was built to commemorate Ontario's first inland pioneers. French settlements had existed along the Detroit River and United Empire Loyalists had settled along the shores of Lake Ontario and Lake Erie. Joseph Schoerg and Samuel Betzner arrived in 1800 and were the vanguard of Ontario's inland pioneers.

By 1805, the German Company had purchased over 24,000 hectares of land along the Grand River from the Mohawks, who had received it as a reward for their service to the British during the American Revolution. Soon, columns of Conestoga wagons were lumbering northward carrying Pennsylvania Dutch and Mennonite settlers. These savvy farmers, with their commitment to farming as a divinely ordained way of life, established one of Ontario's most prolific agricultural communities.

The idea for the tower came more than a century later. To help heal the nationalist wounds caused by the First World War, and to celebrate the German origins of the Waterloo area, William Breithaupt promoted the idea of a pioneer memorial tower.

Designed by Toronto architect W. A. Langton, the tower was officially opened August 28, 1926, and was immediately declared a National Historic Site. The 22-metre-high tower is topped with a copper spire of Swiss influence and a weather vane that commemorates the arrival of the colonists in their Conestoga wagons. The body of the tower is faced with fieldstones to reflect the hardships in clearing the fields. Visitors enter through a doorway of Indiana limestone and climb to an eight-sided observation deck. In 1939, concerned over declining maintenance, the Historic Sites Branch took over the tower and upgraded the grounds, planting grass and adding a parking area.

Farm buildings of the pioneering Betzner and Schoerg families still stand nearby. In the 0.5-hectare park beside the tower, their family graves are the oldest non-Indigenous inland burial grounds in Ontario. The tower is not staffed and has no admission charge. From King Street, follow Deer Ridge Road west to Lookout Lane, which leads to the tower, as well as Kuntz Park, and Schoerg Park. From the tower, a walking trail follows the bank of the river.

This stone tower commemorates the heritage of the German pioneers in the Waterloo region.

51 LAST OF A KIND

Blair's Sheave Tower

THE WOODEN TOWER stands in the middle of the woods near the historic community of Blair, looking like a miniature mining headframe. But this tapering wooden structure, which rises four storeys above a rushing stream, is a rare relic of pioneer Ontario — a sheave tower.

Sheave towers were accessories to grist mills. They used the force of the river to turn a sheave, or grooved wheel, and were connected by a pulley to a water-powered grist mill. A local mill owner named Allan Bowman built the tower at Blair in 1876 to power the nearby Carlisle grist mill. The original mill, a five-storey structure built in 1849, burned in 1928. Following the fire, the power from the sheave tower produced electricity until 1954.

Long a favourite of local artists, photographers and historians, it was partially restored in 1962 by the Waterloo Historical Society. Runoff from nearby housing developments, however, rushed into the creek, where it damaged the foundation and put the building's future at risk.

Blair, however, is one of those heritage-conscious communities. So while the owners of the tower worked to clear the sluiceway of silt, the local council voted, in 1986, to declare it a heritage structure, to help reduce the threat of demolition. In 1994 it was bought, in turn, by the Cambridge chapter of the Architectural Conservancy of Ontario.

Four years later renowned heritage architect Nicholas Hill was hired to restore the crumbling ruin. Hill had been responsible for more than a dozen community heritage plans, as well as restoration of the Kingsville, Ontario, railway station and the University of Guelph's Cruickston Park mansion and grounds.

Because much of the tower's wood had rotted, many original planks required replacing. But in 2000, the restored tower was unveiled to commemorate the village's two hundredth anniversary.

The heritage of Blair goes beyond the sheave tower. The village began life as a milling centre on Blair Creek, close to the Grand River, where today, the urban sprawl from Cambridge creeps ever closer. Yet the historic integrity of Blair continues to survive, as hotels, homes, mills and cemeteries that date from the early days of settlement have been retained. But of all the saved and restored historic buildings, the sheave tower, the only one of its kind left in Ontario, remains the most unusual.

The tower lies in the woods on Mill Lane, west of Blair Road.

Blair's strange sheave tower resembles a miniature mining headframe.

52 FROM NUISANCE TO BEAUTY

The Paris Plains Stone Church

ONTARIO'S CITIES AND countryside contain many magnificent stone buildings, from the huge blocks of red sandstone that form the Queens Park legislative buildings and the old city hall, both in Toronto, to the rubble stone that hardened pioneers gathered from the fields to make the handsome St. Margaret's Church on the Bruce Peninsula. But no stone construction technique is as distinctive or as delightful as the neat rows of cobblestones on the Paris Plains Church near the intersection of Brant County roads 24A and 28, north of Paris, Ontario.

When Levi Boughton migrated from Rochester, New York, to Paris in the late 1840s, he brought with him a construction technique that few Upper Canadians had ever before seen. Originally devised by the ancient Romans during their occupation of England, it was a technique that could utilize common fieldstones, the bane of many farmers in the Paris and Brantford area, to create buildings of rare beauty.

The technique involved gathering thousands of field stones, usually dolomite or limestone, that had been relentlessly ground into spheres by the great glaciers and the swirling of their meltwaters. The stones would then be passed through a standard ring to ensure uniformity of shape and size. Then they would be laid in level "courses" to construct the walls of the buildings. The result was walls of incredibly uniform rows of cobblestones, almost as if they had been handmade.

The contractor for the church, and about a dozen other buildings in the town of Paris itself, was Philo Hull. Here, the technique was applied to a church, fences and several houses of different dimensions, making Paris the centre of this style. Later in the century, when brickmaking made construction so much cheaper, Boughton's cobblestone style died completely. Occasionally it is resurrected in individual homes, not because it is cheaper, but because of its rare beauty and grace. But back in Boughton's day, it was an inventive way to turn a nuisance into a thing of beauty.

Paris, Ontario, is noted for its cobblestone architecture, such as this former store.

53 RUTHVEN

A Mansion in a Ghost Town

RUTHVEN PARK IS a "castle" in a real ghost town. The village of Indiana was, throughout much of the nineteenth century, a bustling mill town that grew up around the mills on the Grand River.

As the banks of the Grand River began to fill with settlers, William Hamilton Merritt, chief promoter of the Welland Canal, began to push for a canal that would link the settlements of the Lower Grand River. One of Merritt's contractors, David Thompson, arrived at lock station one and built two grist mills, a carding mill, a lumber mill and a distillery. The town of Indiana was laid out and, at its peak, could claim more than four hundred residents. A short distance away Thompson built a grand mansion, which he called Ruthven Park.

Built of Ohio limestone between 1845 and 1847, the thirty-six-room structure overlooked the river. Four columns soared the full two storeys to mark the main riverside entrance. Inside were two black marble fireplaces and an oval staircase to the second floor. Surrounding the mansion was Thompson's 450-hectare farm.

By the 1870s, the railways had arrived and the canal fell into disuse. The wooden lock gates rotted and the locks filled with debris. Indiana became a ghost town and, by 1900, would count fewer than two dozen inhabitants. But the mansion remained in the family.

In 1995, the federal government declared the building a National Historic Site and the property was deeded by the family to the Lower Grand River Land Trust, which has undertaken not just the restoration of the mansion but also the conservation of the lands around it. Summer students have excavated the ghost town itself and restored the large Catholic cemetery, which over the years had become heavily overgrown. Of the town, only a pair of buildings survives on the now largely vanished grid network of roads.

The Land Trust leads tours through the mansion, which is located on Highway 54 between the towns of Caledonia and Cayuga. Ruthven Park has long been a bird banding location and offers educational opportunities for students to learn about the region's bird species and their habits.

The grand mansion known as Ruthven Park is almost the only remaining structure in the ghost town of Indiana near Cayuga.

Port Dover's "ghost" mausoleum has long been a roadside curiosity.

54 FROM MOTORCYCLES TO MAUSOLEUMS

Port Dover

MANY ARE THE times that the traveller will quickly discern from the window of a car an eye-catching feature. On Highway 6 west of Port Dover, it's a thing of curiosity — for there, on the north side of the road, stands a peculiar structure. Its columns rise above the overgrown field, with no seeming neighbour or sign to explain what it may be.

The sad structure is in fact a lonely mausoleum built by the Port Dover Cemetery Board in the hopes of encouraging some of the area's wealthier residents to consider interring their deceased loved ones in elegant, and costly, surroundings.

But the cost, $225 to $275 per crypt, did not seem worth the expense in 1927. With its four Doric columns, the entrance was grand enough. Even the evocative words in the ad for the facility could not attract any business: "No matter how inclement the weather, the entrance halls of our mausoleum present a beautiful chapel."

But no takers arrived, and the concrete building remained vacant. It did, however, attract the attention of a Toronto filmmaker. It was here in 2008 that Internext Studios chose to film three scenes from its science fiction movie, *Six Reasons Why*, starring Canadian actor Colm Feore.

Port Dover is well known for considerably more than the abandoned mausoleum. Its long sandy beach and fish food restaurants keep the lakeside town busy most of the year. And whenever a Friday the 13th rolls around, so, too, do the motorcycles. That date has become a call to thousands of motorcycle enthusiasts from across Canada and the United States, making Port Dover the site of some of North America's premier motorcycle rallies.

Friday the 13th in Port Dover is noted far and wide for its gathering of bikers.

55 NORMANDALE

Ontario's First Iron-Making Capital

ASK ANYONE WHERE Ontario's iron industry began, and the answer would more than likely be Hamilton. But Hamilton was a relative latecomer to that industry. Instead, pioneers wanted their needs to be close at hand, and for that reason much of Ontario's early iron-making took place near the larger peat bogs. When burned in a furnace, bog ore produces iron, which can then be moulded into such needed items as stoves, plough shares and axes.

One of Ontario's first such iron furnaces began operation on the shore of Lake Erie in a community called Normandale. In 1816, an English ironmaster named John Mason erected a small furnace on the banks of a small creek that flowed into Lake Erie. In 1821, Mason's widow sold the operation to Joseph Van Norman who, along with Hiram Capron and George Tillson, expanded the operation to include a 30-metre-high brick chimney, a water wheel and a pair of bellows.

The town that grew around the operation took its name from Van Norman. At its peak, Normandale could count four hundred residents. But by 1847, with the supply of timber and bog ore depleted, Van Norman moved to Marmora, where he launched another iron-making industry, and Normandale became a ghost town. The small harbour could not sustain larger fishing vessels, and it soon silted in.

But the place wouldn't remain a true ghost town, as cottagers and those preferring a rural lifestyle began to build along the old village streets. Enough remains of old Normandale to warrant a visit. Mill Street still leads past the site of the furnace and is a trail to the beach. At the main intersection of Normandale Road and Main Street, the Union Hotel, built in the 1840s, still stands — now carefully restored. Adjacent to it is the former post office, with its "boom town" facade. Further along the main street is a regency cottage-style stone residence with its cupola and wraparound porch and French doors, built by Van Norman's son, Romaine.

Many other early buildings mix with the newer homes in this historic gully, where the ghosts of the town's early days yet lurk.

The former Union Hotel in the near "ghost town" of Normandale
dates from the town's iron-making days in the early 1800s.

Ontario's only adobe blacksmith shop is preserved as a museum in Sparta.

56 A BIT OF "OLD MEXICO"

Sparta's Adobe Blacksmith Shop

SPARTA'S MAIN STREET offers one of the most eclectic arrays of main street buildings in the province.

Take, for example, the former tinsmith shop. Built around 1840, it displays the unusual board-and-batten method of siding and boasts the false facade of a "boom town" storefront. Beside it stands a house built in the Quaker style of construction by the village smithy, John Ollie.

Clustered around the main intersection are two former hotels — the Sparta House on the southwest corner, which functioned as a temperance hall now home to The Whistle Stop Peddlers and a popular spa, and the Sparta Hotel on the northwest corner. The Sparta Hotel stands two and a half storeys high with a full-length wooden porch. The building, now the Sparta House Tearoom and Restaurant, is nicely refurbished and provides visitors with light meals or, simply, tea.

The old general store occupies the southeast corner, looking much like many of Ontario's traditional stores. It is now home to Sparta Country Candles.

Sparta dates from the exodus of American Quakers, a pacifist sect, who refused to serve in the American army during the War of 1812. In 1813, Quaker Jonathon Doan acquired some 1,200 hectares on a millstream. Naming the place after the village he was forced to flee south of the border, Doan laid out a townsite. Through the 1830s and '40s, it boomed to include mills, stores and churches. Their historic wooden Quaker meeting house, erected in 1865, stands north of the intersection. But after 1875, when the railways reached St. Thomas several miles to the north, Sparta's growth stagnated.

As a result, many of the structures from Sparta's boom times have survived — among them, a blacksmith shop built unlike any other in Ontario. Like homes and stores more commonly found in older neighbourhoods in Mexico, the shop was built of adobe brick — a mixture of clay and straw all trampled in a pit by a team of horses. Constructed in 1827, the shop has walls two feet thick, which remain exposed to view.

Having ceased operation as a blacksmith shop in 1944, the building now houses Ye Olde Forge and Anvil Museum, operated by the Sparta and District Historical Society. Another house opposite was also constructed of abode brick, but those bricks are now covered over by siding.

Today the blacksmith shop and the other village stores have become a popular day-trip destination for residents of nearby cities like London, Kitchener and Hamilton. Sparta lies along County Road 27, about 25 km southeast of St. Thomas.

The wind farm at Port Burwell reflects a drastic change to Ontario's landscape to provide a greener energy source.

57 WAR OF THE WORLDS

Port Burwell's Wind Farm

LURKING HIGH ABOVE the Ontario farm landscape, they resemble the spacecraft that brought the Martian invaders to Earth in H.G. Wells' realistic radio drama, *The War of the Worlds*.

Despite their otherworldly appearance, Ontario's wind turbines are invaders of a different type: they are the leading edge of renewable electricity.

Wind power has been in use for centuries and provided power to grind wheat for the early settlers of Upper and Lower Canada. Farms across the country used windmills to draw all-important water from the ground. Few of these ancestral relics survived, much less remain in use.

In 1994, the province of Alberta was the first in Canada to apply wind power to enhance its power grid. Ontario joined the trend in 2006 with a wind farm north of Sault Ste. Marie. The largest wind farms are those that capture the strong winds that blow across the "Roof of Ontario" near Shelburne, with a capacity of nearly 200 megawatts. The Wolfe Island Wind Farm, a project that turned a once bucolic landscape as viewed from Kingston into a contentious aesthetic dispute, has a capacity of 198 megawatts.

Ontario currently has almost 40 wind farms pumping out more than 5,200 megawatts of electricity into the province's grid. The Erie Shores Wind Farm, in operation since 2006, on Lake Erie may be one of Ontario's smaller farms — the 66 turbines churn out 99 megawatts, enough to power 25,000 households — it offers an information centre located a short distance west of Port Burwell. In fact, by the end of 2019, Ontario had 95 wind farm projects in operation, with a total of more than 2,600 turbines.

Despite their apparent environmental benefits, the massive turbines have invoked considerable controversy. Many argue that the projects form a health hazard and are a danger to migrating birds. But perhaps the most objected aspect is their visual impact on a once scenic landscape since their presence dwarfs farmlands and forests. The newer turbines are up to 200 metres tall with 45-metre blades. In that sense the monsters are indeed aliens to rural Ontario. The 1-hectare site includes seasonal picnic tables, a short trail and an information kiosk. It lies on Brown Road, a few metres north of CR 42.

58 THE BIG SAND PILE
Houghton's Sand Hill

TOWERING MORE THAN 120 metres above the waters of Lake Erie, Ontario's biggest sandbox, the Houghton Sand Hill, stands higher than even the Scarborough Bluffs. As the glaciers of the last great ice age melted northward, a huge lake, four times the size of Lake Erie, formed along the edge of the ice lobe. As the torrents of meltwater raced into the lake, a huge delta took shape. The glaciers melted back still farther, allowing the great lake to drain away, leaving today's Lake Erie and a monster pile of sand. The winds began to blow across the treeless wasteland, and the sand piled into huge dunes that towered above the lake.

Thousands of years later, as settlers took up land in the nearby forests, this geological phenomenon did not go unnoticed. In 1877, the *Atlas of Norfolk County*, normally a conservative and understated tome, gushed uncharacteristically that there was "nothing more astonishing than the immense mounds of pure sand, standing upon the edge of the precipitous cliffs which border the lake."

One of the first to take advantage of the heights was the United States Lake Survey, which placed an 18-metre observatory on the summit. A similar tower on Long Point, and a third across the lake in Pennsylvania, helped map the navigation charts used by sailors to this day.

The sand hill attracted curiosity seekers as well and has been owned by the Alton family and their descendants since 1854. In the 1890s, George Alton, the owner, charged ten cents a visit. A geological oddity was quickly becoming a tourist attraction. But the hill came perilously close to extinction when a glass manufacturer tried to purchase the sand for export to the United States. Alton resisted, and the sand pile was saved.

Then in 1958 a campground was opened. Constant improvements to the unusual grounds have made it one of the more popular privately owned attractions on Lake Erie. From the roadside, the hill looks like an uninspiring grassy mound. A short walk to the top reveals the dizzying height above the lake below. Pure sand from crest to beach, the bluffs display ever-changing layers and shapes.

Sand Hill Park is located 12 kilometres east of Port Burwell on Regional Road 42.

Ontario's biggest "sandbox" towers 120 metres above Lake Erie.

59 LAKE ERIE'S COLD WAR SUBMARINE

HMCS *Ojibwa*

LAKE ERIE'S HERITAGE is decidedly maritime. Numerous little coves evolved into busy fishing ports, many of which are still active. Shipwrecks abound as do marine museums. But the last thing one would expect to find on the Lake Erie shore is a real Cold War submarine.

Launched in 1964 as the HMS *Onyx*, an Oberon-class submarine, the HMCS *Ojibwa* served as a Canadian Cold War sub under the Marine Forces Atlantic until 1997.

Submerged, the *Ojibwa* could attain speeds in excess of 30 kilometres per hour and could remain submerged for fifty-six days. Although it carried twenty-four torpedoes, none was fired in hostile action. Its only confrontation came with a Spanish fishing vessel caught fishing illegally in Canadian waters during what was known as the "Turbot War."

Cramped sleeping quarters could accommodate sixty-five submariners, although when needed crew might sleep in the torpedo room. Crew members would often share sleeping bags even though they might not wash for up to three months at a time. To pass the time, crew would enjoy games of cribbage or chess, or watch movies projected on a sheet. The *Ojibwa* ended its service in 1997 and was decommissioned the following year. Its proposed fate: the scrapyard.

While looking for a tank for its museum display, the Elgin County Military Museum in St. Thomas saw in the sub an opportunity to celebrate the Canadian Navy's 100th anniversary in 2010, and discussions began in 2008 with the Ministry of National Defence to purchase and move the *Ojibwa*. But negotiations dragged on longer than expected (no surprise there), as did the finalizing of techniques required to move the vessel from Halifax — 1,200 nautical miles up the St. Lawrence River and through the locks of the St. Lawrence Seaway and the Welland Canal — without damage to the sub or the locks. Towing was not an option. To solve the problem a floating dry dock was constructed to carry the *Ojibwa* to its resting place in June 2012. Tours began a year later.

Resting on the river bank below Port Burwell's historic wooden lighthouse, the shiny black hulk extends nearly 90 metres long, while the distance from the hull to the top of the conning tower is equivalent to a five-storey building.

Canada has had submarines as far back as 1913, but the *Ojibwa* was the first to be owned by the Canadian Navy, one of five. The Museum of Naval History is open beside the submarine and offers a variety of escorted tours.

An unlikely place to find a Cold War-era Canadian submarine is on the shores of Lake Erie at Port Burwell.

The flag station at Union, still in use, is North America's smallest "Union Station."

60 THE SIZE OF AN OUTHOUSE

The Smallest Union Station

WHAT IS THE size of a two-hole outhouse and attracts tourists from across the continent? The answer is North America's smallest "Union Station." In railway terminology, a union station is one shared by more than one railway company, and more often than not they are large, urban terminals. Therefore, when train travellers think of Union Station, they picture the high-vaulted concourse of Toronto's Union Station, or the grand facade of that in Washington, D.C. They are not likely to envisage the tiny grey-flag station that guards the track of the Port Stanley Terminal Railway. The station's name derives not from its size or its function, but simply from the name of a nearby hamlet, Union.

Not only is it the oldest building on the once-busy line, but the style and the arched windows reveal that railway architects often paid as much attention to the tiny flag stations as they did to the larger and more elegant city stations.

Today's Port Stanley Terminal Railway was resurrected as a labour of love from the near ruins of the pioneering London and Port Stanley Railway. Originally built to carry lumber and farm products from the southwestern farmlands to the wharves at Port Stanley, and to link with the Grand Trunk Railway in London, it eventually became a busy excursion line. Londoners crowded into the coaches at that city's now long-demolished brick-and-stone station to go to the Lake Erie beaches, or to dance to the big bands that played the internationally renowned Stork Club.

Eventually CN took over the line and, after a few years of dwindling traffic and a washout in 1982, closed it. While other stations were demolished, the little flag station at Union was given little thought. When the line was abandoned, Union Station, deteriorating and overgrown, miraculously still stood.

Local rail enthusiasts purchased the line and, after pouring countless hours and money from their own pockets into its repair, restored passenger rides from Port Stanley to a new replica station in downtown St. Thomas. Awaiting the passengers halfway along is the smallest Union Station, restored, repainted and housing old photos and railway memorabilia. Most of the passenger coaches are actually converted cabooses rebuilt into open and closed cars. The five diesel engines built during the 1940s and 1950s were given nicknames like Stanley, Donald and Winnie.

You can board the excursion trains at the larger station in Port Stanley and travel the few miles up the line to Union and St. Thomas, or, if the trains aren't running that day, you can follow the Golf Club Road west to the little station from Highway 4 in Union.

Once pallisaded, these prehistoric earthworks now appear as grassy mounds.

61 THE SOUTHWOLD EARTHWORKS

A Pre-European-Contact Village Site

THE FLATLANDS OF Elgin County stretch along the shores of Lake Erie, yielding some of Ontario's most fertile farmlands. Where the few forests remain, they contain Carolinian flora species. And farming has removed nearly all traces of early habitations. All except the unusual Southwold Earthworks.

Now a National Historic Site, these barely discernible lumps of earth represent a village site occupied by the Attawandaron prior to European contact, an Indigenous group whose territory stretched from Chatham to Niagara Falls. Built about the time that Christopher Columbus was wandering around the Caribbean, the site consists of two circular mounds of earth separated by an apparent moat structure. The mounds represent the double row of palisades that surrounded the village, with gaps to indicate where a stream meandered through the site.

Research concludes that the outer mound is the older of the two. The palisades were built of tree trunks 4 to 5 metres high, driven into the ground and embanked with earth. The inner, or later, palisade consisted of two rows of trunks, indicating perhaps a concern for greater security. The double palisade is the site's most archaeologically significant component. Inside the compound were a number of the traditional longhouses, while fields of maize and squash surrounded the village.

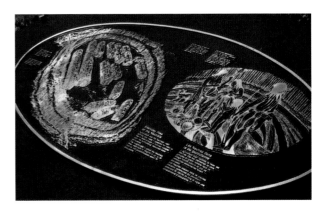

By the time the first Europeans began ploughing the ground, likely during the Thomas Talbot settlements of the 1820s, the tribe had long vanished, possibly having fled the deadly Iroquois incursions of the 1640s. What is most astonishing about the site is that it survived the pioneer period, when homesteaders would not likely have recognized the site for what it was, nor cared. One wonders how many similar heritage treasures were lost to the plough during that time.

Despite its national heritage status, the site is barely developed. The only parking is along a widened shoulder on the road. Informational plaques indicate how the site was arranged, while a grassy pathway leads the quarter-kilometre from the road into the stand of trees where the earthworks can be seen. The Southwold Earthworks are situated just south of Iona on County Road 14, about 3 kilometres south of Highway 3.

62 · POINT PELEE
Where Canada Begins

STAND HERE AND all of Canada is north of you. So, for that matter, is northern California. At 42 degrees north latitude, Point Pelee is the most southerly part of mainland Canada and lies south of much of the continental United States. Such a southern latitude also provides the point with a range of southern vegetation found nowhere else in Canada, vegetation more common, in fact, to the Carolinas. Even prickly pear cactus is found here. Indeed, the rare plant and animal life earned the point its status as one of Canada's first national parks.

But its history goes back far beyond that. Owing to Point Pelee's strategic location, well into Lake Erie and close to American shipping lanes, the British military in the 1790s set the point aside as a naval reserve. That didn't stop a handful of squatters, known as "Pointers," from moving in and starting up fishing and small-time farming.

The sandy soil limited the range of crops, and the point gradually became more popular with hunters and birdwatchers. Then, in 1918, through the efforts of ornithologist Percy Taverner and his bird-lover friend Jack Miner (founder of the nearby Jack Miner Bird Sanctuary), the government of Canada designated the reserve as a national park.

Commercial fishing operations persisted

Point Pelee is Canada's most southerly point of land.

until the last lease expired in 1969, and a few cottagers hung around even after that. Nature lovers now arrive from around the world to enjoy the rare plants and animals, but especially the spectacular fall migration of the beautiful monarch butterfly, during which branches of trees are entirely enveloped in the orange-and-black creatures.

Park planners have made the park's many features easy to see. Boardwalks guide nature lovers through the vast marshes, and pathways lead them to the cactus patch. Even one of the old squatter shacks has been preserved for history buffs.

But the most unusual experience in the park is the point itself. After the trees end, a bare sand spit leads another 1.25 kilometres into the lake. (This, some believe, gave the point its name, the word *Pelee* meaning "bald," or "peeled," in French.) The point narrows until it becomes a pencil point and then fades into waves. But you can walk beyond even that into the shallow waters of Lake Erie and look back on Canada — all of it.

The remarkable landform lies at the end of County Road 33, south of Leamington.

63 OJIBWAY
The Case of the Missing Town

ACROSS ONTARIO, TOWNS were mapped out. Some remained small, some boomed and some never made it off paper. But rarely were the sidewalks, hydrants and roads built only to remain empty and unused.

Windsor, Ontario, grew in a most unusual way. While most towns started small, perhaps around a mill site or a port, Windsor was an amalgamation of planned company towns. The first settlement was known as Sandwich, and grew around a trading post on the Detroit River, later becoming the county seat.

Walkerville was laid out around Hiram Walker's whiskey distillery. Its neighbour, Ford City, was incorporated in 1912 as a residential community for the Ford company's automotive plant.

Then there was Ojibway.

Ojibway differed from Walkerville and Ford City. While these predecessors used a traditional grid network of streets, Ojibway represented the latest in town planning. Streets radiated outward from three central squares, while a four-lane expressway linked it with Windsor, then 7 kilometres away.

Ojibway was to be an 800-hectare company town for the American-Canadian Steel Corporation. Construction started during the First World War and continued into the 1920s. Objections, however, from Canadian steel producers, the effects of the Depression and the presence of massive underground salt deposits beneath the proposed streets halted the project.

Although a few industrial buildings were completed, and the roads and sidewalks built, the population remained below one hundred.

This concrete sidewalk, once slated to serve homes, leads only through a silent woodlot.

Over the rest of the townsite, grass and weeds claimed the streets and sidewalks, while forests took hold of the undeveloped area. By the 1960s, Ojibway had earned the distinction of being Canada's smallest organized municipality, with a population of a mere six.

Following Ojibway's inevitable annexation to Windsor in 1966, suburban growth spread onto the old townsite. New housing appeared on some of the original streets, and a racetrack was built in the middle of the "town." But much remained undeveloped. Grandly named streets like Broadview and Ojibway Parkway curved past open fields, where rusting hydrants poked above the tall grasses, while part of the planned four-lane express route became a local lane named Sandwich Street. But the strangest sights of all in this strangest of towns are the concrete sidewalks that cut straight through mature woodlots.

The former streets and sidewalks of the vanished townsite lie within the woodlands of Brunet Park, which lies along Normandy Street east of Ellis. To reach the forest with the sidewalks, follow Normandy Street east from Malden. The doglegs in the first road following Ellis Street and Washington Boulevard represent the proposed streets, which now lead only through the woods. Concrete sidewalks line these dirt lanes, and at regular intervals cut straight into the forests.

Many of Ontario's communities have a strange history, but there are none so strange as Ojibway, the missing town.

The levee road southwest of Chatham leads past a landscape more reminiscent of the Netherlands than rural Ontario.

64 BELOW THE WATER LINE

The Thames River Levee Road

A CANADIAN HERITAGE RIVER, the Thames is one of Ontario's most historic waterways. After all, it was near the forks of the Thames that Upper Canada's first governor, John Graves Simcoe, originally proposed the establishment of the colony's first capital before opting instead for a swampy harbour at the mouth of the Don River, today's Toronto.

Draining an area of nearly 6,000 kilometres square, the Thames begins as a rivulet near Tavistock and gradually assembles small tributaries on its 273-kilometre journey to Lake St. Clair. But the most unusual landscape through which it flows is the flat farmland between Chatham and Lake St. Clair because much of it lies below the level of the river.

From the earliest settlements led by Alexander Selkirk in the 1820s, the region has long suffered from floods from the river and inundations from the lake. As a result, levees and drainage canals were installed to stem the floods, allowing the rich soil to reach a wide range of vegetables and crops. Originally prairie-like and treeless, the land stretches to a flat horizon where, as on Canada's western prairies, the grain silos by the railway tracks can be seen at great distances.

About 12 kilometres west from downtown Chatham, Grande River Line comes to Jacob Road and the start of the unusual riverside levees. Through the intersection the road soon mounts the top of the levee, one of the only such levee-top roads in Ontario, with the river on one side and the fields below on the other. This continues for 3 kilometres down to Town Line Road and Pain Court Line — a right here leads to the nearby French Village of the same name.

Across the river via Jacob Road, Riverview Line (CR 36) follows the opposite bank of the river and leads to Prairie Siding, a prairie-like village with its trackside feed mill. As CR 36 follows the river it passes the historic St. Peters Church with a view of the river. The church remains the centre of a parish that was created in 1802 when most travel was done on the river. Note that the church, manse and hall all face away from the road and onto the river.

Farther on, the village of Jeannettes Creek, once a sleepy one-time railway village, marks the site of a large prehistoric Attawandaron village, where pottery and house ruins have been discovered.

After 5 kilometres from Jeannettes Creek, CR 2 leads to CR 39 and the mouth of the Thames, with its historic lighthouse located at the confluence of the Thames River and Lake St. Clair. Built in 1818, this circular stone tower was rebuilt in 1973 as a light beacon for both the small recreational craft and the large freighters that glide along the small lake. Once the site of wharfs and taverns, the mouth of the Thames River is now home to condos, cottages and a massive marina development.

65 ONTARIO'S BLACK GOLD
The Petrolia Discovery

So VAST, MODERN and international has today's petroleum industry become that its modest roots have been forgotten. And those roots go back to a little town in Southwestern Ontario aptly named Petrolia, where today a non-profit foundation, Petrolia Discovery, is striving to keep the legacy alive.

And it is succeeding. On the east end of Petrolia, the foundation operates a most unusual park. Here, on one of Canada's original oil fields, you can find oil rigs that date back a century. A central pumping plant known as a Fitzgerald Rig contains the biggest drive wheel ever built for a jerker rod system and has been operating off and on since 1903. From this building, wooden jerker rods slide back and forth across the oil field to operate pumps that urge oil from the ground. You can also see the gum beds that drew the first oil explorers to the area, and a cribbed well that shows how, at first, oil was dug rather than drilled.

Although Oil Springs, home to the Oil Museum of Canada and 12 kilometres south, represents the site of North America's first commercial oil well, dating from 1858, Petrolia contained the larger deposits. By 1866 the town had become a boom town of three thousand and a branch-line terminus for both the Grand Trunk Railway and the Canada Southern Railway.

Then, with the formation of the Imperial Oil Company in 1880, Petrolia became the centre of the British Empire's oil industry, a title it would retain for nearly twenty years. In that period, drillers and riggers travelled to all corners of the world, including countries like Iran and Iraq, to share the knowledge and skills that had quickly become legendary.

After the First World War, new refineries at Sarnia, along with the discovery of vast new reserves in Alberta, turned Petrolia into a near ghost town. But Petrolia Discovery has turned all that around. By bringing to the present a living snapshot of the oil industry's past, the park has revived the town. Local businesses have pumped money into streetscaping, while a costly restoration of the grand Victoria Hall has restored summer theatre to the town. A walking tour takes in the grand mansions of the oil barons, while a 4-kilometre fitness trail follows the ruins of the original oil fields.

From Petrolia, head south to the Oil Springs Museum, the site of North America's first commercial oil well. Then follow Gum Bed Line east to Gypsie Flats Road and amidst the ancient jerker rods of the Fairbank oil operation, look for the sixteen life-size metal sculpture vignettes by artist Murray Watson depicting the various historic oil production techniques.

The Petrolia Discovery theme park near the site of North America's first commercial well contains rigs and derricks that date back to the 19th century.

The forest of stacks in Sarnia makes for an unusual industrial landscape.

66 SURPRISING SARNIA
An Environmental Success Story

FOR MOST OF their existence, Sarnia's petrochemical plants have been vilified as one of Canada's most polluting industries, causing illness among its population, in particular among the children of the Amjiiwnaang First Nations located adjacent to the many stacks and flames.

Originating with the development of North America's first commercial oil well in the town of Oil Springs in 1858, the refineries moved first to Petrolia, where large deposits of oil were found, then to Sarnia to take advantage of access to oil from western Canada and shipping on the St. Clair River. The river also provided water for cooling the refineries.

In 1871, the Dominion Oil Company built Sarnia's first refinery. In 1896, it was rebuilt, becoming the largest oil refinery in the British Empire at the time. The company became Imperial Oil one year later. The boom years of Chemical Valley, as the region came to be known, began in 1942 when the federal government created the Polymer Corporation to coordinate the production of synthetic rubber, necessary for the war effort. The supply of natural rubber was shut off by the Japanese invasions across the south Pacific in World War II. Without the vital supply of synthetic rubber produced in the valley, the war's outcome may have been tragically different.

Following the war, more than sixty refineries and chemical operations became established in a tract of land south along the river between Sarnia and the First Nations land. The two biggest projects completed in the 1960s were the CIL fertilizer complex and the Lambton coal-fired generating station, located on the river at Corunna. CIL was attracted by the availability of natural gas and access to the American market for fertilizers and, in 1965, built a world-scale ammonia plant on a 650-hectare site south of Courtright.

However, the unabated sulphur-laden fumes created air that was so vile that a CBC documentary in the 1960s labelled the atmosphere in the Sarnia area as "The Air of Death."

In 1967, thirteen of the chemical companies formed the Lambton Industrial Society whose aim was to reduce their pollution. Thirty years on, the air quality had improved enough to meet government environmental standards. Today, the former "chemical valley" is now on the leading edge of green technology and in 2021, Ontario Power Generation began to disassemble its coal-fired generating station.

In partnership with Western University, the chemical valley community has formed the Bioindustrial Innovation Canada/Sustainable Chemistry Alliance as the basis for a successful business cluster that integrates green and sustainable chemistry to create opportunities for further industrial growth.

Fossil hunters can dig ancient critters right out of the mud.

67 FOSSIL HUNTERS' FANTASY
The Rock Glen Gorge

WHILE NO ONE is going to find any dinosaur bones in the Rock Glen Gorge, they will find hundreds of equally ancient creatures. Located in the Rock Glen Conservation Area, the gorge was created by the relentless erosion of the Ausable River into layers of limestone and shale. As the ancestors of today's shellfish died they drifted to the bottom of an early ocean, where they hardened into rock. Above them, more layers were deposited, and they also hardened. When the last glaciers finally melted, the water of today's Ausable River eroded into the soil and then into bedrock to gradually expose the former seabeds and their trove of early critters.

Fossils appear in much of Ontario's bedrock, and most usually require a pick to remove. But what makes the fossils in the damp little gully so unusual is that, during rainfalls, the shale turns soft enough to allow the shells to be removed by hand. The most common fossils found here are the branch-like staghorn coral or plant-like crinoids. Less common are the snail-like trilobites. The most interesting are the butterfly-shaped brachiopods, which the Chinese call "stone butterflies." While the fossils can be found throughout the little valley, the footing is tricky. The hunting grounds lie deep in the 25-metre chasm, where the stream trickles around boulders.

Rock Glen Conservation Authority has a few rules. Picks and shovels are not permitted, nor is collecting from the valley walls themselves. Loose sediments, however, are everywhere, and here you can help yourself. The park has a museum and staff with helpful brochures. The 25-hectare conservation area is on Lambton County Road 12, close to the village of Arkona, in Southwestern Ontario.

68 THE ST. THOMAS TRAIN STATION
Ontario's Longest Small Town Station

THE VAST FIELD of weeds gives scant indication that here once sprawled southwestern Ontario's most extensive rail yards. In 1873, a railway line known as the Canada Southern Railway (CSR), in reality an American-owned shortcut between Buffalo and Michigan, selected St. Thomas as a major divisional yard and repair facility. It lay halfway along the Ontario portion of its line. Beside the yards, the CSR added engine shops and a stunning railway station.

Although only 12 metres wide, the brick building stretched 120 metres along the tracks. Inside were offices for the general superintendent, paymaster, solicitor and freight agents as well as sleeping quarters for the train crews and the station's restaurant staff. On the ground floor were the restaurant and waiting rooms for the passengers. Italianate in style, the station was designed by a local contractor named Edgar Berryman. The building used 400,000 bricks and contained eight chimneys. Each end boasted four pilasters that led to a temple-like gable. A row of fifty windows lined the upper floor, while the ground level was broken by two archways. The station was the only one in Ontario that was segregated, not for the passengers but for the train crews, whose quarters were racially separated.

It was here in 1885 that one of North America's most notable railway accidents occurred,

The interior of the historic St. Thomas railway station has been restored and now houses the North America Railway Hall of Fame. Opposite: The restored St. Thomas station faces the home of the Elgin County Railroad Museum.

when the famous Barnum & Bailey circus elephant, Jumbo, was killed in the face of a sudden and unexpected onrushing freight train. A statue in the town recalls the story.

Across the wide yard full of tracks and sidings, the repair shops were the largest in the region. But by 1968 the rail line had become part of Penn Central and then Conrail, before being incorporated into the Canadian National Railway. But the line duplicated existing trackage, and the company closed down the operation. Eventually, it removed all the tracks to the dismay of the Elgin County Railway Museum, which continues to offer one of the most extensive collections of historic railway rolling stock in Ontario.

Thanks to On Track St. Thomas and the North America Railway Hall of Fame, the building has been preserved and restored and now serves as an event venue, offices and a gallery of Hall of Fame inductees including singer/songwriter Gordon Lightfoot, composer of "The Canadian Railroad Trilogy." Cementing its reputation as Railway City, St. Thomas now claims Canada's only elevated park, the conversion of the 1929 Michigan Central Railway bridge across Kettle Creek into a pedestrian park. The bridge spans 280 metres, rests on 12 piers and rises a dizzying 28 metres above the valley floor.

69 THE TRAGEDY OF JUMBO

ST. THOMAS, ONTARIO, calls itself "Ontario's Railway City" with good reason. It is the site of the revitalized terminal for the Port Stanley Terminal Railway tour train and the massive Canada Southern Railway station, built in 1873, hosts the North America Railway Hall of Fame. Nearby, the locomotive shop, built in 1913, contains the Elgin County Railway Museum and one of Canada's best collections of historic railway locomotives and rolling stock. More recently, a high-level disused railway bridge which spans Kettle Creek has become Canada's first elevated park.

However, the tragic demise of Jumbo the elephant forms a sad chapter in the city's railway legacy. It was September 15, 1885, and the popular Barnum & Bailey circus had just finished its evening performance. Its star attraction, Jumbo the elephant, was walking along the track to the circus train with his minder. An unscheduled freight train suddenly loomed out of the darkness, startling the giant pachyderm who stumbled forward, driving a massive tusk into his head. He died soon after.

Even his arrival was sad. Captured when young, Jumbo spent three years in the Paris zoo in France before being exchanged with England's London zoo for a rhinoceros. There, in his new home, the 4-metre-high gentle giant soon endeared himself to all who saw him and acquired a female mate. But his fame also came to the attention of P.T. Barnum, an American circus magnate who purchased him from the zoo for $10,000. Outrage over the sale quickly followed and included a lawsuit, and a plea from Queen Victoria herself, to leave him in London. But it was all to no avail. Profit proved paramount.

Jumbo soon became as popular in North America as he was in London, filling the streets and, even more important, the tents. But that all ended on that fateful night in St. Thomas, Ontario. For three years afterward, Barnum continued to ghoulishly display Jumbo's hide, before giving it to Tufts University in Boston, where it remained until 1975 when it was destroyed in a fire. His bones now rest in the Museum of Natural History in New York City. But his presence survives in the town where he died.

In 1985, to commemorate the 100th anniversary of Jumbo's tragic demise, the St. Thomas Jumbo Foundation commissioned sculptor Thomas Bronnum of New Brunswick to create a life-sized statue in Jumbo's likeness. So massive was the form that it required two trucks to transport it from New Brunswick to St. Thomas. It now sits beside the Tourist Information Booth on Talbot Street, close to that fateful rail line, still drawing awestruck visitors.

It was along these tracks that an unexpected freight train took the life of Jumbo.

Left: The City of St. Thomas commissioned a statue of Jumbo, now beside the tourist centre.

London's Blackfriars Bridge is Canada's only arched iron bridge
and the largest to survive in all of North America.

70 LONDON'S BLACKFRIARS BRIDGE

The Only Single-Span Iron Bowstring Bridge in Canada

AMONG ONTARIO'S MANY vanishing heritage features, bridges are the most threatened. Generally, we drive over them and under them but rarely stop to pay attention to them, possibly because they are not easy to see from a moving car. We are just too anxious to get where we are going.

Iron bridges were the first to begin replacing the wooden bridges that connected pioneer Ontario. While the older wooden structures were quicker and cheaper to build, and often strong, they were prone to rot and fire. Truss bridges made of wrought iron were far stronger and more durable.

Iron bridges owed their popularity to the railway. Because sparks from steam engines would all too often set the wooden bridges ablaze, iron bridges soon began to replace them. Road bridges simply drew upon the designs used by the railway.

In Ontario, the earliest iron road bridges appeared in Brantford, Paris, Peterborough and London. That also describes London's Blackfriars Bridge. Named after its more famous counterpart in London, England, Ontario's Blackfriars Bridge is, at 68.6 metres, the longest single-span iron bowstring bridge in North America, and the only one in Canada. Built in 1875 to cross the north branch of the Thames River, Blackfriars Bridge was the work of Isaac Crouse, a contractor employed by the Wrought Iron Bridge Company of Ohio. The feature that sets this iron bridge apart from others in Ontario is the bowstring, or arched shape. Bowstrings are very rare in iron bridges, and because they were limited in the weight they could carry, iron bowstring bridges were often replaced. But the graceful, curving superstructure gave them an appeal no other iron truss bridge could match.

In 2013 it was revealed that major repairs were needed. Traffic was restricted to pedestrians and bicycles and, in 2017, Blackfriars was lifted from its site. It was returned a year later, ready to serve for another 150 years. In 1992, the Ontario government declared it as an Ontario Heritage Structure, and it also appears on the Ontario Heritage Bridge list, as well as on the Canadian Register of Heritage Places.

Ontario still claims a bountiful supply of heritage bridges, from the oldest stone bridge in Lyndhurst to the sole surviving suspension bridge on Sewell's Road in Scarborough. Many graceful concrete bowstring bridges still cross the Grand River in many locations, including Caledonia, which boasts one with eight arches. Ontario has had many historic bridges, but with the more stringent engineering and safety demands and higher maintenance costs, they are a threatened heritage feature that is disappearing from our landscape.

71 TRIBUTE TO A FALLEN CHIEF
The Tecumseh Monument

IN ONTARIO, YOU sometimes find monuments in unlikely locations. On a lonely stretch of Highway 11 in northern Ontario rises the Reesor Monument, commemorating workers killed during a violent labour dispute in 1963 near Kapuskasing. In the silent woodlands north of Huntsville you will find the Dyer Memorial, a tribute by William Dyer to his deceased wife. Both of these features are described elsewhere in this volume. And then there is the relatively little-known memorial to a Shawnee chief named Tecumseh.

Tecumseh was born in the Ohio Valley in 1768. As a youth he witnessed the stream of Americans swarming into the area from what were then the former British colonies on the Atlantic coast. Although, following independence, the new American government had promised the Indigenous people ownership of their traditional lands north of the Ohio Valley, pressure from settlers and land speculators, along with anti-Indigenous racism, rendered those promises useless. Determined to keep their traditional lands, Tecumseh and his brother, known as "the Prophet," rallied the tribes to unite and stand firm.

Then, with the outbreak of the War of 1812, Tecumseh found an ally in the British who promised him that his people would retain their lands in exchange for helping the British stem the American invasion of Canada (then known as the Colony of Upper Canada).

Tecumseh and his allies were instrumental in the British victory over the Americans at Fort Detroit. Then, following a disastrous naval defeat on Lake Erie in 1813, the British forces began a retreat up the Thames Valley. On October 5th, the pursuing Americans caught up with the British and defeated them at the Battle of the Thames. As the redcoats fled, Tecumseh and his warriors stood their ground. However, during his brave stand, the chief was killed. Without his inspired leadership, the confederacy he had cobbled together fell apart, and their territory was lost.

To honour the chief and the place near where he fell, the National Historic Sites and Monuments Board of Canada declared a National Historic Site across the river and erected a monument to Tecumseh. The monument lies along the Longwoods Road, 4.5 kilometres east of Thamesville. It consists of a bronze mould of his profile and a First Nations petroglyph etched into a large granite boulder. This section of the Longwoods Road is now known as the Tecumseh Parkway.

In 2014, Indigenous sculptor Gordon Reeve added to the site a stunning sculpture of arching stainless steel bands, which he called *Wisdoms*. It measures 18 metres by 15 metres and resembles the shape of a turtle. The First Nations call the Earth "Turtle Island." Outlines of animals that are sacred to the Indigenous peoples are etched into the

Gordon Reeve's stunning sculpture of stainless steel bands speaks to Indigenous traditions.

beams. The memorial grounds consist of a 4-hectare green space along the Thames River and include gardens, walkways and picnic tables. Two rows of banners depict the life of the chief and the stories of his accomplishments and of the battle which took his life.

To find the monument, exit the 401 at County Road 21 (exit 109) and drive north to Thamesville, and then go east for 4.5 kilometres on County Road 2, Longwoods Road, to the monument.

The Oxford County jail in Woodstock is one of Ontario's most stunning architecturally.

Opposite: Thomas Cook was the unfortunate victim of a hangman
who made the rope too long. The image of his decapitated head now
forms a "death mask" beside the one-time jail's entrance.

72 WOODSTOCK'S DEATH MASK

The Hanging of Thomas Cook

PERHAPS IT IS because their stories are sordid or gruesome that Ontario's heritage jails are among the province's least appreciated heritage buildings. From the time Upper Canada governor John Graves Simcoe created Ontario's first four administrative districts, courthouses and their requisite jails began to make their appearance. No town could become a district capital without these buildings.

By 1850, Ontario had evolved into a system of counties. As in the case of Simcoe's districts, each county town — the county's administrative capital — needed to build a courthouse, a registry office and a jail before it could receive the coveted designation. In 1849, the County of Oxford was carved out of the earlier District of London, and Woodstock became its administrative centre. Here a magnificent courthouse was erected and, behind it, an equally stunning jail. Built of yellow brick in an Italianate style, the jail consisted of an octagonal central guard tower from which four long cellblocks radiated.

The first of five felons to be executed in the county jail was Thomas Cook, who in 1862 was convicted for beating his wife to death. It would turn out to be a most bloody hanging.

The duty of an executioner is to ensure that the length of the fateful rope is consistent with the weight of the condemned prisoner. Should the rope be too short for the convict's weight, the unfortunate person would simply dangle until he strangled to death. However, should the rope be too long and the convict too portly, the felon would plunge through the trap, gaining speed until, at the end of the rope, the excessive weight would keep the torso going while the head remained tight in the noose. In such cases public spectators were treated to a grisly decapitation. That is the fate that befell the unfortunate Cook.

For reasons that remain unknown — perhaps to prevent a similar occurrence — Cook's likeness has been sculpted into the arch that marks the entrance to the jail. It is Woodstock's death mask.

In 1977, the jail was closed and slated for demolition. However, a spirited fundraising drive by the town's heritage-conscious citizens saved the building, and it now serves as a local health office. And Cook's gaze continues to greet its visitors. The former county jail lies on Buller Street, two blocks north of the main street.

The Donnelly tombstone still sees many visitors.

73 THE TELLTALE GRAVE

The Donnelly Tombstone

IT'S OKAY TO go to Lucan these days and talk about the Donnellys. But a century ago all of North America was talking about the "Black Donnellys" and their untimely demise.

On a bitterly cold night in February 1880, a local vigilante gang attacked two homes belonging to a family of Irish immigrants named the Donnellys, and brutally butchered five of their number. Members of several prominent local families stood accused of the grisly slaughter, among them the sheriff.

Daily newspaper reports of the trial kept the English-speaking world transfixed for months. The first trial resulted in a hung jury. In the second, the judge, allegedly following instructions from his political masters who were seeking re-election, ordered the jury to disregard the testimony of a youthful witness, and the vigilantes went free.

The massacre was the result of an ancient Irish feud and a bitter business rivalry, all played out in an era when drunkenness and violence were part of pioneer life. Eventually the feud reached such a fever pitch that beatings and burnings became routine, and many of them were blamed on the large Donnelly clan.

Lucan is one of those down-to-earth towns where many residents can still trace their roots back to the first pioneers. Several had grandparents or great-grandparents who were part of the simmering feud, and even a few who were part of the mob. Time has eased, if not altogether erased, the bitterness. The Lucan Area Heritage and Donnelly Museum at 171 Main Street in Lucan recounts the tragedy, while the current owner of the homestead property hosts group tours (by appointment only), vividly re-enacting the events of that deadly night. The house on the site now was built by one of the surviving sons after the original cabin crashed in flames the night of the murders, marked only by stones laid at the cabin's four corners.

The "Swamp Schoolhouse" where the vigilantes hatched their plot still stands, used now as a storage shed. But the strongest reminder of that night lies in the graveyard of St. Patrick's Roman Catholic Church, the very church where the sworn enemies had even worshipped together. That reminder is the marble headstone listing all the names of the family members who were cut down that night.

The original marker, now secreted away in a northern Ontario basement, used the word "murdered" to describe their demise, but vandalism forced its removal. Today's stone says simply "died." The graveyard lies at the corner of Highway 4 and the Roman Line, about 25 kilometres north of London, Ontario. The homestead itself is about 6 kilometres north of that.

74 THE GHOST SQUIRRELS OF EXETER

A Town's Fluffy Mascot

A WHITE APPARITION SCAMPERS across the grass and leaps into a tree. No, it is not a Halloween prank nor is it an optical illusion. Rather it is one of Exeter's white squirrels.

First reported by local hunters in 1912, the white squirrels in this Southwestern Ontario town have become a tourist attraction in a prosperous community that can claim few tourist draws.

In fact, the town has gone to great lengths to adopt the furry balls of white. In 2001, council passed a bylaw prohibiting the harming or hunting of wild squirrels. And the town's Business Improvement Area has incorporated the animal as its logo. So, even if you don't see any white squirrels in the town parks or neighbourhood yards, you can spot them on street signs, trash receptacles and town banners. And while you can't take one home with you, you can drop in to the visitor centre at the south end of the main street and purchase white squirrel key chains, fluffy dolls, earrings or candles.

According to Ontario biologists, the critters are not albinos as one might initially assume, nor are they a separate species. Rather, they are a genetic variation of the more common grey squirrel but with different amounts of melanin. The town is said to have more than a hundred of the animals.

But Exeter is not North America's only home to the white squirrel. This author has witnessed white squirrels in the eastern Ontario community of Chaffeys Lock, and populations exist in Olney, Illinois, and in Brevard, North Carolina.

West of downtown Toronto, a small group of white squirrels inhabits Trinity-Bellwoods Park on Queen Street West, but in fact they are true albinos with the typical pink eyes. A nearby Queen Street West coffee shop displays an image of the white squirrel.

Exeter is situated on Highway 4, about an hour north of London.

An unusual population of white squirrels finds a home in the parks and yards of Exeter. (Photo by David Bishop, supplied courtesy of the Exeter BIA.)

The Town of Exeter's Business Improvement Area has incorporated the resident white squirrels in their logos and street furniture.

75 A TOUCH OF HOLLAND
The Bayfield Windmill

A FIELD OF TALL grass bends before the warm summer wind. Above the field, four huge wooden wind sails creak in a slow circle. They belong to North America's only wind-powered saw and grist mill. Located near the Lake Huron port village of Bayfield, it is known as the Folmar Windmill.

Frank de Jong was descended from generations of Dutch millers. Wind-powered sawmills, though rare in Canada, were part of his family heritage and remained in his blood when he migrated to Canada following the Second World War. When he purchased a parcel of land beside the Bayfield River, southeast of Goderich, Ontario, he set about to re-create his own touch of Holland — a saw and grist mill that would be powered by wind alone. Eighteen years went into creating the mill pond on the Bayfield River, and thirteen into building the mill. Its design was based on an actual mill in Holland known as "the Arend." When it was finished, the mill, wind cap and sails towered 29 metres above the Bayfield River marshlands. Although the mill remains privately owned, it is open to the public on a seasonal basis, and indeed has become one of the area's best-known attractions.

For a society accustomed to the ceaseless roar of cars and trucks, the only sounds here are the creaking of the sails. On the main floor of the mill, cables and hooks drag the logs up onto the slipway, where they are pulled slowly forward to the saw blades. These can number from two to twelve. Above the mill, a balcony encircles the wind cap. Above that are the four 22-metre wind sails, which rotate slowly in the wind. The windmill changed hands in 2013, and underwent a complete restoration under the direction of a Dutch "windmill whisperer." Although the mill remains privately owned, while further restoration is underway, the mill is closed to the general public, although tours can be arranged with the landowners. Keep in mind that the mill is on private land although it can be viewed from the road. It is a good example of how thoughtful private ownership can celebrate the unusual and historic features of Ontario's landscape.

The entire area offers plenty to see, from the beautiful and busy tree-lined streets of Bayfield to the strange octagonal main street of Goderich (almost completely rebuilt after the devastating 2011 tornado), and the heritage park in the ghost town of St. Joseph. The Folmar Mill is located on the south side of Huron County Road 13, about 3 kilometres east of Highway 21.

Bayfield's wind-powered sawmill.

76 SLOMAN'S SCHOOL CAR
The Schoolhouse that Rode the Rails

Between 1880 and 1914, five railway lines made their way through the forests of New Ontario, as the north was then called. At railside there grew a string of mill towns and hamlets for railway maintenance workers. But only a handful of towns grew large enough to support their own schools.

By 1922, the population of these outposts was substantial, yet they had few facilities, no luxuries and no schools. A North Bay school superintendent named J. B. McDougall pleaded with the then Ontario premier, G. Howard Ferguson, to initiate a six-month experiment that would bring to the settlements a school in the back of a train.

Passenger cars were altered into classrooms containing desks, books, blackboards and a small apartment for the teacher. In 1926, the first two cars departed their display areas at the Canadian National Exhibition for northeastern Ontario. The experiment proved so successful that it was quickly made into a permanent program, and by 1938 seven such cars were operating across the northland. On board the first of the travelling classrooms was Clinton school teacher Fred Sloman, his wife and five children. His route covered the 240-kilometre portion of the line between Capreol and Foleyet, a route he would follow throughout most of his 41-year teaching career.

For four days at a time the cars would rest at a siding in the tiny settlements, while children hiked or sledded for several kilometres for their precious education. Night school was provided for adults, and the schoolcars became social gathering places for the area.

However, during the 1950s, the trackside settlements faded. The advent of diesel and a massive highway-building program turned them into ghost towns, and the schoolcars were no longer needed. One of the last, CNR No. 15089, was shunted unceremoniously into a Toronto railyard in 1967.

After spending a few years with the Ontario Rail Association, car 15089 was put up for sale. A former student noticed the ad and eagerly phoned the family of the car's last teacher, Fred Sloman.

To their credit, the people of Clinton, the home of Fred Sloman's widow, Cela, rallied behind the cause and brought the car to Clinton, where it was restored to its appearance as a schoolcar and opened as a museum. While many a country schoolhouse has received new life as a residence, the schoolhouse that rode on rails is one of a kind, and retells a story of northern life that would otherwise be forgotten.

To reach the museum, follow Highway 4 south from Highway 8 within the town of Clinton.

The School on Wheels, Clinton, Ontario.

77 CARVED IN STONE
The Apple Park Farm Statues

I F YOU STOP to buy apple cider, apple butter or even plain old apples at the Apple Park Farm, don't be surprised if you get the feeling that you are being watched. Surrounding this attractive brick farmhouse on Highway 8 just east of Goderich are more than fifty stone figures that depict pioneer life in Ontario, or at least one man's view of it.

George Laithwaite moved to the farm from nearby Holmesville in 1895, and for the next forty years carved from local limestone his depiction of the people and scenes that he saw around him. In pioneer Ontario, with no radio or TV shows to sap the imagination, reading the Bible was a popular pastime. Accordingly, Laithwaite drew from the scriptures scenes for his sculptures of a lion with a lamb and of the Queen of Sheba. He satirized politicians with his portrayal of Sir John A. Macdonald and Sir Robert Borden turning swords into ploughshares. The more raucous aspects of pioneer life appear in the caricatures of a drunken farmhand staggering home supported by his braying donkey, and in four drunken fishermen tottering home from a "fishing" trip. Few of today's generation would remember the cartoon characters Jiggs and Maggie from *Bringing Up Father* but you can see them here as well.

Early travellers to Goderich soon began to go out of their way to see Laithwaite's sculptures, and at one point they were so popular that he sold postcards from his studio. Although Laithwaite died in 1956, the farm remains in the family. The statues are placed around a 1.25-hectare lawn, while apples, apple cider and apple butter are produced from the 350 trees on the farm.

The farm is on the west side of Highway 8, a short distance southeast of Goderich.

Borden and Macdonald have turned their "swords" into ploughshares.

Opposite: One of the more rollicking of the Park Farm statues.

Goderich's eight-sided main street is based on an early Roman town plan by architect Marcus Vitruvius Pollio.

78 GOING AROUND IN CIRCLES

Goderich's Eight-Sided Street

IF YOU SPEND any time driving on Goderich's main street, you soon get the sense that you've been going around in circles. Goderich has an unusual main street. Designed to accommodate the convergence of eight radiating streets onto a market square, it is a perfect octagon.

John Galt, the first commissioner of the Canada Company (a pioneer land settlement company), designed it because he wanted the town that was his headquarters to be unique. Drawing on the city planning concepts of Roman architect Marcus Vitruvius Pollio, he laid his eight-sided town down in the uncleared forests of pioneer Ontario. Few other examples of the style exist anywhere in the world and none are as exact as that in Goderich.

With the arrival of the Buffalo, Brantford and Goderich Railway in 1858, and the Guelph and Goderich Railway in 1908, the town boomed. A grand courthouse replaced the market in the centre of the square, and hotels and stores of yellow brick filled in the eight sides.

Although some have been lost to redevelopment, a number of the more outstanding buildings have survived. One of the most imposing is the recently renovated three-storey Bedford Hotel, built in 1896 and located between South and Kingston streets.

With its corner entrance and magnificent domed roof, it visually dominates that side of the square. Near the corner of Kingston Street stands the former Victoria Opera House.

On August 21, 2011, a dark wall of clouds and rain advanced on the port town, unleashing a deadly tornado which cut a swath of devastation destroying many homes and historic main street business and flattening the stand of mature hardwoods which surrounded the courthouse. But within a few short years, trees had reappeared on the courthouse lawn and most businesses had re-opened, although a number of gaps remain to testify to the storm's ferocity.

Goderich has more to offer the heritage enthusiast than just the square. The unusual octagonal jailhouse, located north of the square on Victoria Street, is now a museum. West Street leads to the lake and takes you past the Port of Goderich town hall. By the shore, the Romanesque former CPR station now sits closer to the water as a restaurant.

Another one-time railway station sits four blocks east of the square at the corner of East and Maitland. This former CNR station, with its two attractive towers, has been recently sold to private owners who are committed to its restoration.

Once visitors stop going around in circles, Goderich does indeed have plenty to offer.

CENTRAL ONTARIO & TORONTO AREA

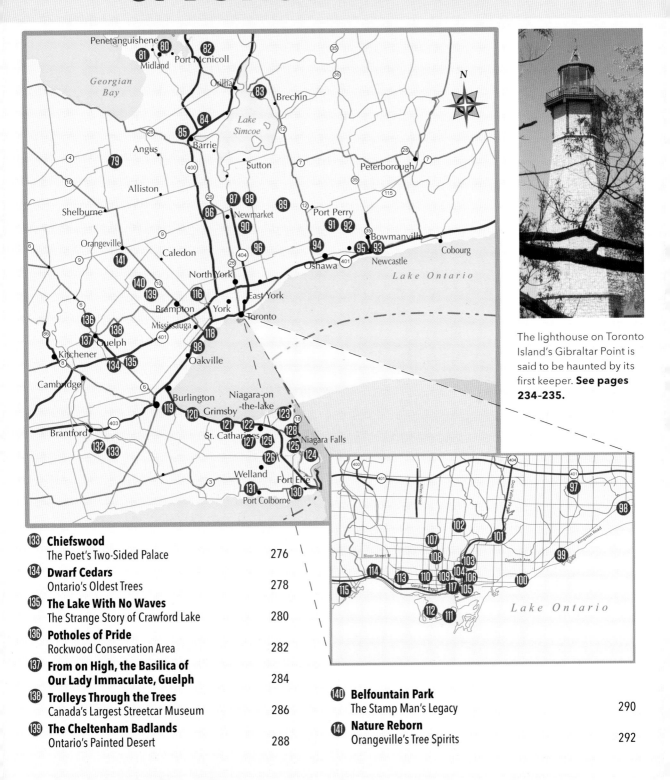

The lighthouse on Toronto Island's Gibraltar Point is said to be haunted by its first keeper. **See pages 234-235.**

79 SIZE MATTERS

The Battle over the Country's Smallest Jail

FOR MANY YEARS, tourist brochures for the village of Tweed boasted of its having North America's smallest jail. The little stone lockup, then serving as a tourist information centre, measured a mere 4.9 metres by 6.1 metres. And for years the claim went unchallenged. Then several other communities began to discover that they, too, had little heritage jails, sometimes literally in their own backyards.

Creemore jumped in with its jail of 4.5 metres by 6.0 metres. Located beside the library, a block east of the main street, it now serves as a museum. The tiny cells remain as they were when they held the local town drunk (or, in one case, a cow).

Down a small side street in Coboconk, a little stone building was scheduled for demolition. A local seniors' group lobbied for its preservation, and so the "Coby" jail was saved. Its dimensions, however, proved to be a few centimetres shorter than that in Creemore, and today it functions as a gift shop run by the same seniors' group.

Deep in Southwestern Ontario, the little railway town of Rodney also has its own tiny claim to fame — a brick jail beside the fairgrounds that measures a mere 4.5 metres by 5.4 metres. After serving as a book drop for many years, it is now a tourist information centre, although only seldom open.

Port Dalhousie, near St. Catharines, was not to be outdone and submitted its own candidate with measurements almost identical to those of the Rodney jail. It is now part of a bar. Also, almost forgotten, and unacclaimed, is the former jail in Providence Bay on Manitoulin Island, which is now converted to a cabin for tourists. Many of Ontario's towns and villages harboured tiny lockups. The Beaverton gaol, a three-cell stone building has been relocated to the town's museum grounds. The building from Woodslee has been moved to the grounds of the Southwest Ontario Heritage Village. Both buildings are restored to their original condition. Similarly, on Manitoulin Island, the former lockup in Manitouwaning is part of a local museum. The one in Little Current serves as a library. The one-time district jail in Gore Bay portrays prison life in that old stone building. Others in Silver Islet, Bruce Mines and Madoc still survive, but are privately owned.

The tiny Creemore lockup is one of several claiming to be North America's smallest.

80 THE *KEEWATIN* IS HOME

Port McNicoll

AFTER NEARLY FOUR decades in American waters, the CPR steamship the SS *Keewatin* is back home in Port McNicoll.

Built in Scotland in 1907, the *Keewatin* went into service the next year. Along with four other ships, the *Keewatin* linked the ports of southern Georgian Bay with the lakehead at Port Arthur for sixty years.

Operating originally from Owen Sound, where the CPR's Georgian Bay terminus lay, the ship relocated to Port McNicoll in 1912, once the CPR had completed its Sudbury main line.

More than 120 metres long, the mighty Titanic-like vessel could accommodate 280 passengers and carried a crew of 86. From Port McNicoll, the cruise took two and a half days and often stopped in various north Georgian Bay ports to off-load freight as well as local residents.

But times and regulations were changing. Following the tragic *Noronic* fire of 1949, where nearly 120 passengers burned to death or drowned while jumping to safety as the ship lay berthed in Toronto harbour, the government began to tighten regulations. In 1965, the *Keewatin* sailed its last cruise.

After fire consumed its sister ship the *Assiniboia* in 1968, the *Keewatin* became the last Edwardian ship afloat on the Great Lakes

and it, too, appeared destined for the scrapyard. But in 1967, a Great Lakes historian, R.J. Patterson of Douglas, Michigan, rescued the historic ship, towing it to the Kalamazoo River on Lake Michigan. There he converted it to a floating museum.

Then, in 2012, a Port McNicoll group, the Friends of the *Keewatin*, purchased the ship and began preparations for its return to Port McNicoll. Later that year, the ship opened for tours.

Comparisons to the *Titanic* were not out of place. Elaborate staircases with railings of carved wood lead from the main deck to the flower pot lounge at stateroom level.

All features are now displayed on the volunteer-led tour. Those tours include all portions of the mighty ship. Everything remains original to its later years, including staterooms, crew quarters, the wheelhouse and even the grain holds and the mighty boilers. Be sure to stand on the bow and gaze out toward the endless waters of Georgian Bay, much as the passengers might have done in the ship's bustling heyday.

In 2021, the curators of the mighty vessel announced that the property owners, regrettably, have refused to allow the museum to re-open in its current location, thereby threatening a unique piece of Ontario's maritime heritage.

Launched in 1907, the majestic *Keewatin* is now home in Port McNicoll. It displayed luxurious trappings (inset) similar to those of the ill-fated *Titanic*.

Midland's collection of outdoor murals includes even the grain elevators.

81 SAVED THROUGH ART
Midland's Giant Outdoor Art Gallery

THEY SAVED A B.C. town from becoming a ghost town, and now they have turned the bustling port of Midland into a tourist attraction. They are giant outdoor murals.

During the 1970s, the sawmill town of Chemainus, on Vancouver Island, faced the loss of its sole industry. Disaster seemed imminent. To cushion the blow, the town hired leading muralists to turn their central streets into an outdoor art gallery. The paintings, which depict scenes from local history and culture, proved successful beyond the residents' grandest hopes, and today the little town draws more tourists than any other Island attraction outside Victoria.

The idea was quickly copied by towns in Ontario that were facing similar downturns. Beginning in the 1950s, the Georgian Bay port of Midland began to lose its industries. The key shipyards closed, followed by the grain elevators and finally, in the 1980s, the Canadian National Railway removed its line into the town.

In 1991, the town commissioned renowned artist Fred Lenz to paint a series of murals throughout the downtown area. As the murals gained in popularity, the town hired other artists, including Dan Sawatsky, who had created some of Chemainus' finer works. Today more than thirty murals look out over Midland's downtown core.

Most of the murals lie along King Street — the main drag — between Elizabeth Street and the waterfront. They portray Midland's early history, with images of schooners, mills and stores. A three-panel mural shows a steam engine puffing into the town's railway station, while another depicts wildlife at the nearby Wye Marsh.

The grandest mural, however, decorates the side of the former Ogilvie grain elevator that looms above the water, across the harbour from the foot of the main street. Here the viewer can admire Fred Lenz's rendering of an early Jesuit missionary meeting members of the Huron tribe.

While working on the mural, Lenz suffered a heart attack and died. Family and friends took up his brushes and finished the work.

While several other towns across Ontario have tried to emulate Midland's success, the tiny port's murals remain one of Ontario's finest outdoor art galleries.

The preserved mill at Coldwater was built in 1833 for a nearby First Nations band.

82 THE COLDWATER MILL
A First Nations Gift

ONTARIO HAS BEEN very active in preserving its many heritage mills. In fact, the authoritative book, *Ontario's Historic Mills* by George Fischer and Mark Harris (Firefly Books), lists more than 100 — be they operational, restored, preserved or simply lying in ruin.

The Backus Mill, the Bayfield Windmill, the Bell Rock Mill and the Tyrone Mill are identified elsewhere in this book. But the Coldwater Mill, which lies north of Orillia near Highway 12, is one of the province's oldest and the only mill to have been built for a local First Nations band. It also remains in a near-perfect state of preservation.

The government built the structure in 1833 for the nearby Ojibwa band, which later moved to Rama and Beausoleil Island and sold the mill in 1849. Sir John Colborne had originally created the reserve in gratitude for the band's help in defending York against the American attack in 1813. It continued to grind out grain until 1994, first using an undershot waterwheel, then turbines and finally electricity. It is still in operation.

In 2008, to commemorate the origin of the mill, a "doodem" or totem pole, carved by Pamela Rawliuk in consultation with the Mnjikaning First Nation (the Rama band), was erected on the mill grounds.

Today, thanks to the Coldwater Mill Heritage Foundation, visitors can explore the old wooden interior. The three-storey board-and-batten building, situated by the Coldwater River, is a photographer's delight due to the beautiful scenery surrounding it.

Today, the mill is known as The Coldwater Mill and Artisan Boutique. The building has added more space, while a First Nations gallery occupies the renovated second floor. Although the mill is open May to November, events may occur year-round. Another new addition to the site is the Musical Barn, a replica of an 1866 barn which stood near the nearby hamlet of Eady.

83 THE HURON FISHING WEIRS

The Birth of the Name "Toronto"

BENEATH THE 4-LANE bridge in Orillia that carries Highway 12 traffic across The Narrows, a link between Lakes Simcoe and Couchiching, lays the birthplace of "Toronto" — not the city, but simply the name.

For centuries, the Huron First Nations and their predecessors, who had moved into the lush lands south of Georgian Bay, used the narrow channel that carries Lake Simcoe's water into the smaller Lake Couchiching to place their nets to catch the abundant fish. Here, in the shallow waters, they crammed heavy logs into the rocky bed and laced them with branches and nets.

They called it the "place of the fishing weirs" or "gathering place." In the Mohawk language, that word was "Taranto." Today the location is known by its Indigenous name as the "Mnjikaning Weirs."

When French explorer Samuel de Champlain visited the site in 1615 as part of his exploration of today's Ontario, he named the large lake Lac Toronto, after the place of the fishing weirs. It was later renamed by Upper Canada's new governor, John Graves Simcoe, to honour his father Captain John Simcoe of the Royal Navy. The portage that led to it from Lake Ontario became the "Toronto Carrying Place." Later the French erected a trading post at the Lake Ontario end of the portage calling it Fort Toronto. When the British purchased the Lake Ontario lands from the Mississauga band, they called it the Toronto Purchase. And so the name "Toronto" migrated to the shores of Lake Ontario.

Today the location of those ancient fishing weirs is a protected national heritage site, although they are rarely visible except at low water. However, beneath the busy bridge sits a heritage plaque and the sacred "grandfather rock," a large boulder of banded granite which the First Nations hold sacred, as they do the site itself.

Access to the site is along Bridge Street, a short road that begins at Queen Street, west of the Tim Hortons that sits on the southwest side of the Creighton Street traffic lights on Highway 12 in the village of Atherley.

The "grandfather" rock at the site of the Mjikaning fishing weirs symbolizes the religious significance of this historic First Nations National Historic Site.

Right: A graphic illustration of the Mjikaning weirs is displayed at the site, as the weirs themselves are seldom visible above water.

Shanty Bay's Anglican church is perhaps North America's only example of a "mud church."

84 THE MUD CHURCH OF SHANTY BAY

St. Thomas Anglican Church

CANADIANS HAVE LONG looked to nature for building material. Bark and skins were used by Indigenous inhabitants. The first shanties of the European arrivals were hastily erected from logs, while prairie pioneers were noted for their early sod huts. And where stones were plentiful they were used for homes, churches and schools.

While adobe brick was commonly used in the southwestern United States, it was rarely employed in Canada, owing largely to its vulnerability to rain. But one ingredient was so rarely used that only one building of any significance in Canada is known to have used it, and that ingredient is mud.

Common in medieval Europe, it is also known as cob, or "rammed earth" construction, and consists of a mixture of clay, sand and straw. The three ingredients are mixed into a dough-like substance and pressed, or rammed, into a wall mould. It is then covered with plaster or wood. The only building of such size to be made of the mud, some say in all of North America, is St. Thomas Anglican Church in a hamlet on Lake Simcoe named Shanty Bay.

The church was started in 1838 on land donated by the founder of the Shanty Bay settlement, Colonel Edward O'Brien. The mud walls, 1 metre thick, were laid on a stone foundation. Wood was hand hewn from local supplies of pine, ash and cedar — the axe marks remain visible to this day. The original square pews are still used as well.

Despite the unusual construction technique, you wouldn't know it to look at it. With its stucco finish, it resembles many a church of the era, solid and Gothic, with a handsome steeple. In only a few sections of the lower wall is the mud exposed. The church, which remains in full use, lies south of Ridge Road in the centre of the village, about 8 kilometres east of Barrie.

The name Shanty Bay itself dates to the 1830s, when the community was a jumping-off point for Black settlers en route to farm lots north of the lake. Their settlement also left its religious imprint by way of the Oro African Church, built in 1849 and located on the Old Barrie Road at the east end of the village of Edgar, about 10 kilometres from Shanty Bay.

The City of Barrie has carried out extensive repairs to its historic Allandale Grand Trunk station.

85 BARRIE'S ALLANDALE TRAIN STATION
Ontario's Grandest Wooden Station

CURVING ALONG THE western shore of Lake Simcoe's Kempenfelt Bay stretches what is, simply put, Ontario's grandest wooden railway station.

Railway activity here dates to the building of Ontario's first railway line — the Ontario, Simcoe and Huron Railway, which opened in 1853. When the line was extended to Collingwood, it became the Northern Railway. Then the Northern and Pacific Junction Railway was extended from Allandale northward to Callander, Allandale became a bustling railway junction — so bustling, in fact, that in 1905 the new owners, the Grand Trunk Railway, decided that a new station was needed.

The elegant new station offered a rounded waiting room at the south, from which passengers could enjoy views of the scenic lake. Attached to the waiting room was one of the GTR's finest dining rooms, with twinned pillars that led to a grand hall where uniformed wait staff could attend to as many as fifty patrons. Attached to the grand hall was a brick structure that housed offices for railway staff.

In the 1950s CNR closed the yards, moving staff to Capreol and the restaurant became a soda bar. In the 1980s, the waiting room was closed and passengers relegated to a small shelter.

Passenger trains such as VIA Rail's Canadian and the ONR's Northlander continued to use the station until the 1990s, when the CNR removed the tracks between Barrie and Orillia. Following its designation as a heritage station by the federal government, the station was briefly occupied by a local radio station.

In 2011, the City of Barrie acquired the property and began restoration work. With the exterior complete, work was halted by a certificate of pending litigation brought by a developer, later removed by the courts. As of 2021, further development awaits the completion of an archaeological review.

Nearby Station Park, which contains the foundation of the old turntable and the former mechanical shop for the divisional yards, is now a tourist office and event venue.

86 THE SWAMP THAT FEEDS THE WORLD

The Amazing Holland Marsh

LIKE MUCH THAT is interesting in Ontario, the Holland Marsh is paid scant attention by travellers. To most, the marsh is little more than the flat, black fields that flash past along Highway 400. Yet, for the driver who exits at Canal Road, the marsh becomes one of the most interesting bits of landscape, not just in Ontario, but in Canada. It is the country's largest vegetable garden.

That wasn't the case around the turn of the twentieth century, when this post-glacial lake bed, with decayed plants 30 metres deep, was good for little else than growing marsh grasses to stuff into mattresses. Then, in 1904, a Bradford grocer named Watson convinced professor W.H. Day of the Ontario Agricultural College in Guelph to investigate the possibility of draining the swamp for vegetable production. All his studies and experiments pointed to the same thing — the swamp could become one of Canada's premier market-gardens.

In 1925, the Ontario Department of Agriculture began to drain the bog. Canals and dikes enclosed both sides of the wide valley like huge brackets, diverting the water to Lake Simcoe.

**A view across the Holland Marsh
as harvest season approaches.**

By 1930, the rich black soil was drained and ready for farming. The first farmers to arrive were eighteen Dutch families from Hamilton, Ontario, in 1934. Many others, including Russians and Poles, followed, and within a few years the one-time swamp had become one of North America's leading vegetable-producing areas. (The name "Holland" does not come from the Dutch settlers, but rather from Major A. Holland, the British surveyor who laid out the land in 1830.)

Canal Road, which skirts the northern rim of the marsh, provides the best look at the 2,900-hectare marsh. From Highway 9 to Yonge Street in Bradford, Canal Road follows the northerly of the two canals through a world of overhanging willows and still canal waters. It passes sprawling modern backsplits that contrast with the cabins and trailers that house the seasonal workers who pick the lettuce, potatoes, celery, parsnips, cabbage, cauliflower and the 120,000 tonnes of carrots that sprout each year from the fertile earth.

87 TEMPLE OF LIGHT
The Sharon Temple

GROUPS LIKE THE Quakers and the Shakers, the Mormons and the Mennonites, all originated with "visionaries" who led a group of dedicated followers away from the mainstream denominations. While all were present in pioneer Ontario, none left so prominent a landmark as did David Willson and his Children of Peace.

In 1801, Willson, a Quaker, migrated from New York to the Newmarket area of Upper Canada, where his Society of Friends brethren (as the Quakers were called) were particularly active. However, Willson grew impatient with the local leadership and decided to have a vision of his own. His vision was to restore his form of Christianity to its Judaic roots.

In 1825, Willson and his Children of Peace began construction of an elaborate and highly symbolic temple. When finished, the three-storey structure resembled a windowed wedding cake and totally dominated the landscape of simple pioneer buildings. Centre doors on each side symbolized the equal acceptance of people from all directions, while the square shape, it is said, meant the group dealt "squarely" with everyone. Inside, twelve pillars represented the twelve apostles.

Then, as now, religious leaders displayed a strong sense of self. Inside the temple Willson placed a decorative altar that was partially enclosed, while on the grounds outside the temple he built his small but equally ornate personal study. The Children of Peace celebrated two festivals, Willson's own birthday, dubbed the "Feast of the Passover," and the fall "Feast of Illumination," when the Children placed 116 candles in their temple windows.

Willson's death in 1866 signalled the downfall of the Children of Peace. By 1890 they were extinct, and the temple vacant. But in 1919, a far-sighted York Pioneer and Historical Society acquired the temple and converted it into a museum.

And so it remains today. On the outskirts of Sharon, now a Toronto bedroom community, visitors may view the temple, little changed in a century and a half. Although other pioneer buildings, including an 1852 township hall, have been moved onto the grounds, the story of David Willson and his Children of Peace brings to life a small but highly unusual chapter of our pioneer past. The stunning temple is on Leslie Street in Newmarket, a short distance north of Green Lane.

One of the most unusual churches ever constructed in Ontario is Sharon Temple, built by the equally unusual Quaker sect known as the Children of Peace.

This Holland Landing lock on the Newmarket Canal never saw water.

88 THE CANAL THAT NEVER WAS

Newmarket's Ghost Canal

THE WALL OF concrete looks enough like a canal lock, but 8 metres below your feet, where water and boats should be, you see grass and trees. You are standing beside the remains of a canal that never saw water: the Newmarket Canal.

The early decades of the nineteenth century were the canal era. At a time when railways were little more than science fiction and roads little better than quagmires, water was the only highway. The remarkable success of the Erie Canal in New York State sparked a spate of canal building in Ontario. The Welland, Rideau and Grand canals, parts of the St. Lawrence and Trent, had all made their appearance by the 1840s. And as early as 1800, Surveyor General Smith produced a map showing a canal linking Lake Ontario with Lake Simcoe along the Rouge and Holland river systems.

But by the time the smoke of steam engines ushered in the railway era around 1850, the Newmarket Canal still existed only on paper. With canals in decline, there seemed little point in proceeding. Then, in 1904, the Trent Canal was completed to Lake Simcoe and politicians from the Newmarket area, led by their Liberal MP William Mulock, pushed once more for a link to that system. The engineers, however, cautioned that the watershed might not contain enough flow of water to properly operate the system. But with an election looming, the federal government went ahead anyway.

The canal was to be built in three sections. The first was from Lake Simcoe to Holland Landing, a distance of 15 kilometres, and wouldn't require any lock structures since it would be at lake level. The second was from Holland Landing to Newmarket, a distance of 7 kilometres, and would require three locks to cover the 14-metre rise in elevation. The third section would carry the canal to its completion at Aurora.

After the first two sections were finished, the First World War intervened, and in 1916 the canal project was cancelled. The engineers were proven right — there was too little water. One lock structure, minus gates, still stands in Holland Landing where old Yonge Street enters the village. Between here and the south end of Newmarket, the Nokida Bike Path and Hiking Trail runs parallel to the river and canal. The trail leads you to Lock 2 where you can find parking, the former swing bridge beside Green Lane (there is parking here too) and on to Newmarket and the location of Lock 3 in a municipal park.

Although many Ontario canal projects either failed outright or declined economically, the Newmarket Canal remains as it began, high and dry.

89 ONTARIO'S TAJ MAHAL
The Thomas Foster Memorial

YOU DON'T NEED to spend a lot of time looking for this one; it dominates the countryside on County Road 1 about 5 kilometres north of Uxbridge. Thomas Foster was born near Toronto in 1852 and moved to the hamlet of Leaskdale, north of Uxbridge, where he ran the local hotel. He later moved back to Toronto, where he was elected a member of Parliament and later mayor of the city. One of his oddest acts was to offer a prize to the woman who could bear the most children in a ten-year period. He made his fortune by investing in real estate.

Following the death of his wife, he travelled the world. While visiting India he gazed in wonder at the beautiful Taj Mahal, built in 1628 by Shah Jahan as a monument to his wife, Mumtaz Mahal. Foster decided that he, too, would build a Taj-like temple for his own wife. The location he chose was a hilltop just north of Uxbridge and not far from his home town of Leaskdale.

In 1934 he commissioned architects J.H. Craig and H.H. Madill to design the memorial. Workers cleared away the hilltop and then began carefully laying limestone and marble according to the intricate plan. When they were done, the strange Byzantine monument rose more than 18 metres into the air. The onion dome was built of copper and allowed the sun to filter through twelve stained-glass windows. The coloured rays fell upon marble mosaics, lighting up the pink, green and black inlays on the walls and floor. Surrounding the floor are marble pillars, each different from the other. Against one wall stand the three crypts: his, that of his wife and the third containing his daughter.

Maintained by the Foster Memorial Committee, and designated as a heritage building, the memorial plays host to weddings and plays, and is open to the public Wednesday through Sunday during July and August between 11:30 and 4:30. Tours are available Wednesday through Sunday during July and August. Concerts take place every Friday evening from May to September. For information, visit www.fostermemorial.com.

Thomas Foster modelled his memorial to his wife after India's Taj Mahal.

90 LIVING ON THE WATER
The Floating Mansions of Lemonville

IT'S A WATERY wonderland, but one that's a long way from any river or lake. Lemonville sits on the slope of a sandy hill, the grey apartment towers and suburban glass offices of northeastern Toronto looming on the hazy horizon. An undistinguished hamlet that dates from pioneer days, Lemonville has seen a most unusual housing boom — mansions that float on water, or so they appear.

The water comes not from a river or a lake, but from a massive and mysterious underground reservoir. The ridge that looms behind the mansions is known as the Oak Ridges Moraine. A line of sandy hills, it was formed when the great glaciers that once covered Ontario cracked and began to melt. The icy meltwater carried sand and rocks into a long fissure in the ice, and by the time the glacier had melted, all that remained was the long ridge.

Because the soil in the hills is so porous, rainwater drains right through it, creating a high water table at the foot of the hills. That is not unusual, but the Lemonville area sits on a geological anomaly. While the water seeps quickly through the light, sandy upper soils of the ridge, the flow suddenly encounters a hard subsurface layer of clay. This propels it even faster toward the flats below and keeps the water near the surface like a massive underground lake contained only by the soil above it. Because of the downward force of the water in the hills behind, whenever the surface of the flats is broken, the water gushes upward like a geyser unleashed.

But house builders have turned what could have been a curse into a blessing. By digging carefully into the underground lake, they have landscaped the large housing lots into a miniature lake land. Surrounded by ponds, some more than a hectare in area, are mansions in styles that range from "California ranch" to "Woodbridge Italianate," or simply to "Scarborough suburban."

The land of the floating mansions extends along Bethesda Road for about 2 kilometres between Kennedy Road and McCowan Road. Many of the mansions are obscured by thick hedges although the most visible display lies at the intersection of Bethesda and McCowan Roads.

Lemonville's mansions are set in a watery wonderland.

91 THE "MODEL A ACRES" BED AND BREAKFAST

The Ultimate Recycler

IAN BARON WILL tell you his remarkable collection is not a museum; it is "yard art." That is because the Model A cars, the classic WWI and WWII fighter aircraft, tank, and submarine conning tower are made entirely from spare and recycled parts.

Fans of the *Peanuts* comic strip will recognize Snoopy at the entrance to the property standing proudly beside his Sopwith Camel biplane. Constructed over a period of nine months, the full-scale replica consists of such recycled parts as apple juice cans and buggy wheels, while the skin of the aircraft comes from the aluminum sides of above-ground swimming pools. In fact, more than 33 swimming pools have gone into the creations.

Appropriately sitting next to the Sopwith is the Red Baron's own design, the Fokker D. VII biplane.

The far side of the lawn takes the visitor to WWII, where the Battle of Britain is commemorated with replicas of a British Spitfire Mk IX and a German Messerschmitt ME 109 G, both with mannequin pilots in WWII pilot's headgear. The Messerschmitt represents the one flown by celebrated German fighter pilot Adolph Galland, noted for his love of large cigars. Hitler's own fascination with Walt Disney characters shows up in the form a cigar chomping Mickey Mouse logo on the side of the aircraft.

Again, Baron created both pieces entirely from recycled materials.

Near the rear of the spacious yard, a Sherman Firefly tank and a conning tower from the German U-boat *U-505* face off against each other, their cannons fully capable of hurling projectiles at each other. (The capture of the German U-boat by the Americans was kept a careful secret from the Germans until after the war. The submarine now rests in the Chicago Museum of Science.)

Baron used information from his father's war album to create the tank, which consists mostly of a Chevy Silverado pickup truck.

But it is the theme of the Model A Ford that marks the entrance to this gallery and which carries on to the rooms of the B & B itself — the headboards are Model A Ford fronts with working headlights as reading lamps.

Around the property lay glass cylinder gas pumps, a Model A racing car circa 1931 and a penny farthing bicycle (with the oversized front wheel).

So if anyone has a spare TV antenna, teeter-totter or even a doghouse, Ian Baron could likely convert these items into other bits of heritage transportation yard art.

(The property located near Clarington is open to the public for an admission, but advance notice is needed. See www.modelaacres.com.)

Left: A train stops suddenly at the end of the tracks.

Bottom right: The entrance to the Model A B&B is marked with, what else, a replica Model A Ford.

Bottom left: Snoopy stands guard by his replica Sopwith Camel.

92 THE LAST OF THE WATER MILLS

The Tyrone Mill

WITHIN THE SPRAWLING Greater Toronto Area, there remains a tranquil oasis where visitors can return to simpler pleasures of pioneer Ontario. That retreat, one of the last commercially operated water-powered mills in the province, is found in the historic village of Tyrone.

In 1846, as pioneer settlers pushed inland from Lake Ontario, James McFeeters and John Gray built a flour mill on the waters of Bowmanville Creek, about 18 kilometres north of Bowmanville. It became the main industry in the growing little community. In 1908, with most of Canada's wheat-growing having moved west, then owner Thomas Goodman converted the building to a feed mill to provide feed for the growing dairy cattle industry.

But even that operation began to flag, bringing in less than $50 a year by the 1970s. At this point, most mills would have either burned or been converted to a restaurant. But Bob Shafer, a relocated American, had other plans. And that was to continue operating it as a mill, and not just any mill. It would be one that continued to use water. At first, he focused on custom-cutting logs provided by local farmers. However, after locating a compatible turbine, he restored the mill's original role to that of grinding grain.

Today, the Tyrone mill has become a popular day-trip destination for families and history lovers who wish to flee the maddening world of ceaseless traffic and the tedium of urban sprawl. The mill offers not just its own grain but also fresh apple cider (in season) and its specialty, hot and tender freshly baked doughnuts.

Visitors may also climb the wooden steps to the second floor to view the woodworking room, where a system of pulleys is also run by water power. At the rear of the mill, a small lookout over the millpond may reveal ducks, geese and, possibly, a pair of swans.

Meanwhile, Tyrone's main street offers up other vestiges of Ontario's pioneer days, including an early schoolhouse, churches and a stone blacksmith shop.

The Tyrone mill near Bowmanville may be Ontario's last commercially operated water-powered mill.

This structure housed the more senior German POWs.

Top: When prisoners tried to tunnel out of Bowmanville's POW Camp 30, the dirt they stored in the roof of the structure brought down the ceiling and foiled the attempt.

93 THE BATTLE OF BOWMANVILLE

Canada's POW Camp

WITHIN THE GREATER Toronto Area there remains the only surviving intact Second World War prisoner of war camp in any of the former Allied countries.

In 1925 the property opened as a boys' training school. At the onset of the Second World War, facilities were needed to house captured prisoners of war. Winston Churchill asked Canada to house the highest-ranking German officers. He wanted them kept as far as possible from the front, lest they escape and rejoin their units.

And so it was that, in November 1941, the three hundred boys were moved out and eight hundred high-ranking German officers, including generals, were escorted in. Because of the rules that governed captured soldiers, the prisoners were allowed to keep their uniforms and their ranks. Within the camp, prisoners did their own cooking, used the recreational facilities, formed a theatre group and orchestra, and even were allowed off the property to tend their own farm. While most of the eight hundred POWs were crammed into dorms designed for three hundred boys, the highest-ranking generals enjoyed the exclusive use of what had been built as a hospital for the juveniles. The most noted of the generals was von Ravenstein, who had served under Rommel on the African front.

Then in October 1942 came the "Battle of Bowmanville." On learning that the Allies had shackled a number of German POWs following the failed raid on Dieppe, the Germans retaliated by shackling Allied POWs. A furious Churchill sent orders to Bowmanville to similarly bind the high-ranking officers there. But the Germans would have none of it and barricaded themselves in the various buildings. Finally, after three days, the Canadian guards stormed through the upper windows, armed only with baseball bats. After a furious free-for-all, the POWs relented and agreed to the shackles. However, to maintain order and morale, the Canadians allowed the shackles to remain loosely applied and for the men to take turns wearing them.

Following the war, Camp 30 reverted to a training school — a role it played until 1979, when the property was sold to a religious order and subsequently left vacant.

In 2013, Parks Canada designated Camp 30 as a National Historic Site. The grounds are part of the Ehrenwort Trail in Clarington and tours of the site are available through the Jury Lands Foundation. Still, the site remains derelict and overgrown while awaiting repurposing.

94 OSHAWA'S "TANK MUSEUM"

IN A CITY best known for automobile manufacturing, Oshawa is also renowned for having North America's largest collection of operational armoured military vehicles. Located in the northwestern corner of Oshawa, adjacent to the municipal airport, sits the Ontario Regiment RCAC (Royal Canadian Armoured Corps) Museum, with more than 100 tanks and armoured vehicles, dating from the Second World War right up to the modern-era tragedy in Afghanistan.

Known at first as the Ontario Regiment Ferret Club, the organization began in 1976 when Colonel Norm Wilton purchased nine Ferret military scout cars to use on ceremonial occasions. Over the years, military enthusiasts joined in and began acquiring and restoring tanks and armoured military vehicles wherever they could find them. And today they number more than 100 and have a home in Oshawa's Ontario Regiment Museum.

The use of tanks in wartime began in 1916. Before that, experimental armoured vehicles proved to be cumbersome and impractical. With trench warfare leading to a muddy stalemate in the First World War, the allies needed a way to get the infantry through the trenches. Horses were tried but were not up to the task. Finally, in 1915, W.G. Wilson designed an armoured vehicle with a gun and wheels that ran on caterpillar tracks and, more important, was maneuverable. During manufacturing, in order to disguise its real military purpose, the military described the vehicle as a "water carrier." The workers simply called it a "water tank." It was then that the term "tank" came into usage and has remained the name of the vehicle ever since.

By 1916, more than 600 tanks were ready to roll and first saw deployment in the Battle of the Somme. During the Second World War, more than 100,000 of these monsters were manufactured. The oldest tank in the museum is the 1942 Canadian-made Leopard, although the best known is the iconic Sherman Tank, named by the British for American Civil War general William Tecumseh Sherman. It saw its inaugural combat in the Battle of El Alamein in North Africa in 1942 and has remained a legend ever since. And, yes, the museum has one of these as well.

The newly constructed Military Vehicle Conservation Centre has added 100 square metres for the display and maintenance of the vast and growing collection. Visitors can visit anytime during the year and possibly climb into a real tank for a ride. Be sure to check times on the Museum website and try to visit on special days. One special day is Tank Saturdays, when the vehicles are rolled out on display in the tank arena. Another is the two-day Aquino Weekend when tank battles are staged.

Oshawa's tank museum is the largest of its kind in North America.

Other than the monument, little remains of Camp X, the top-secret war facility where James Bond was born in the mind of author Ian Fleming.

95 JAMES BOND AND THE SECRET OF CAMP X
A WWII Training Facility for Spies

CLOAK-AND-DAGGER MOVIES AND spy thrillers like the James Bond books conjure images of stealth, danger and sultry temptresses. In reality, undercover work was humdrum. Most espionage work involved censoring mail, breaking codes and forging diplomatic documents. Canada's most secret Second World War spy-training facility was known simply as Camp X.

Located on a then-isolated Lake Ontario shoreline, midway between Oshawa and Whitby, Camp X was the responsibility of a man called "Intrepid." In real life he was William (later Sir William) Stephenson. Born in Winnipeg, the decorated First World War flying ace was put in charge of British counterespionage at the camp.

The camp consisted of two components. One was the Special Training School, or STS 103, focused on spy training. A second, even more secret activity, code-named Hydra, involved top-secret messages sent between the United States and Canada. So sensitive was the work that any outsiders who ventured near it were to be shot on sight.

After the war, Camp X continued as a government communications centre until 1969. Even then its wartime secrets remained locked away. Only after the buildings were demolished or removed were the secret activities at Camp X finally revealed.

While Stephenson became the subject of books (*A Man Called Intrepid*), another Camp X visitor went on to write them. Ian Fleming, a commander of British naval intelligence, used his spy training to create a fictional super spy named James Bond.

When the legends of Camp X finally became public, a park was opened on the site of the camp. Created in 1984, Intrepid Park features a large monument erected to commemorate those who worked there. On the base of the monument, photographs and text depict the story of the camp and its contribution to the Allied victory. From the monument, trails lead to an isolated beach on Lake Ontario, where camp artifacts that had been dumped into the lake wash ashore from time to time.

While most of the camp's buildings were demolished, some were removed to other sites. A former barracks is located at the Whitby Humane Society, on Thickson Road. Rare Camp X artifacts, formerly on display at Oshawa's Robert Stuart Museum, were auctioned off in 2011. However, many Camp X photos may be found at www.camp-x.com. No longer isolated, Camp X today is surrounded by industrial sprawl. The park and monument can be found on Boundary Road, on the Oshawa-Whitby border.

The subdivision's wide streets give the historic community a modern appearance.

96 MARKHAM HERITAGE ESTATES

A Suburb of Last Resort

WHERE DO CENTURY-OLD farm-houses go when urban sprawl engulfs the cornfields? Sadly, most fall beneath the wrecker's ball to be replaced by an endless sea of look-alike new homes. But in the heritage-conscious community of Markham, historic houses are given a new lease on life.

Markham, a fast-growing area of big-box stores, endless malls and gridlocked traffic, sits on the northeastern fringe of the Greater Toronto Area. But despite this unchecked growth, Markham retains much of its built heritage.

That heritage dates back to the 1790s, when William Berczy led a group of colonizers from the United States to the headwaters of the Rouge and Don rivers. In the years that followed, farm villages and mill towns appeared across the landscape. One of the most successful was Markham. In 1871, the Toronto and Nipissing Railway built a station a short distance north of Markham's mills, and the community boomed.

And thanks to Markham's citizens and politicians, much of that heritage has been retained. The historic main street, like that in the smaller village of Unionville a few kilometres west, has been historically refurbished, and new development must be compatible with the historic theme. North of the main street, the original station has been restored to its original appearance and reopened as a GO commuter station and community facility.

And then there are the Markham Heritage Estates. Faced with the loss of countless historic farmhouses and village homes to urban sprawl, the Town of Markham gave the houses a home. In 1996, Markham created, adjacent to its museum village, a plan of a subdivision, with thirty-eight lots, solely for the purpose of relocating threatened heritage houses. Under the plan, the Town of Markham sells the lots at less than market value to owners of heritage homes that are threatened with demolition. The amount saved on the price of the lot provides the owners with the incentive to relocate and restore the house in the new location.

Among the oldest of the relocated houses are the David Leek Houses built in 1840 and formerly located in the vanished village of Dollar, and the 1845 house built by Richard Lewis in the community of Gormley. For its heritage initiatives, Markham was awarded the coveted Prince of Wales Prize in 1999.

Markham Heritage Estates is located next to 16th Avenue, west of Highway 48.

97 TORONTO'S MOST UNUSUAL CEMETERY
The Taber Hill Ossuary

I N THE HEART of suburban Scarborough, surrounded by curving streets and 1960s-era back-splits, there rises Taber Hill, an unusual smooth mound, with a large granite boulder resting on top. It is not a natural feature. Rather, the mound contains the remains of nearly 500 Iroquois buried sometime during the fourteenth century, well before the first Europeans landed on mainland Canada.

Fast forward six centuries, and the farm fields of the rural township of Scarborough were in the throes of a suburban boom. Corn fields were being bulldozed for new homes, and Highway 401 was making its way around the then northern limits of Toronto. While digging up earth in 1956 for a 401 overpass and to make way for new housing, a steam shovel operator looked in surprise to see parts of human skeletons on his shovel.

Province of Ontario archaeologists quickly made their way to the scene and recommended the province acquire the site and declare it a cemetery. Although Iroquois left their dead in trees, they would later collect the bodies for a mass burial. Another

documented ossuary lies north of Barrie, Ontario, while the remains of an Iroquois village were unearthed close by the Taber Hill site.

In 1961, local dignitaries and First Nations representatives participated in a Feast of the Dead ceremony. Today, a large granite boulder with an historical plaque on one side and an Iroquois prayer dominates the hilltop. The ossuary is prominently situated on Bellamy Road, between Eglinton Avenue and Lawrence Avenue.

An unusual mound in the heart of suburban Scarborough is in fact an ancient Indigenous ossuary or burial mound.

Inset: A plaque atop the Taber Hill.

The rescued remains of Toronto's demolished buildings decorate the Guild Inn's gardens.

Right: Terracotta turrets from the Produce Exchange Building have become the rear gates to the Garden of Ruins.

98 THE GUILD INN'S GARDEN OF RUINS

Part of Toronto's Lost Heritage

IN 1914, GENERAL Harold C. Bickford built a country home on the Scarborough Bluffs. He called his two-and-a-half-storey house Ranelagh Park. In 1932, Rosa and Spencer Clark bought the home with its 162 hectares and established the Guild of All Arts. Here the Clarks hoped to help artists survive the difficult Depression years by giving them a home where they could practise their crafts. As the guild expanded, a dining room and more guest rooms were added, turning the facility into a popular resort under a new name — the Guild Inn.

After 1947, the couple became alarmed at the rate at which Toronto's many heritage buildings were being demolished. To help preserve part of this vanishing heritage, they began to acquire remnants of these elegant structures. And so began the garden of ruins.

In the garden, which stretches between the inn and the lake, lurk the vestiges of banks, homes, schools and industrial buildings: a white marble facade from the Imperial Bank of Canada (1875); a cornerstone and cornice from the Imperial Oil Company building; white terracotta Ionic capitals from the University of Toronto's Faculty of Medicine building; bas-relief panels from the Bank of Montreal buildings at King and Bay, from the Toronto Globe and Mail building (1938) and from the Toronto Star building (1929); as well as stone carvings and keystones from the O'Keefe Brewery (1840), the Ontario Bank (1868) and the Toronto General Post Office (1873).

Pillars and columns survive from the 1895 Temple Building, the 1915 Registry of Deeds and Lands Titles building and the 1913 Bank of Nova Scotia building. But the most photographed relic is the Greek Theatre built in 1981 from eight of the original twenty-one Corinthian capitals and columns belonging to the Bank of Toronto. The bank was built in 1912 and demolished in 1966.

In all, nearly sixty ruins and remnants lie scattered throughout a formal garden setting. The Inn has been restored and expanded to become a popular event venue and fine dining bistro. The garden of ruins is now part of Toronto's system of attractive parks and remains a popular setting for wedding photography, providing a unique opportunity to witness part of Toronto's lost heritage. The Guild Inn is located on the Guildwood Parkway, south of Kingston Road.

99 THE DUTCH CHAPEL
The Pillars of the Scarborough Bluffs

AMONG SOUTHERN ONTARIO's more unusual natural features are the Scarborough Bluffs. Not only do the craggy 20-kilometre-long forms loom up to 100 metres over Lake Ontario between the eastern end of the Beaches and the Rouge River, but their fractured and ever-eroding face reveals to scientists and laymen alike the mysteries of central Ontario's prehistoric past.

Unlike the tiny trickle that is today's Don River, Toronto was once the site of a mighty pre-glacial torrent, greater than the St. Lawrence. Here, more than seventy thousand years ago, these rushing waters poured into a great lake and there deposited an extensive delta. Then the ice age, with glaciers often more than 2 kilometres thick, deposited more boulder clay on top of the delta.

As the last ice sheets melted away twelve thousand years ago, and the lakes behind them drained, the delta stood like a mighty mesa above what was then a barren landscape. Wind, water and frost then began to eat away at its southern face. The alternating layers of soft, pure sand and rock-hard clay created oddly shaped pinnacles and buttresses. So closely did the rugged shoreline resemble her beloved Yorkshire homeland, that the wife of Upper Canada's first governor, John Graves Simcoe, named them the Scarborough Bluffs.

In a quiet gully at the foot of Scarborough's Midland Avenue, erosion has created a series of buttresses somewhat like the architecture found in medieval European chapels, and geologists have named the area the Dutch Chapel.

Today, most visit "the Bluffs," as they are called locally, to picnic in the popular Bluffers Park located at the foot of Brimley Road. Here are beaches, restaurants, yachts, houseboats and unsightly marinas.

A few steep and lengthy walking trails will get you down as well, but don't expect to find any facilities. The Doris McCarthy Trail, named for the famed Canadian painter, starts from the foot of Bellamy Road and descends to the lake where a sculpture pays tribute to the painter. Another trail leads from the Guildwood Parkway adjacent to the Guild Inn and a third is next to Scarborough Heights Park. The lands along the top of the Bluffs offer a few intriguing sights as well. The beautiful clifftop Rosetta McLean Gardens, once a private estate, provides a walk through a series of attractive seasonal gardens. The Guild Inn features remnants from many of Toronto's demolished historic buildings. A plaque at the end of Meadowcliffe Drive celebrates the life of McCarthy, where her former home, which she called "Fool's Paradise," is now a retreat for artists. You can also view the bluffs from a string of lofty cliff-top vistas located in a series of small parks scattered along its length.

The unusual formations along the Scarborough Bluffs are a popular geological attraction.

100 A UTILITARIAN BEAUTY

The R.C. Harris Filtration Plant

IN THE EAST end of Toronto, on a grassy slope overlooking Lake Ontario, sits one of the city's most attractive and least-known buildings — a filtration plant. Buildings housing public utilities seldom inspire either architectural elegance or public interest. But this one is different, and its difference is attributed to its namesake, Rowland Cole Harris.

Designed by Thomas Pomphrey, the building was constructed between 1932 and 1941. A second building was added in the early 1950s. It was named after Harris, who was at the time Toronto's commissioner of works, and was a man who appreciated grand public buildings. The style that Harris chose for his filtration plant was Art Deco, an attractive modern style in vogue during the 1920s and '30s and often used for skyscrapers and other grand buildings.

Characterized by streamlined curves and shapes, Art Deco is also a style that was relatively short-lived. After the Second World War, the tastes of a generation railed against the recent past, the years of war and Depression. Architects moved to a simpler form known simply as the International style.

The R.C. Harris Filtration Plant occupies an extensive grassy park. The older structure, closer to the lake, is the pumping station, which draws water from over 2 kilometres out in the lake, while the higher building does the filtering and chlorinating.

While sleek lines dominate the exterior, herringbone tiles of marble imported from Siena decorate the foyer and vast halls. In these halls the plant can process 950 million litres of water each day. Like the Distillery District, the R.C. Harris plant, which provides a modernistic set for movies, is popular with film companies.

The exterior grounds are open to the public on weekdays, while the interior is open to public tours during Toronto's Annual Doors Open weekend held in the spring-summer.

The plant is located on Queen Street East at Neville Park Boulevard, the eastern terminus of the Queen Street streetcar line. It also marks the eastern end of the popular Toronto neighbourhood known as the Beach, with its lakeside boardwalk, trendy cafés and eclectic mix of stores.

The Art Deco R. C. Harris water filtration plant.

⑩ PERFECT PURIFICATION
The Elevated Wetlands of the Don Valley

THE ELEVATED WETLANDS of the Don Valley have drivers on the busy Don Valley Parkway blinking in disbelief. At the Don Mills Road exit are a half-dozen massive plant pots. To some, they may look more like giant topless teapots; to others, grotesque mastodons performing some form of daisy chain. They are in fact an innovative system of purifying the waters of the Don River using only plastic.

In 1995, the Canadian Plastics Industry Association hired artist Noel Harding to create a public work of art that would help illustrate the artistic potential of that industrial material. Harding, a sculptor who pushes the limits of both sculpture and material, is well known for his Potato Eaters sculpture. This series of metal structures is 12 to 25 metres high, each containing a living tree, and helped earn him international attention at the Atlanta Olympics.

Inside the giant pots in the Don Valley are various types of plastic, all shredded, including bottles, resins, auto fluff and geo textiles. A cluster of solar panels pumps water from the Don River into the highest of the pots. Here, plants, shrubs and trees draw the pollutants and toxins from the water and return it perfectly pure. More than seventy different industries helped sponsor the unusual project, including fifty plastics industries. The sculptures, which measure between 8 and 15 metres high, were created between 1997 and 1998 and developed from a prototype developed at the University of Lethbridge.

Harding's is not the only effort to clean up the river. A short distance downstream, the Friends of the Don won a $100,000 grant from the Ontario government to excavate a century and a half of industrial residue from the floodplain. They replaced the landfill with a natural wetland ecosystem which, like the elevated wetlands, provides free water purification.

The strange sculptures can be seen up close from Taylor Creek Park on Don Mills Road, just north of the Don Valley Parkway. The marshland lies to the south of the Bloor Viaduct and can be accessed from the bike trail that follows the valley.

The Don Valley Parkway's elevated wetlands.

⑩ MOUNT PLEASANT CEMETERY

A Who's Who of the Rich and Not-so-Famous

NOWHERE IN ONTARIO do so many figures from history gather together as in Toronto's Mount Pleasant Cemetery. There are grand mausoleums for the rich and famous, as well as simple monuments that honour those who contributed to the country's history. Some are as large as houses, designed by the leading architects of the day, while others are modest stones or plaques. One is even shaped like a truck tire.

Surrounded now by a busy city, when it first opened over a century ago, it was far off in the country.

As York began to grow it needed a place to bury its dead. At first only those who adhered to the Catholic or Anglican Churches were guaranteed a place in which to rest in peace. Then, in 1826, a three-hectare parcel of land on the northwest corner of today's Yonge and Bloor was set aside as a non-denominational graveyard. By 1855, Potter's Field, as it came to be called, contained 6,000 bodies.

But the village of Yorkville to the north and west needed to expand and the cemetery stood in the way. To allow the growth, the remains were exhumed and reburied in the Necropolis on Winchester Avenue. But in less than 20 years, it too was full and the city's fathers needed to look to the country.

An 80-hectare farm north of the hamlet of Deer Park (Yonge and St. Clair today) seemed to be the right answer. A German-born landscape architect named Henry Engelhardt designed the grounds, drawing inspiration from Boston's Mt. Auburn Cemetery. In 1876, when Mount Pleasant Cemetery opened, its first interments were some still-unclaimed remains from the old Potter's Field with a plaque to mark the spot.

But along with these unnamed poor are monuments to the rich and famous, such as the Simpson family's mausoleum and the massive temple-like tomb of the Eatons, both families of department store fame. Nearby, and easily the most impressive of the mammoth monuments, is that of the Massey family, multi-millionaire scions of the Massey-Harris farm implement manufacturing empire. Designed by Toronto's leading architect, Edward James Lennox, also famous for Old City Hall, it towers 10 metres above the cemetery grounds.

Among the most compelling memorials are those to victims of some of Canada's most horrific disasters, such as the 1,477 victims of the ocean liner *Empress of Ireland*, which sank in just 15 minutes after colliding with a coal boat in 1914; the 119 victims of the *Noronic* that burned in 1950 while docked at the Toronto waterfront; and the 109 victims of Air Canada Flight 621, which crashed and burned at Toronto airport in 1970.

Besides the politicians and prime ministers are the graves of Frederick Banting and

James Best, co-inventors of insulin; Alexander Muir, who composed *The Maple Leaf Forever*; and Foster Hewitt, whose voice remains forever in the memories of Toronto hockey fans from the 1930s to the 1970s. The strangest monument of all honours Wallace Gordon Chalmers, the inventor of a revolutionary suspension system for trucks, trailers and wheel chairs. His grave marker is in the shape of a large radial truck tire.

Visitors can follow Toronto's self-guided Discovery Walk tour or the more detailed and delightfully anecdotal guide written by Mike Filey.

Top right: The Massey family mausoleum is one the grandest structures in the Mount Pleasant cemetery.

Right: As his monument may indicate, Gordon Chalmers was an inventor of wheel suspension systems.

⑩③ THE LUMINOUS VEIL
A Bridge Ahead of Its Time

THE MASSIVE ARCHING bridge that carries Bloor Street across Toronto's wide Don Valley was a bridge ahead of its time. As Works Commissioner from 1912 to 1945 (the longest serving commissioner in the city's history), R.C. Harris envisioned a bridge for the future.

In 1914, Toronto extended east only to the Don Valley. The wide chasm was until then breached only by a small bridge across the river. Transit users were forced to use Broadview Avenue south to Queen Street before they reached a bridge over the river.

But as pressure to expand grew, Harris realized that the city needed to open up the area east of the valley. And so he proposed the Prince Edward Viaduct. But it wouldn't be a simple bridge — it would be wide enough to accommodate four lanes of motor traffic with streetcar tracks along the middle. Then, in a far-sighted initiative, he added a lower substructure to accommodate rail traffic. Subways were becoming a major means of public transit in such places as London and New York. But Toronto politicians are notorious for not rushing their decisions and another half-century would pass before the bridge saw its first subway train.

With the opening of the bridge, growth quickly leapt the gap, spurring commercial growth along Danforth Avenue and residential development along the side streets leading off of it.

True to his artistic instincts, Harris also insisted on an elegant design for his structure (Harris was most famous for his art deco water filtration plant at the foot of Victoria Park Avenue). The final design is the work of Edmund Burke and consists of three arching spans that extend for nearly 500 metres and rise 40 metres above the flat valley land below.

But the bridge tragically attracted more than development. It also lured those determined to end their lives as a platform from which to plunge to their fate. In fact, the suicide rate in the 1990s exceeded one per month. This led to the design and installation of a suicide barrier known as the "luminous veil." The design by Derek Revington consists of 9,000 aluminum rods 5 metres long and positioned 12.7 centimetres apart.

Completed in 2003, the design has earned the Canadian Architect Award of Excellence. Revington's vision also included lighting, but it took the advent of the Pan Am and Para Pan Am Games in July of 2015 for the usually obstinate Toronto City Council to allocate the $2.8 million to finish the 450-metre long LED lighting system. The system, which begins after dark, casts a blue glow over the veil while moving coloured lights illuminate the frame.

The Bloor Viaduct's luminous veil has 9,000 rods to prevent suicides.

(104) TINY TOWN

Toronto's Smallest Houses

TORONTO'S LITTLE NOOKS and crannies hide many surprises. While its older and architecturally more splendid buildings are widely known, smaller and simpler structures are often even more interesting because their odds of surviving demolition or alteration are comparatively slim. That's the case with Cabbagetown's tiny Wellesley Cottages, located just north of Wellesley Street at Sackville.

During the 1870s and '80s, Ontario's railway boom years, labourers' cottages, as they were called, were hastily built to house the influx of workers. Between then and the 1890s, thousands were constructed in working-class neighbourhoods all across Toronto. The Wellesley Cottages were built around 1886–87.

Constructed of wood, usually with no foundations, these tiny one-and-a-half-storey cabins all boasted a centre plan, and many had a trademark gable over the front door. The style earned its designers an architectural award for workmen's cottage design at the Crystal Palace Exhibit in England in 1851.

Over the years, demands for bigger and safer housing meant the end of a housing era in Toronto and the gradual disappearance of these simple abodes. Throughout the city only a few isolated examples survive, and the Wellesley Cottages are a remarkable row of seven. They are located not on a main residential street, but on a narrow lane behind the backyards of the principal row of houses. After being used for a time as low-cost rental units, they were sold to a developer who upgraded them.

Much of Old Cabbagetown is equally interesting. A stroll along Wellesley, Sumach (Cabbagetown's old-timers pronounce it "shoo-mack"), Spruce and Winchester streets reveals a residential neighbourhood of eclectic houses that date to the days when the area's low-income residents planted cabbages in their front yards, giving the community its unusual name. In this area you will also find the former Riverdale Zoo, now an animal farm for children.

For many years a 2.5-metre-wide house on Shuter Street, now enlarged, was considered Toronto's narrowest. However, an even narrower dwelling on Day Street in Toronto's west end now claims that title, being wedged between two larger two-storey homes.

Farther west of Shuter, another row of tiny nineteenth-century homes lines a narrow lane a block west of McCaul Street and a short distance north of Queen Street.

Toronto's tiniest house is dwarfed between two regular-sized homes in Toronto's west end.

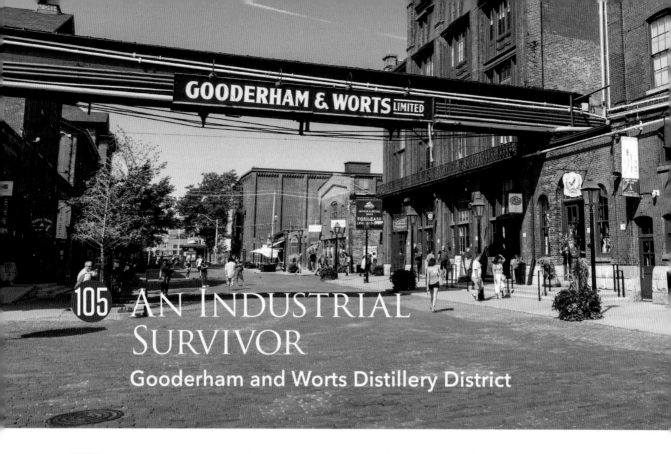

105 AN INDUSTRIAL SURVIVOR
Gooderham and Worts Distillery District

DESPITE A HISTORY of insensitive and often unnecessary demolitions, Toronto can still claim a remarkable collection of heritage buildings. While structures like Old City Hall, Casa Loma and Union Station are widely known grand buildings, gritty industrial survivors are just as compelling and sometimes even more so.

Of paramount importance to Toronto's industrial heritage is the Gooderham and Worts complex at Parliament and Mill streets, in what was once the industrial heartland of east-end Toronto. Today it has been rechristened as "the Distillery District," and is Toronto's newest major tourist attraction. It is also considered Canada's oldest and most complete early-nineteenth-century industrial complex.

In the 1830s, English miller James Worts chose the confluence of the Don River with Toronto's harbour to erect a wind-powered flour mill, eastern Toronto's first industry. He was later joined by his brother-in-law, William Gooderham. It was common in pioneer Canada to use second-grade grain from grist-mill operations to produce whiskey. And the Gooderham and Worts mill did just that.

In the 1850s both the Great Western Railway and Grand Trunk Railway completed their lines into Toronto, and the waterfront boomed with industry. In 1859, Gooderham and Worts added a magnificent limestone distillery, the beginning of an expansion phase that lasted until 1890. By 1861 the company was producing 25,000 litres of whiskey a day, and by 1870 it was responsible for one third of Canada's rye whiskey production. Extensive sections of the waterfront were filled in, the Don River was straightened and soon the

The Gooderham and Worts industrial complex, a candidate for World Heritage designation.

plant was nowhere near the lake. But with a railway siding beside the distillery, water transport was no longer needed.

In 1928 the firm merged with Hiram Walker of Windsor, and the Gooderham and Worts facility became a secondary production plant. In 1986 it was purchased by Allied Lyons of England. Four years later it was declared obsolete and closed. A century and a half of liquor production had ended.

Because it had been relegated to a lesser role in its later years, the entire complex was little altered, and remained much as it had appeared in the 1890s. Its size and age make it one of Canada's most remarkable historic industrial complexes, earning it recognition as a National Historic Site.

Still, for fifteen years the site sat vacant, although popular for movie shoots. Its brick streets and authentic facades provided set pieces for period movies such as *X-Men*, *The Hurricane* and the Academy Award-winning *Chicago*, as well as dozens of sketches in the television show *Kids in the Hall*. It is claimed that more than eight hundred movies and commercials have used the grounds for film sets.

In 2002, the entire complex was purchased by a group called Cityscape, which converted the two dozen buildings into a haven for artists and galleries, and in May of 2003, the "Distillery District" was formally opened. Various rooms, including the smoke house, the boiler house, the malting plant and the pure-spirits building, are now occupied by galleries, studios, bars and cafés. Where possible, early machinery has been left in place.

106 FROM BRICKS TO BROCCOLI

Toronto's Evergreen Brickworks

THERE IS OFTEN a long line waiting to enter the farmers' market at the iconic Evergreen Brickworks on the Bayview Extension in Toronto's Don Valley. It is one of the many attractions which has opened in what was once one of Canada's largest and longest-lasting brickmaking operations. And it almost didn't happen.

The many fine clays which lie beneath Toronto proved ideal for the making of bricks. As Toronto's growth boomed through the nineteenth century, demand for building materials exploded and by the century's end, Toronto could count thirty-two brickyards among its many industries. The largest of them all was the Don Valley Pressed Brick Company.

The company was launched in 1891 by John, William and George Taylor whose family, over the years, had created a milling empire along the Don Valley. The site was ideal, situated at the base of the valley wall where deep layers of red and yellow clay abounded. And it was right beside a main railway line. Within a few years, the Taylors were operating eight kilns and producing 114,000 bricks each day, including more than 400 different types of brick. Their sixty-five employees lived on the east side of the valley in communities like Chester and Todmorden.

By 1901, the Taylors went bankrupt and in 1909 sold the operation to the Davies family.

By 1920, then known as the Don Valley Brick Works Ltd., the kilns were pressing more than 25 million bricks each year, its four chimneys dominating the valley's landscape.

Renovations through the 1950s and '60s included the arrival of a massive brick press from the then-closed John Price brickyards on Greenwood Avenue. In 1984, production halted and a developer, Torvalley, acquired the site with plans to demolish the historic buildings and erect apartments. However, opposition began to grow and the plans for apartments were abandoned when the Conservation Authority designated the site as a flood plain where no development could occur.

The Conservation Authority then expropriated the entire site, turning the pit area over to the Toronto parks department and leasing the buildings to Evergreen Brick Works.

Today, this unusual industrial survivor has become one of Toronto's most popular daytrip destinations. The buildings contain a large farmers' market and a garden market, while in the kiln building, the TD Cities Centre offers displays and exhibits. Here too the John Price brick press sits on display, described by the Ontario Heritage Trust as the most significant industrial artifact of the many on site.

When not exploring the buildings or shopping or enjoying a snack, families can explore the park behind the buildings with trails, a

222

children's garden, herb garden and a pond which becomes a skating rink during the winter, or climb to a look-out point above the site. A few souls might wander to the rear of the property where the varved clays, which supplied the brickworks for nearly a century, remain exposed along with interpretative signage.

Visitors often arrive by bicycle along the Don Valley bike path or by a shuttle bus from the TTC's Broadview subway station. A large, and somewhat confusing, pay parking lot caters to drivers arriving via the Bayview Extension roadway.

Toronto's Evergreen Brickworks is now one of Toronto's more popular daytrip destinations.

⑩⑦ A Horse Palace

Casa Loma and Its Stables

CASA LOMA DOMINATES Toronto's brochures, has felt the footsteps of millions of tourists and has been the location of dozens of movie shoots. Toronto's best-known landmark is also its only castle. Less well known are the incredible Casa Loma stables. In fact, these elegant barns were finished a full four years before construction on the Casa even started. With their castle-like towers and turrets, their design owes much to the stables of large European houses.

The castle's owner and builder was Sir Henry Pellatt. A multimillionaire, Pellatt earned his riches by investing in land along the newly built Canadian Pacific Railway to the west. He used those earnings to build Canada's first hydro generating station at Niagara Falls.

But he also loved the military and castles, and in 1905 he purchased twenty residential lots on top of the Davenport Escarpment. He then hired architect Edward James Lennox, designer of the city's most prominent buildings (including the old city hall), to design his castle. By 1914, the dream castle was complete on the outside. Huge cost overruns, however, prevented him from finishing the interior. After ten years, his wife's illness and financial ruin forced him to flee the castle.

Interestingly, the lesser-known stables more truly reflect the lifestyle and tastes of this mysterious man. Described as the most lavish anywhere on the continent, the buildings were completed in 1906. Inside, the stalls are of mahogany, with the horses' names spelled out in gold lettering above each. The floors were covered in Spanish tiles, laid in a herringbone pattern so that horses would not slip. Pellatt's favourite horse, named Prince, was even outfitted with a set of false teeth. The entrance is framed in white stone to contrast with the red brick of the building.

Adjoining the stables, the carriage house boasts a room larger even than the castle's main hall. Here, Pellatt stored his magnificent collection of carriages and Toronto's first electric car. The stables and carriage room are connected to the castle by a 150-metre-long tunnel.

Casa Loma and its stables are located on Spadina Road, north of Davenport Road.

Casa Loma's stables are as grand as the "castle" itself.

The Yorkville Rock sparked controversy when it was moved from Gravenhurst to Toronto.

108 THE YORKVILLE ROCK
A Piece of the Canadian Shield in Toronto

THE ROCK IS more than a billion years old, weighs 650 tonnes and cost $300,000, yet it contains no precious metals or minerals. Plunked right in the middle of Toronto's priciest shopping district, it is known, somewhat derogatorily, as the "Yorkville Rock."

In 1966, Toronto's new east-west subway slashed through the hippy haven known as Yorkville Village, a collection of coffee houses tucked into a row of nineteenth-century homes. Although the little neighbourhood evolved into an ever-pricier shopping area, the subway route had left a no-man's land on which nothing heavy could be built. For years the strip of land remained an unsightly parking lot.

Finally, in 1991 the City of Toronto and the local business association hired architect Olesand Worland to create a park to befit both the context and the history of the area. In just one city block, his park would display the ecological variety of the entire province. While the trees and the flowers presented no problem, Toronto offered nothing that resembled Ontario's most extensive landscape element, the Canadian Shield, whose hard, rounded rocks are the oldest on Earth. The nearest outcrops were over 150 kilometres away.

The solution he proposed was to move a granite outcrop from Gravenhurst to Toronto, a procedure that would cost more than a quarter of a million dollars. The first reaction was ridicule and outrage; however, the park not only proceeded but opened in 1994 to widespread acclaim from architects and users alike. In one city block the visitor can travel from a garden with bluebells and trilliums to an alder grove, a wetland and a herb garden. At the end of the provincial mini-tour, the visitor has lunch or reads a book on top of a billion-year-old rock. The park stretches along the south side of Cumberland Avenue, between Avenue Road and Bellair Street.

Although equally acclaimed, the award-winning Cloud Gardens, in the heart of Toronto's financial district, has fared less well. In contrast to the much-visited Yorkville park, Cloud Gardens is little more than a haven for the homeless and a gathering place for downtown bike couriers.

Designed by Margaret Priest, the small lot on Temperance Street between Yonge and Bay contains urban woodland, waterfalls and an observation platform. Situated over the entrance to a parking garage is a glass-enclosed "Cloud Forest" conservatory, with its re-creation of a tropical rain forest. Surrounded by the glass towers of the Bay Street brokers, this intriguing urban park won a Governor-General's Medal for Architecture in 1994 and a merit award from the Canadian Society of Landscape Architects the next year.

The faces of Old City Hall.

109 THE FEELING OF BEING WATCHED

Toronto's Old City Hall Gargoyles

HAVE YOU EVER had the feeling that you're being watched? Stand in front of Toronto's Old City Hall and you are — by its gargoyles!

Old City Hall is a remarkable example of the Victorian Romanesque Revival architectural style. Completed in 1899, it was one of those grand municipal buildings typical of the period. With its tall clock tower dominating Bay Street, each nook and cranny — and there are many — of its sandstone exterior seems to offer a different architectural surprise, especially the gargoyles. While such grotesque faces were common on medieval buildings, some of those on Old City Hall carried a special meaning.

City architect E.J. Lennox had staked much of his reputation on what he hoped would be his masterpiece. But when the Toronto city council of the day short-changed him, or so he thought, he decided to even the score.

There, above the grand entrance, sits E.J. Lennox's revenge: the gargoyles are the distorted faces of the councillors themselves. In a final act of defiance, Lennox added, contrary to instructions, his own name and a caricature said to resemble himself. Old City Hall is festooned with dozens of the more traditional gargoyles — grotesque animal-like faces. But the faces of the Toronto council of the day will live on in a way none had likely intended.

Much of Victorian Toronto has vanished. Fine old buildings of stone or brick have fallen victim to insensitive redevelopment, and to builders whose bottom line doesn't include a respect for heritage. Even Old City Hall itself was threatened when the Eaton Centre was proposed. But citizen outrage saved the building, which today functions as a court. And so, amid modern glass and concrete towers, the gargoyles of Toronto's Old City Hall still keep watch.

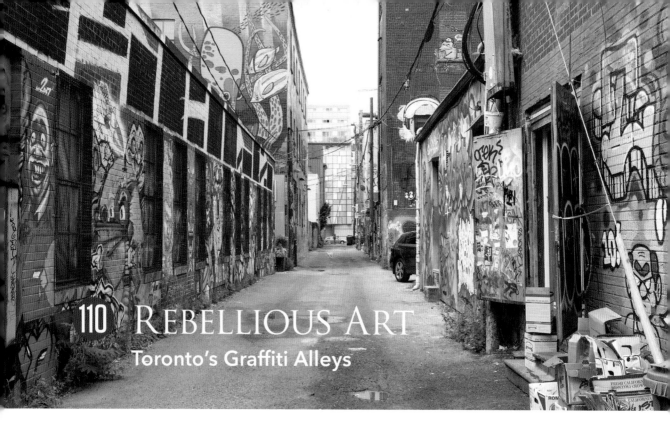

110 REBELLIOUS ART
Toronto's Graffiti Alleys

WALL ART HAS existed in Ontario for thousands of years. The earliest known examples were created by First Nations inhabitants using ochre and animal grease to depict myths and events that formed parts of their daily lives.

But graffiti evolved from rebellion, not mythology. Originally, disenchanted New York City youths would simply spray their names or "tags" on whatever was handy, a symbolic representation of themselves or their group as a defiance of authority. For the most part these lacked any aesthetic sense and were considered vandalism to be quickly painted over or whitewashed.

As the graffiti artists grew more competitive, the art grew more elaborate. Eventually tags became more like murals. Graffiti artists became increasingly well known, even famous, such as the British artist Banksy. Many of Toronto's graffiti depictions were

the work of KWEST, Peru 143, EGR, Skam, Elicser and Sensr.

Despite efforts by misguided city politicians to declare "war" on graffiti, Toronto has come to embrace the phenomenon. The Graffiti Management Plan funds street art, and StreetARToronto has a directory, which lists more than 100 street artists. Organized tours include the more popular graffiti walls, while comedian Rick Mercer used graffiti backdrops for the "rant" portion of his weekly CBC television show, "The Mercer Report."

Even Toronto Tourism now promotes the graffiti attractions, while a local Business Improvement Area offers free summer tours of Graffiti Alley. In Toronto's bustling Chinatown, merchants commissioned local artists to paint the walls in their area.

The most visited of Toronto's mural collection is aptly known as Graffiti Alley, a laneway that runs between Spadina Avenue and

Graffiti has gone from vandalism to art in Toronto's "Graffiti Alley,"
as well as in several other locations around the city.

Bathurst Street, just south of Queen Street. The Kensington Market area, just west of Spadina and north of Dundas, is another well-visited graffiti attraction. In 2012, twenty local graffiti artists collaborated on a series of murals along a laneway near Ossington Avenue, where dozens of garage doors now sport their creations.

Subway riders travelling between Dundas West and Keele stations, where the tracks emerge from the tunnel, will encounter a large graffiti wall on the rear of a row of stores. Other popular graffiti locations include laneways near Pape and Danforth behind Eaton Avenue, Woodycrest and Langford Avenues, and also along Milky Way, a laneway in Toronto's Parkdale neighbourhood. Fortunately Toronto's transit vehicles, unlike those in most American cities, have remained free of the controversial art form.

Sadly, many fine creations do not last, as successions of later graffiti artists may cover more elegant depictions with crude tags. This often leads to the question about where graffiti art and historic outdoor murals overlap. Many business groups have commissioned mural artists to create exterior wall murals that depict the history of their business area, such as those found along Islington Avenue and Kingston Road. Indeed, communities across Ontario have become famous for their downtown murals, including Midland, Welland and St. Thomas.

Toronto, however, has quickly attained the status of being the graffiti capital of Canada. (For tour information, see www.tourguys.ca.)

Tiny cottages with no roads, only sidewalks, make for an unusual landscape on Toronto's islands. Many island cottages enjoy a harbourside view of Toronto's skyline.

⑪ Cottage Country South
The Toronto Island Community

O N THE EAST end of the island archipelago known collectively as the Toronto Islands are cottages unlike any that are found elsewhere in Ontario. In fact, they are no longer real "cottages" but have become permanent homes.

The island chain was at one time a sandy spit of land jutting into the lake. In 1858 a vicious storm sent waves hurtling across the narrow isthmus, so strong that they opened a new channel, turning the sand spit into a chain of islands.

Several amusement parks sprang up along the lake at spots both east and west of the industrial core, including Hanlan's Point on the Toronto Islands. Hotels, dance halls and rides drew Torontonians to the island haven. There was for a time a baseball stadium located where today's island airport is situated.

At the same time on Ward's Island, down at the east end of the chain, a campground appeared. Campers originally paid $10 for the season to pitch their tents. But the demand grew to such an extent that the government laid out "streets" and designated lots for each tent. As time went by, floors were added, as were kitchens and then porches. Finally permanent buildings replaced the tents. Then in 1953, the newly amalgamated Metropolitan Toronto government assumed ownership of the island and set about removing the buildings. But the government hadn't counted upon the tenacity of the cottage owners, who by now were occupying their dwellings year-round.

Despite ongoing efforts by the Metro government to have them evicted, cottage owners were eventually granted 99-year leases. And so there they stay.

The island allows no cars; residents move about by foot or bicycle. The lots on which the buildings stand remain the size of a tent site. No roads run between them, simply sidewalks. More than 260 homes crowd the islands, a smaller number of them on nearby Algonquin Island. The styles and methods of decorating are eclectic, with statuary, sculptures and vines all adorning the tiny homes. Islanders work, shop and play for the most part on the mainland, connected by frequent ferry service.

Beyond Ward's Island lie luxurious yacht clubs and the concrete steps and foundations of those homes that were removed earlier on. Other historic structures include the 1809 Gibraltar Point lighthouse, said to be haunted by its first keeper; a church rectory that now serves as a delightful restaurant; the lovely white, wooden St. Andrews-by-the-Lake Anglican Church; and the historic airport terminal building.

112 A GHOST ON WATCH

Toronto Island's Haunted Lighthouse

ONTARIO'S OLDEST STANDING lighthouse is haunted, some say, by the ghost of its first keeper. Constructed of huge limestone blocks, the hexagonal 16-metre structure was built in 1808 at Gibraltar Point, on what is now the Toronto Island archipelago, before there was a Toronto, and even before there were islands. (In 1834 the Town of York became the City of Toronto. The islands were actually a peninsula until 1858, when a vicious storm hurled waves across its narrow, sandy neck, severing it from the mainland.)

When the lighthouse was completed, John Paul Radan Muller was appointed its keeper and he moved into a small log cabin beside it. In April 1813, he watched helplessly as Colonel Pearce guided fourteen American ships past the lighthouse and landed the troops that would capture York, in one of the few American victories of the War of 1812.

Just two years later, Radan Muller disappeared in circumstances that the *York Gazette* described as "moral proof of having been murdered." It would later add that there was "no conviction of the supposed murder." Was he murdered by drunken companions? Did he renege on a bootlegging operation then being run from the military base?

Although the former whale-oil lamp has been replaced by modern navigational aids, the lighthouse remains virtually unaltered. Yet, around it, an entire chapter in Toronto's history has started and finished. By the 1920s, the islands had become a popular recreational complex of amusement parks, hotels and private cottages. It was here in the island baseball stadium that baseball legend Babe Ruth hit his first professional home run into the waters of the lake.

Today, Gibraltar Point is a passive recreational area where trees, grass and trails have replaced the buildings of a bygone day. And the changes are all carefully watched over by the lighthouse and its keeper.

The old stone lighthouse on Toronto Island's Gibraltar Point is said to be haunted by its first keeper.

113 HIGH PARK'S RARE BLACK OAK SAVANNAHS

HIGH PARK, IN the west end of Toronto, is a blissful oasis in this congested and sprawling city. We can thank a landowner named John Howard for the park. In 1836, Howard purchased a 66-hectare property where he built his home, Colborne Lodge. He lived there with his wife, Jemima, until her passing in 1876. In 1873 he donated the land to the citizens of Toronto to maintain as a "Public Park for the free use, benefit and enjoyment of the citizens of the City of Toronto forever."

Following the donation, the city acquired a further 69 hectares in 1876 and a final 29 hectares around Grenadier Pond in 1930. As city growth engulfed the natural area, planners began adding recreational features such as a swimming pool, tennis courts, skating rink and picnic grounds, as well as a zoo. Finally, in the 1990s, the city and the province embarked on studies to help preserve and maintain the ecosystem of the park, including the rare Black Oak savannahs which have survived there.

The parkland originally lay on the shores of Lake Ontario. Here, the sloping sandy soils were ideal for the evolution of a Black Oak savannah ecosystem. While visitors can enjoy High Park's playing fields, the zoo, the gardens or the seasonal splendour of the Japanese cherry blossoms, only a few may be aware of its rare natural features, like the Black Oak savannahs and even prairie grasslands. Experts consider the oak savannahs at High Park to be "continentally significant" as they represent the last 0.1% of the two million hectares of savannah which once existed in southern Ontario.

This rare landscape covers about ⅓ of the park's area and is found largely on its western and northern reaches, although a small stand lies along the east side. The savannah landscape is one of large widely spaced black oak trees, interspersed with a variety of grasses and flowering shrubs, such as mulberry, sunflower, milkweed and wild raspberries and blueberries. The Western Woodlands Trail offers the best opportunity to view the oak savannah ecosystem. A small Prairie ecosystem is found on the park's highest point, known as Hawk Hill.

While there are three vehicle entrances to the park, there is also the High Park subway station on the north side of Bloor Street.

High Park's rare Black Oak savannahs are among the few such remaining ecosystems in Canada.

Right: High Park's cherry blossoms are a popular springtime draw.

114 ODE TO JOY
The Last Joy Gas Station

ARCHITECTURE AND GAS stations just don't seem to go together. Mention the latter and one thinks of gas pumps, the smell of old oil and a building whose architecture is better left unmentioned.

But that wasn't the case during the 1920s and '30s, when the auto age was unfolding and gas stations were becoming part of the neighbourhood landscape. While price wars and gimmicks were the most common forms of competition, another method, undertaken first by the Hercules Oil Company of Detroit, was to create an attractive style of gas station.

Ironically, the style that Hercules chose was that which the Canadian Pacific Railway had introduced more than thirty years earlier when its stations were designed to attract passengers to the rail service. Known as the "chateau style," it incorporated steep bell-cast roofs and high towers. The Joy Oil Company introduced them to Toronto in 1936, and with their high red roofs and white stucco siding, these mini-chateaux soon became landmarks in many areas of the city. A total of sixteen red-roofed Joy Oil gas stations were built throughout Toronto.

Following the war, architectural styles changed. North America wanted to forget the hard years of war and the Depression that preceded it. Decorative features such as turrets and steep roofs were discarded in favour of the airiness and simplicity of flat roofs and large windows. Cars became bigger, so to keep up, the gas stations needed to be larger and more efficient. The tiny Joy gas stations were inadequate to meet the economic and environmental needs of the new auto age. Corporate image was important too, and the subsequent owners of the Joy stations replaced them with the newest styles.

The old Joy stations quickly began to disappear from the landscape. By the mid-1980s only four remained in Toronto and by 1992 there was just one. Located at the northwest corner of Lakeshore Boulevard West and Windermere Avenue, this solitary station was built while the Queen Elizabeth Way was under construction, which, until the Gardiner Expressway opened in the 1950s, connected directly to the lakeshore.

In 1989, the city of Toronto designated the unlikely little structure as a heritage building. In 2000, Olco, then the station's operator, finally closed the pumps and sold the site for affordable housing. The station was relocated to the south side of Lakeshore Boulevard where it has been renovated. As of 2021, an option to allow a restaurant in the building is caught up in red tape between the City of Toronto and the food service company which owns exclusive food service rights to the entire Sir Casimir Gzowski Park in which the building is located.

Toronto's last Joy gas station has been relocated
and restored on the south side of Lakeshore Boulevard.

Now a Humber College campus, buildings originally designed for the Mimico "lunatic asylum" offered early residents a more rural feel than did the previous hospital settings.

⑪⑤ A NEW LEASE ON LIFE

The Mimico Asylum

THERE LIES AT the foot of Toronto's Kipling Avenue, where it meets Lakeshore Boulevard, a stunning set of brick and stone buildings. Now a part of the Humber College campus, it may be difficult to believe that they once housed a population of individuals who a century ago were categorized as "lunatics."

It all began with Dr. Daniel Clark, the superintendent of the then Queen Street Asylum for the insane in Toronto. He believed that institutionalization was of little benefit to its residents, and a village-style setting would aid in their rehabilitation. Along with provincial architect Kivas Tully and a landscape gardener named Samuel Matheson, Dr. Clark created such an environment on a 20-hectare parcel of land overlooking Lake Ontario in an area that at the time was farmland.

In 1889 the first residents moved to the new facility. The "village" consisted of a series of dormitories and an assembly hall. The asylum residents formed their own cricket team and farmed the land.

In 1911 it became the Mimico Hospital for the Insane. Soon the designation "insane" was removed, and it became the Ontario Hospital (New Toronto) and then the Lakeshore Psychiatric Hospital.

Then in 1979, badly overcrowded, the hospital closed its doors and became a popular location for the filming of movies, including *Police Academy*.

Because of the buildings' remarkable architecture and historic institutional role, the Ontario government designated them a provincial heritage district. In 1999 the assembly hall was renovated to become a community facility, and the remaining buildings redesigned to become a campus for Humber College.

116 AN INDIAN JEWEL

Toronto's Shri Swaminarayan Mandir

YES, IT IS quite a mouthful. Rising above the industrial sprawl of north Etobicoke, this Hindu temple is as sudden and surprising as coming upon the Taj Mahal. Here, a series of delicate white towers and turrets rise above the surrounding sprawl of faceless industries. While it looks as though it belongs in 15th century India, it is very much a modern addition to Toronto's landscape.

Opened in 2007, the temple employed more than 1,800 craftsmen who worked for 18 months sculpting 24,000 pieces of Turkish white limestone, Carrara marble and Indian pink sandstone, using ancient Hindu carving techniques. So precise was their workmanship that the building was completed with no steel, no mortar and not a single nail. The largest of the intricately carved stones weighs 5.6 tonnes, the smallest 50 grams. There are 18 domes and, inside, visitors will pass 340 carved pillars and more than 130 archways. The entire structure was built according to ancient Hindu proscriptions for religious architecture. Gardens and fountains mark the entrance.

The main worship hall, with its labyrinth of pillars and enclaves, contains gilded statues of the various Hindu deities, who are given a ritual daily feeding, part of the lighting ceremony that members of the public are invited to join. Many festivals occur throughout the year including Diwali, the festival of the lights, one of Hinduism's most important events.

Volunteer devotees give guided tours of the Mandir. There are a few rules of which visitors should be aware: shoes may not be worn inside, although cloth slippers are provided; there is no photography inside; and men and women sit separately during the lighting ceremony.

The complex also includes a museum and large community hall.

The BAPS Swaminarayan Santhsa, which oversees this and other mandirs around the world, is a global branch of Hinduism headed by Pramukh Swami Maharaj. The mandir is located at 61 Claireville Drive, just north of Finch Avenue and Highway 427. You may want to compare this temple with the very modern architecture of the Hindu Sabha temple a few kilometres away on Gore Road.

The Shri Swaminarayan Mandir looks like a miniature
Taj Mahal set amid Etobicoke's industrial wasteland.

(117) WELCOME TO CHINATOWN

Toronto's Most Colourful Streets

A WALK ALONG SPADINA Ave and Dundas Streets in downtown Toronto is like a stroll through the bustling markets of China itself. Vegetable stands crowd the sidewalks as customers with shopping carts laden with produce jostle for space. Overhead, colourful signs of yellow and red announce markets and gift shops.

Canada's Chinese immigrants arrived in the thousands to build the Canadian Pacific Railway, enduring low wages and harsh working conditions. When the railway was completed the Canadian government proceeded to make the immigration of Chinese difficult by barring family members and introducing the hated head tax.

The Chinese arrivals made their way eastward, where job opportunities were mostly limited to restaurants and laundries. And that is how Toronto's Chinatowns, the largest in North America, first grew along Dundas and Elizabeth Streets between University and Bay Streets, at first the city's Chinese population numbered only around 200.

Urban redevelopment through the 1960s, notably the building of Toronto's new city hall, destroyed much of the old neighbourhood, merchants moved west along Dundas and set up shop along Spadina Avenue. Over the following decades, as China became a leading source of new immigrants, Chinese traditional welcome gates were added. Even traditional Canadian businesses like banks and drug stores sported signs with their names in Chinese characters. Today, downtown Chinatown extends over several city blocks stretching north to College Street and both east and west along Dundas.

Sleek new streetcars trundle down a tree-lined boulevard in the centre of Spadina Avenue dominated by red columns, each boasting a figure from Chinese mythology at the top including a phoenix, unicorn, dragon and monkey. Chinese New Year attracts people from all over the city to witness traditional dragon dances and fireworks.

As Chinatown over-spilled its boundaries, a new community grew around Gerrard and Broadview. Later communities were established in Scarborough, Markham and Mississauga but it is still the crowded sidewalks of the Downtown Chinatown that evoke the atmosphere of China itself.

Dragon dancers parade on the streets of Toronto's Chinatown.

118 THE HOOKERS OF PORT CREDIT

(Stone Hookers, That Is)

UNLIKE THAT OTHER profession, the stone-hooking trade in Ontario is now all but forgotten. After the middle of the nineteenth century, demand for construction material skyrocketed. Cities and towns, especially those around the growing city of Toronto, were expanding along with demand for more roads and rail lines. The most readily available materials for construction were the many rocks and boulders, particularly well rounded and often flat shale, that lined the shore of Lake Ontario.

Beginning in the 1840s, stone hooker boats would depart the many ports along Lake Ontario from Whitby to Port Credit. These would usually be manned by four men with grappling hooks to lift the stones onto the barge. The stone loads, known as toises, were then transferred onto schooners for the trip to the wharfs in Toronto, where they would be sorted by size according to use. Smaller stones would be used for road ballast, flat stones for pavement, while large round rocks would end up in building foundations.

By the 1850s, more than thirty stone boats were wrenching the rocks from the waters. With their shallow drafts, the boats could manoeuvre close to the shore — too close, it seems. Farmers began to complain that the operations were causing their farmland to erode and, in 1857, the Three Rod Law was passed prohibiting stonehookers from taking stone less than 15 metres from shore.

But concrete soon replaced the stones in construction and, by the outbreak of the First World War, fewer than a half-dozen stone boats remained in use.

Nearly all vestiges of the trade have vanished. One exception is a small stone building at 49 Bronte Road in the old village of Bronte, formerly a popular restaurant known as Stoneboats and constructed from these stones by a one-time stone boat captain. Other buildings in the vicinity, such as the historic Glendella House, display those lake stone foundations.

Stones grappled from the waters of Lake Ontario have been used in local buildings in the Bronte area.

⑲ BURLINGTON HEIGHTS
How a Sandbar Changed History

To drivers entering Hamilton from Burlington along the Burlington Heights, York Boulevard is just another four-lane road. But anyone who takes a second look and delves into the story of this unusual ridge will realize it is no ordinary pile of dirt. Dropping down to Hamilton Harbour on one side and the waters of Cootes Paradise on the other, this 50-metre high and 3-kilometre long ridge owes its origins to the Ice Age.

Twenty thousand years ago, enormous ice sheets covered Ontario and much of the northeastern United States. As they gradually began to recede about 12,000 years ago, the ice blocked the east end of what is today Lake Ontario, forming an inland sea about 50 metres higher than today's lake. The swirling currents of that historic lake formed a sandbar near its western limits. As the ice jam melted, the waters of what geologists called Lake Iroquois began to erode the shoreline creating a shore bluff. Meanwhile the waters behind the sandbar found an outlet of their own through the ridge, Grindstone Creek, resulting in the lagoon called Cootes Paradise.

Centuries later, the strategic significance of the ridge became apparent; first for the First Nations who were often at war; and later for the British in their defence of Canada in the War of 1812. On these heights they erected earthworks, a supply depot and a barracks. It was from this vantage point that the British launched their attack against the Americans camped at Stoney Creek, surprising and routing them in a nighttime raid.

The ridge is visible from both the grounds of Dundurn Castle, which sits atop the ridge, and from below where the Desjardins Canal was completed in 1837 to allow passage to Dundas and the start of the Governor's Road to London. Stairs lead to the base of the ridge from York Boulevard, and a walking and cycling trail also leads to the base of the ridge from Bayfront Park in Hamilton.

The remnant beach ridge, which divides Hamilton Harbour from Cootes Paradise, is an unusual relic of the last Ice Age.

⑫ MONUMENT TO A BATTLE
The Stoney Creek Pillar

HISTORIANS BELIEVE THAT the Battle of Stoney Creek turned the tide in favour of the British during the War of 1812. And one of Ontario's most unusual monuments is there to mark the occasion.

The Americans were soundly sleeping on June 6, 1813, when a little after two in the morning, Lieutenant Ephraim Shaler of the American 25th infantry heard a piercing shriek. A sentry had been shot with an arrow and was perhaps being tortured by some of Major John Norton's Mohawks. Britain's Mohawk allies were noted for their ferocity and less than gentle handling of those who fell within their grasp, so any indication that the First Nations fighters were close at hand terrified the Yankee troops. In short order, the 700 British troops along with volunteers and John Norton's Mohawks managed to rout more than 3,000 American infantry.

Until then, the Americans had been stationed in the Gage House, a wooden two-storey home at the foot of the Niagara Escarpment near Stoney Creek. In 1894, to commemorate the battle and the lifestyles of the times, the Wentworth Women's Historical Society launched a fundraising drive to create a museum in the historic house, which opened in 1899.

But it is not the house that dominates the grounds; rather it is the soaring Battlefield Monument. Following the opening of the museum, the WWHS along with the Wentworth Historic Society began to raise more funds, this time for a monument to the battle itself and those on both sides who fell. In 1900, the firm of Rastrick and Sons submitted a design for a lofty limestone monument to be located in the adjacent park.

Finished in 1913, it was unveiled by Queen Mary via transatlantic cable on June 6th 1913, the 100th anniversary of the battle. Based upon the Nelson monument in Edinburgh, the monument begins with a square base that leads to an octagonal tapering tower stretching more than 30.5 metres in the air. Using various types of limestone sheathing a concrete core, the Tudor Gothic structure features a spiral staircase, heavy oak doors and a castle-like roof.

Although it lies on the grounds of one of the fiercest battles in the War of 1812, the monument is intended to represent the enduring peace that has prevailed since then. The museum and monument lie at the intersection of Centennial Parkway South and King Street West in Stoney Creek.

The 1812 war monument is a prominent landmark in Stoney Creek.

⑫1 GRIMSBY PARK
Ontario's Chautauqua

SURPRISES OFTEN WAIT in unexpected places. One of those places lies only a few metres from the busy Queen Elizabeth Highway near Grimsby. Along a labyrinth of narrow lanes is a cluster of colourful cabins and cottages. A cairn in their midst announces that here was the 1859 beginning of a Methodist meeting ground, where John Bowslaugh donated a parcel of his land on the shore of Lake Ontario. People gathered from throughout the Niagara Peninsula to listen to lectures and enjoy the lakeside breezes.

Then in 1874, the grounds evolved into the Ontario Methodist Campground Company, which created fifty-five cottage lots and added a wharf and a pair of hotels, while the Great Western Railway placed a small station on its line to serve the park. In 1888, a large domed temple arose in the midst of the cottages. Many of the cabins boasted decorative fretwork and colourful wooden exteriors. The popularity of the grounds set the template for the development of a similar but much grander institution in upper New York State. That institution was Chautauqua.

But by 1912, the campground company was bankrupt and sold the property for an amusement park with a carousel, miniature railway, roller coaster and shooting gallery. In 1916, Canada Steamship Lines bought the park and added it to its growing list of amusement grounds.

But time has taken its toll. Canada Steamship Lines dropped its park system in the 1950s, fires destroyed the hotels and many of the tiny cottages, and the temple was demolished. In 1939 the QEW opened its four limited-access lanes to through traffic, and tourists began to bypass the site en route to more colourful places like Niagara Falls.

Although the narrow lanes with names like Auditorium Circle and Temple Lane, lined with tiny colourful houses, are now part of Grimsby's urban area, they remain an unusual enclave that recalls an earlier, simpler era. Access is via Bartlett Avenue from the QEW.

Decorative cottages recall the early days of historic
Grimsby Park when it was the prototype for Chautauqua.

(122) SHIPWRECKED

The Ghost Ship of Jordan Harbour

FORGET NIAGARA FALLS and forget the wineries; perhaps the most arresting sight of the Niagara Peninsula is the bizarre shipwreck that rests on the rocks at Jordan Harbour, in full view of drivers on the busy Queen Elizabeth Way.

It looks like it's straight out of a pirate movie, with its three tall masts leaning towards the waves. *La Grande Hermine*, as it was later known, was in fact built in 1914 in Lauzon, Quebec, and served as a ferry called *Le Progress* to cross the St. Lawrence River, later serving as a cargo ship. In 1991 it became a floating restaurant, redesigned to resemble one of Jacques Cartier's ships, *La Grande Hermine*, which brought the explorer to Canada in 1535.

It is alleged that the owners, in an effort to avoid unpaid moorage fees in Quebec, towed the vessel to Lake Ontario in 1997 to turn it into a restaurant again. However, neither funds nor permission were forthcoming, and so it was simply left. Six years later it was gutted by fire. Today, the 50-metre-long relic still lists on the rocks, in plain view of the six lanes of speeding traffic on the QEW.

The best views and photo ops are from a small dirt parking lot beside the Beacon Harbourside Hotel and Suites on Beacon Boulevard. On the opposite bluff sits the popular fine dining restaurant, the Lakehouse.

To reach the location, exit the QEW at Victoria Street in Vineland.

Like a pirate ship of old, *La Grande Hermine* makes for an unusual
landmark beside the QEW in the Niagara Peninsula.

Once neglected and forgotten, Niagara-on-the-Lake's Fort Mississauga now endures a barrage of golf balls from the course on which it sits.

Right: A musket demonstration in nearby Fort George.

⑫③ FORT MISSISSAUGA

The Forgotten Fort

ROUND AND HARD, the missiles speed through the air, crashing against the walls of the ancient fort. Bricks and mortar splatter into the air and fall to the ground.

Niagara-on-the-Lake's Fort Mississauga is being assaulted, not by enemy batteries, but rather by errant golfers on the golf course that now surrounds it. The fort was hurriedly built between 1814 and 1816 on the site of an earlier Seneca fishing village from the rubble of an old lighthouse to stave off a repeat of an earlier American attack.

It sits on the site of the original Fort George which the Americans destroyed during their attack on Niagara on the Lake. In 1837, Fort George was re-established further inland and is now a key historic attraction.

The fort sustained a garrison only until 1826. It was re-manned in 1837 during the Upper Canada rebellion of that year, and again during the American Civil War and the Fenian troubles. Later, it was used as a training camp during the various wars of the twentieth century. For all that, Fort Mississauga never had a hostile shot fired at it.

Although small, the site remains the only example of a star-shaped military earthwork in Canada. In addition to the brick tower and the tunnel to the lake that you see today, the fort originally consisted of a barracks, guardroom and cells as well.

In 1976 when Parks Canada, which had so masterfully restored the much larger Fort George a short distance away, indicated its intention to restore Fort Mississauga, the golfers temporarily rebelled and won the day. Although Parks Canada has retained ownership and has stabilized the walls and roof, they have left the fort a ruin. And that is what makes the fort unusual and enhances its appeal.

It is accessible along a trail from the corner of Front and Simcoe streets in the historic heart of Niagara-on-the-Lake. The town, of course, has much to offer the history lover, for it has retained its nineteenth-century ambience though careful preservation and restoration of many of its early buildings. Restorations of Fort George began in 1937 and were completed in 1940. However, the restoration retained only one original building, the stone powder magazine. Costumed staff replicate military drills, including musket firing, and music from a fife and drum corps. The town is best noted for its annual Shaw Festival, an event that brings theatre lovers to share the history of this picturesque Lake Ontario town.

(124) LIGHTING UP THE NIGHT
Niagara Parks Power Station Light Show

HOW READILY WE take for granted our dependency upon electricity. Without it, all illumination and communication as we know it would cease, as massive blackouts over the last half-century have amply demonstrated. Yet, in 1905 when electricity was first turned on in much of the province, nervous homeowners were known to literally flee outdoors for fear of an explosion. But the only explosion was in usage when the Niagara Falls Electrical Generating Station began spinning its turbines.

The power plant was the culmination of a dream of William Rankine, chairman of the Canadian Niagara Power Company. In 1901, excavation began on a 600-metre tailrace tunnel to divert water from the Niagara River above Niagara Falls, to a 60-metre vertical shaft down which the water would cascade to spin the turbines, which would power the generators and create electricity. When it finally opened in 1905, the generating hall measured 60 metres long and 20 metres high and contained five generators. The length was doubled in 1913, when five more generators were added. Another generator was added in 1924.

In 2006, the Niagara Falls Power Station was decommissioned and three years later acquired by the Niagara Parks Commission. In 2018, the NPC, recognizing the educational potential of the power station, launched a plan to convert the historic structure into a museum. Opened as a museum in 2020, the revitalized Niagara Parks Power Station was designed by the Ventin Group of Architects, specialists in heritage repurposing. Tour guides explain the story of electricity, the use of the generators and the construction of the plant, and then lead visitors through the tailrace tunnel.

In 2021, the Parks Commission introduced a nighttime sound and light show called *Currents* a display that fills the entire interior of the hall — walls, ceiling, generators and even the floor. The interior becomes the river itself, drawing viewers into the age of the glaciers, the feel of the falls and the growth of electricity. The spectacle was created by the Thinkwell Group, described as a "global experience design company."

Niagara Falls is all about the lights: the stunning illumination of the falls, the glitter of Clifton Hill and the popular Christmas light displays. However, this newest light show, *Currents*, is the only one that is true to the electrical legacy of the falls itself. After the tour and show, guests may enjoy a bite in the cafeteria and possibly acquire a souvenir in the gift shop.

The Niagara Parks Power Station is about 550 metres south of the Table Rock Welcome Centre on the Niagara Parkway.

The *Currents* light show in the Niagara Parks Power Station
is one of the falls' newest attractions.

"Frankenstein" enjoys a bite on Clifton Hill in Niagara Falls.

(125) CANADA'S MIDWAY

Clifton Hill in Niagara Falls

THE GREAT CATARACT known as Niagara Falls has long generated awe and wonder in all who behold it. Indigenous visitors attached mythical legends to the falls. As European settlers began to invade the Niagara Frontier, visits to the falls grew in popularity.

But it took the arrival of the railways to really usher in the tourist era.

Meanwhile, Ferry Road, an older, well-travelled pioneer route which led to the ferry landing on the Niagara River, attracted the attention of wealthy landowners. Captain Ogden Creighton in 1832 built his Clifton Cottage, named for his home in England, on a hill facing the river and laid out the streets that today embrace the amusements of Clifton Hill. In 1833, the first Clifton Hotel appeared at the foot of the street. In 1842, Samuel Zimmerman laid out his 15-hectare estate, which he called Clifton Place, adding gardens and a fountain as well as his mansion. The fountain still survives at the north end of Queen Victoria Park.

As the tourists began to flood in, so did the hucksters, and the road along the rim of the gorge became known as The Front.

Soon a conservation movement took root; in 1887, the Niagara Parks Commission was created and acquired the lands known as The Front, establishing today's Queen Victoria Park, a landscaped road and walkway stretching from Table Rock to Clifton Hill.

The next surge of tourists arrived with the auto age in the 1950s. Clifton Hill, as Ferry Road came to be called, soon offered places of amusement like the Houdini Hall of Fame, Ripley's Believe It or Not, Louis Tussaud's Wax Museum (he was the grandson of Mme. Tussaud), the Hollywood Wax Museum and the House of Frankenstein.

While some ventures came and went, such as the Legends of Rock and Roll Wax Museum and the Criminals Hall of Fame, the bright lights and attractions continued to grow and have spilled over to side streets as well. Tourists now flock to ride the 53-metre high Skywheel or play on the world's largest mini-golf course — the 70,000-square-foot Dinosaur Miniature Golf — ride the go-carts at the Niagara Speedway or play at the Great Canadian Midway with more than 300 interactive games. The scares are still there, too: the Screaming Tunnels, Alien Encounter, Dino Rampage, the Haunted Castle, the Nightmare's Fear Factory and the old standby, the House of Frankenstein. By contrast, the foot of the Hill is highlighted with the historic and elegant Oakes Garden Theatre. As the mists of the Falls swirl around the historic Table Rock, the lights and sounds of Clifton Hill seem like a world away.

Clifton Hill is hard to miss. It runs between Victoria Avenue and Falls Road in Niagara Falls, a few metres south of the Rainbow Bridge.

⑫⑥ THE COMFORT GIANT
Canada's Biggest Sugar Maple Tree

ONE SPECIMEN OF the tree that symbolizes Canada may be older than the nation itself. The Comfort Maple squats wide and solid beside a field near Welland, Ontario. It had been there for three hundred years when, in 1816, the Comfort family first settled the land. And there it has remained, its survival defying all the odds.

Ontario once boasted a magnificent forest cover. Oak, hemlock, beech and maple provided a cooling leafy canopy that assured a high water table, which in turn allowed the many rivers and streams to flow year-round — cascading streams that powered the countless pioneer mills. But that forest quickly vanished, for what fire and old age didn't claim, pioneer wood hewers did.

With the forest gone, the water table lowered and the streams dried up, turning the once-vibrant mill towns into ghost towns.

But the Comfort Maple survived. With its girth of 6 metres and crown width of almost 40 metres, the 30-metre-high giant became a local attraction, and owner Earl Hampton Comfort set aside a piece of land solely for the preservation of his tree. In 1961, his sister Edna donated the tree and 4 hectares of land around it to the Niagara Region Conservation Authority.

Today the authority maintains about a half hectare of land, a parking lot and a few benches. As the ancient tree ages, it has become necessary to support some of the branches with guy wires. The Comfort Maple lies at the end of a short lane which leads south from Metler Street, about 3 kilometres west of Effingham Street. Described as "the oldest and finest maple tree in Canada," it was added as a heritage tree under the *Ontario Heritage Act* in 2000.

The Comfort Maple is said to be Canada's largest sugar maple.

The ghost town of St. Johns West in Pelham contains Ontario's' oldest and tiniest schoolhouse.

⑫⑦ ONTARIO'S TINIEST SCHOOLHOUSE

OTHER CHAPTERS IN this book tell the story of the Smallest Union Station, Ontario's smallest car ferry and its smallest jails. This is the story of the province's tiniest schoolhouse. It may also be its oldest. Built in 1799, in the fledgling industrial settlement known as St. Johns West, it was the first home of pioneer John Darling, who lived in it until 1804 when he built a new home. His original cabin then became a schoolhouse.

Smaller than today's average two-car garage, the schoolhouse measures a mere 6 metres by 6 metres. Its first teacher was John Birdsall, teaching as many as 29 pupils crammed into the tiny room. It remained in use until 1844 when a new school was built.

Industrial activity began in the little valley in 1792, when pioneer settler Benjamin Canby built a sawmill on Twelve Mile Creek. The creek was noted for its consistent flow, even during dry summers. Several more mills soon followed. By the turn of the nineteenth century, St. Johns West, as it was called, was becoming a booming industrial centre for the entire Niagara Peninsula with saw- and grist mills and foundries, many of which were situated in the hollow, while stores and other businesses lined Holland Road on top of the valley wall.

According to the local archives, the diminutive schoolhouse building was of "frame construction, clapboard over hand-hewn timbers, mortised and tendoned, and held together with wooden pegs. Each side wall and the back wall of the one room classroom contained two small windows, while the front had only one window and the building only one door." After its school days ended, the little building reverted to a residence and then, for a time, it was used as a grocery store, before once more becoming a residence. It is also famous because in 1804 it was the first true public school in Upper Canada. The right to attend a public school did not extend to all students in Ontario until 1846.

In 1973, the school board restored the building and now uses it to demonstrate, for today's generation of students, school life in early Ontario. On the hill above the tiny house of learning, the former main street of St. Johns West, today's Holland Road, now consists of little more than a cemetery and a series of cellar holes. Down below the hill, Ontario's tiniest school stands at the junction of Hollow Road with Orchard Road, a hundred metres south of Holland Road. To reach Holland Road, take exit 14 south from Highway 406 and follow Regional Road 67 to RR 50 south, which leads to Holland Road.

(128) NIAGARA BEYOND THE FALLS

The Secret Gorges of the Niagara Peninsula

NIAGARA FALLS IS one of the world's most spectacular waterfalls. For more than 10, 000 years, erosion has carved this stunning gorge on the Niagara Escarpment. But this is only one of dozens of other steep, rocky gorges, many with waterfalls nearly as high as the more famous neighbour.

Overlooking the City of St. Catharines, the historic stone Morningstar Mill marks the plunge of 12 Mile Creek as it falls 20 metres into the perilous gorge below where a second cascade drops another 11 metres. A picturesque stone mill, blacksmith shop, and, the early home of the miller, sit atop a hill overlooking the site that lies on Decew Road south of St. Catharines

Further west, 15 Mile Creek, the upper Rockway Falls plunges 20 metres while the lower falls plunges a further 12 metres. Trails follow the rim of the canyon in the Rockway Conservation Area, offering dizzying views into the rock-walled gorge. The upper falls lies by Regional Road 89, while the conservation area parking lot and trail head lie off Reginal Road 81.

Twenty Mile Creek provides a rewarding view as the upper and lower falls, combined, drop 38 metres. The town of Ball's Falls grew around the mills but became a ghost town after the arrival of the railways in 1853. Today the Ball brothers' family home, a grist mill which now houses a museum, overlooks the lower falls. The road to the site leads east from Regional Road 24, south of Vineland.

Beamers Memorial Conservation Area, near Grimsby, is the location of Beamers Falls which plunges 12 metres into a deep canyon. A small parking lot is located on Ridge Road just west of Regional Road 12.

The Devil's Punchbowl at the south end of Stoney Creek is famous for its rounded bowl-shaped canyon where the layers of stone reveal the geological history of the Escarpment itself. A pay parking lot is located on Ridge Road east of Centennial Parkway in Stoney Creek.

Two falls adjacent to Hamilton, Tews Falls and Webster's Falls, are connected by a wooded trail and plunging 41 and 21 metres, respectively, into the Spencer Gorge. The falls lie along Webster's Falls Road east of Reginal Road 8 and north of the historic community of Dundas.

Sometimes only a trickle of water makes it into the distinctive Devil's Punchbowl at Stoney Creek.

The Welland Canal's three rare twin-flight locks ease massive ocean and Great Lakes vessels up and down the Niagara Escarpment.

⑫⑨ NEPTUNE'S STAIRCASE
The Welland Canal's Twin-Flight Locks

WHEN THE ERIE Canal opened in 1826, it linked Lake Erie with the Atlantic Ocean at New York City. Meanwhile, the only all-Canadian route meant struggling up the rapids-strewn St. Lawrence River, and then overland to reach the upper lakes. It was quickly evident to William Hamilton Merritt that an all-Canadian canal was needed. By 1828, Merritt's canal opened between Port Dalhousie on Lake Ontario and Port Colborne on Lake Erie, and the all-Canadian alternative to the Erie Canal was bringing ships from Lake Ontario to Lake Erie.

But while construction between Lake Ontario and the Niagara Escarpment and from the top of the escarpment to Lake Erie was relatively straightforward, the problem lay with the 100-metre limestone cliff that formed the face of the escarpment. In the first version of the canal, of the forty locks, more than half were needed to climb the escarpment alone. Because of the step-like appearance of this series of locks, they earned the nickname "Neptune's Staircase."

Fifteen years later, a second canal replaced the narrow wooden locks of the first, reducing the number of locks from forty to twenty-seven. But again, a dozen locks were still needed to reach the limestone summit.

Although the third canal, completed in 1887, succeeded in widening and deepening the locks, it failed to reduce the number required to climb the cliff. That did not occur until the fourth version of the canal opened to traffic in 1932, when a mere eight locks operated through the entire length — three at the cliff face itself.

As with the earlier structures, those three today are an engineering marvel. As the locks, 4, 5 and 6, feed into each other like a flight of stairs, they have also been twinned to allow vessels to pass through in each direction at the same time. Over a stretch of 1,250 metres, the twin-flight locks lift or lower enormous ships by almost 43 metres, each operation requiring the draining and filling of more than 91 million litres of water. Yet incredibly, the entire process requires only 10 minutes per lock.

The lock areas themselves are off limits, but a canal side road and trail allow visitors to pause and watch the passing of the ships as they inch into and out of the locks, often with less than a metre to spare on either side. Although the twin-flight locks are situated in the town of Thorold, a canal interpretive centre offers visitors a canal museum and platform from which to view the operations of lock 3 in the city of St. Catharines.

⑬⓪ FATHER OF THE PEACE BRIDGE

Fort Erie's Mather Monument

As the Niagara frontiers began to grow and boom on both sides of the churning Niagara River, among the only links between the two nations were the ferries that shuttled between Black Rock (near Buffalo) on the U.S. side and Fort Erie on the Canadian. Finally in 1873, the great Canadian railway builder, Casimir Gzowski, designed a railway bridge to carry trains across the border. But that still left out pedestrians and vehicular traffic, although the auto age was still some years away.

Then in 1899, Alonzo Clark Mather, a Chicago inventor whose inventions had included a humanely designed railway car for transporting cattle and horses, saw the need for a bridge that not only would allow both rail and road traffic, but would also harness the power from the swift currents of the Niagara River sweeping below it. While railways would travel the central section, and pedestrians and wagon would use outer lanes, beneath the structure a series of water wheels, or dynamos, would convert the water power into electrical power.

Although his plan did get as far as Albany, the state capital, Alonzo's dream did not materialize. But he did not give up, and in 1919 was pushing for what he called a "peace" bridge — one that would symbolically link two peaceful neighbours. In 1927, the 1,700-metre, five-span Peace Bridge opened for traffic and soon became the busiest border crossing between the two countries. In 1992, a plan to build a new structure that would have increased traffic flow by 33 percent, fell victim to court challenges, with motorists continuing to face numbing line-ups to cross.

To honour the man whose vision of the peaceful link between neighbours finally found form in the Peace Bridge, in 1939 the Niagara Parks Commission constructed a triple-arch stone monument in Fort Erie near the western entrance to the Peace Bridge. Dedicated in 1940, the monument is surrounded by a garden within view of Mather's bridge. Mather died in California in 1941. He was 97.

A memorial arch in Fort Erie dedicated to Alonzo Mather frames the Peace Bridge, which he had promoted.

⑬① GUIDING LIGHT
Beautiful Point Abino Lighthouse

PERHAPS IT IS because most of them lie on isolated shorelines, out of view of most landlubbers, that lighthouses are among the least appreciated of Ontario's heritage structures.

Some are small and squat, made of wood; others are tall and elegant, constructed of stone or brick. Then there is the lighthouse at Point Abino. Built of poured concrete, it is unlike any other lighthouse in Ontario. Constructed in a form of architecture known as Greek Revival, it is easily the most elegant lighthouse along the Ontario side of the Great Lakes. Except that, for the most part, you are not allowed to see it.

Point Abino is located on Lake Erie just west of Fort Erie. With the urban boom that engulfed southern Ontario and upper New York State in the late 1800s, increasing numbers of city dwellers sought out the beaches and breezes of the nearest lakeshores. These numbers swelled following the opening of the Peace Bridge between Buffalo and Fort Erie in 1927. While more modest cottages and cabins crowded the beaches in nearby Crystal Beach, the forested peninsula at Point Abino became the exclusive enclave of wealthy industrialists. Other historic homes came to this location from their display at the Buffalo World's Fair of 1901.

In 1892, a wealthy Buffalo developer bought the entire point, subdividing it and selling the lots to twenty-one wealthy Buffalo businessmen who turned it into an exclusive cottage community. Despite the later completion of a road to the point, it has remained a private gated community.

The lighthouse was completed in 1918, built to replace a light ship that was destroyed in the devastating November storm of 1913 which took hundreds of sailors' lives throughout the Great Lakes, including all on board. A light-keeper's residence was added in 1921. Prior to the light ship, the dangerous shelf of rock, which creeps out from the point into the lake, was marked only by buoys. Because the light was surrounded by water and private homes, the keepers had to access the dwelling by wading through the shallows.

The lighthouse was decommissioned in 1995 and, three years later, it was declared a National Historic Site of Canada. However, the road to it remains private and gated. Even though the Town of Fort Erie acquired the unused lighthouse in 2001, and even though the federal government put $425,000 toward its restoration which began in 2011, it has remained out of bounds for visitors. Following vigorous negotiations with the Point Abino Light Station Preservation Society, the owners agreed to allow visitors to the lighthouse but limited visits to twice a month and only during the summer months. Check the Town of Fort Erie website for tour times.

The Point Abino lighthouse is easily the most elegant on the Ontario Great Lakes.

In 2017, the preservation society negotiated permission to re-light the lighthouse lamp for the celebration of its 100th anniversary with the federal government. It is now lit each year between May and October. Still, despite the efforts and accomplishment of the preservation society, it remains regrettable that a group of wealthy Americans can continue to limit the ability of Canadians, and other visitors, to access one of the country's more stunning and unusual National Historic Sites.

Ontario has a mixed legacy of lighthouse preservation. Of the six Imperial Towers, lofty stone structures erected around the shore of Lake Huron in the late 1800s, some are in dubious states of repair while others have been preserved as historic sites. Some have become museums; others remain in private hands. The preserved wooden lighthouse in Port Burwell, built in 1842, is the oldest of its kind in the province; Toronto's Gibraltar Point Lighthouse dates from 1808 and is said to be haunted by its first keeper. The Province of Quebec promotes a Lighthouse Route driving tour of heritage lighthouses along the south shore of the lower St. Lawrence River which could be an example for Ontario as well.

The partially finished town of Townsend can be seen behind the welcome sign.

⑬² A Peculiar Place to Live

The Townsend Experiment

THERE IS SOMETHING peculiar about Townsend.

Along Highway 3, about 50 kilometres southwest of Hamilton, you come to Nanticoke Creek Parkway. After you drive a short distance down that side road, passing fields and barns as you travel, you suddenly find yourself on a four-lane boulevard. Branching off to the side are streets that twist and curve, lined with modern homes. Further on, you find a substantial seniors' residence and a town centre overlooking a pond. And then Townsend ends as abruptly as it began.

But look more closely. You will find that those suburban streets end in overgrown fields, that the avenues are strangely free of traffic and that the town centre contains little more than drab offices. Welcome to Townsend, once touted as Ontario's grand community of the future.

In the 1970s, government planners decided that the sprawl engulfing the Toronto-Hamilton-Oshawa area was out of control and should be redirected to a series of regional growth centres. The decentralization, theorized the planners, would also help spread the prosperity of those years to less populated and less prosperous regions.

The planners chose an area of flat farmland near the shores of Lake Erie to build a modern new town. By 1976 coloured maps showed a proposed community of 100,000, with areas for recreation, housing and industry.

Tree-lined trails would welcome hikers, cyclists, horseback riders and cross-country skiers. There would be high schools, hospitals and supermarkets, all connected by public transit.

But at the centre of it all would be the community showcase — the town centre. Built to overlook a landscaped lake, the centre would contain four department stores, specialty shops, restaurants, churches, cinemas, an art gallery and a hotel. An apartment complex would house 6,000 residents and sports lovers from throughout the region would travel to a stadium and fields. The first phase would start in 1978 and accommodate 5,000 people.

But somehow the dream city turned into a nightmare. When the Canadian economy plunged into a recession and inflation skyrocketed, industry stayed away. So did most of the 100,000 future residents. In fact, Townsend never expanded beyond that first phase. The recreation trails are overgrown, no buses rumble along the streets and the town centre contains the offices of Haldimand-Norfolk REACH, a support service for children with mental health challenges and families experiencing legal issues. The grandly named Town Centre Road ends abruptly in an overgrown farm field.

While Townsend is no ghost town and looks much like any other well-maintained suburb, the sudden dead-ends, silence and odd location in the midst of fields and barns are all evidence that the "dream city" never came true.

(133) CHIEFSWOOD

The Poet's Two-Sided Palace

OVERLOOKING ONTARIO'S HISTORIC Grand River looms one of the area's most unusual mansions. Known as Chiefswood and home to legendary Canadian poet Pauline Johnson, it contains two front doors and no back door. Both facades — the front and the back — of the handsome building are identical.

Pauline Johnson's father, George Johnson, was an important chief of the Mohawks of the Six Nations. Overcoming family objections, he married an English woman, Emily Howell.

Shortly after their marriage, he built a fine mansion for his wife and future family. High on a bank overlooking the swirling waters of the wide Grand River, a route busy with not only Indigenous canoes but barges and schooners plying the Grand River canal, he built Chiefswood. The fine two-storey structure was built from 1853 to 1856, and was unlike the log or wattle cabins most of the population inhabited. Doors were centred on both the side of the house that faced the river and on the opposite side, which faced the road.

The door facing the river was to accommodate the traditions of his Mohawk kin, who travelled by river, while the door facing the road was for the convenience of his wife's English friends and family, who travelled by road. It was probably Canada's first multicultural domicile.

It was in this unusual abode that Pauline Johnson was born and later started school. Despite a mere seven years of formal studies, she read constantly, absorbing works by Shakespeare, Milton and Scott. When George Johnson died in 1884, Pauline Johnson's family could no longer afford Chiefswood and moved into the nearby city of Brantford. There she began to write poems for publication in the local *Brantford Expositor*.

Soon Johnson began to appear before audiences to recite her poems, such as "Cry from an Indian Wife" and "The Song My Paddle Sings." Displaying an uncanny sense of the stage, she performed in both English and "Indian" costume and displayed such articles as hunting knives, animal pelts and — a grotesque choice — human scalps.

For seventeen years, Johnson toured North America and Europe, finally settling in Vancouver. There, sadly, she succumbed to breast cancer and died in 1913.

To commemorate the famous poet, Pauline Johnson's birth home was made a historic site. Now a museum, it is open for visits and tours. Inside, the simple furniture of the day is on display, and the exhibits tell the story of the poet herself and the story of the mansion with two front doors.

This historic site overlooks the Grand River on County Road 54, 12 kilometres east of Brantford.

Pauline Johnson's home, Chiefswood, has two entrance doors, to accommodate the cultures of her mixed Mohawk and English parentage.

134 DWARF CEDARS
Ontario's Oldest Trees

THINK OF AN old-growth forest and you think of redwood trees that soar upward until their tops disappear in a canopy of green. You don't envisage gnarly little cedars that twist out of the side of a rock and extend only 3 or 4 metres into the air. Yet these spindly little survivors are Ontario's oldest trees.

Normally a swamp species, the eastern white cedars are found along the lip of the Niagara Escarpment, some of them dating back more than six hundred years, and one nearly a thousand years. Dating such a tree is not an easy job. It requires boring into the trunk and then counting, often with the aid of a microscope, the hundreds of nearly invisible rings concentrated into the span of a hand.

Starting as seeds lodged in the limestone crevices centuries ago, the saplings edged slowly outward and then bent upward to face the warm and nutritious sunlight. Anchored in the stony depths, with no soil to feed them, the trees grew imperceptibly. But at least they grew. Their inaccessible location on the side of the cliff spared them from loggers, farmers and browsing animals, and even from the encroachment of other tree species. While original forests were falling all across Canada, the sturdy little white cedars sat firm and continued their slow growth skyward.

Thanks to the creation of a series of provincial parks, and a UNESCO designation as a World Biosphere Reserve, much of the Niagara Escarpment is finally available to the public. One of the best sites from which to view the ancient trees is in the conservation area at Rattlesnake Point. A short path leads from the parking area to the trail along the brink, where a stone fence protects careless walkers from a dangerous and likely deadly tumble over the precipice.

The trees can be identified by their light green, flat cedar needles, and by their trademark origin in the side of the cliff face. But as for the age of those that you see, only a bore sample and tedious tally of the tiny rings can tell you if the tree is sixty or six hundred years old.

A good location to view the gnarled old cedars is in Rattlesnake Point Conservation Area off Derry Road, west of Milton.

Ontario's oldest trees are also among its smallest.

135 THE LAKE WITH NO WAVES

The Strange Story of Crawford Lake

THE CRAWFORD LAKE Conservation Area is a rare find. It sits atop the Niagara Escarpment with wonderful views and trails that wind through a hardwood forest. It also has a small lake, but this is a lake with no waves.

Geologists even have a special name for it, a meromectic lake, which means that, relative to its surface area, it is disproportionately deeper than most lakes, to the point that waves seldom occur and the bottom sediments remain undisturbed. In effect, it is ecologically like two lakes, one on top of the other. The lower levels are deprived of the oxygen that would normally come from the air above, thus preserving the material on the bottom.

Such preservation allows scientists to read this debris and determine with much more certainty what the area around it was like thousands of years ago. Lake Crawford is estimated to be at least fifteen thousand years old.

Among the layers of silt that cover the bottom, scientists uncovered evidence of early Huron habitation. This discovery sent archaeologists searching the area around the lake, where they uncovered the remains of a previously unknown Huron village. The village contained nine longhouses for a population of about 450, and dates from around AD 1430. Numerous other village sites were subsequently recorded in the surrounding hills and valleys.

Not only are the shape and morphology of the lake unusual, so too is its origin. Unlike other lakes, which form along existing rivers or in lowlands, this one occurred, some theorize, when a cave beneath the upper limestone layer suddenly collapsed. Water rushed in from underground streams, quickly filling the cavity. Another theory suggests that the lake fills an ancient post-glacial spillway.

In 1969 the land was sold to the Halton Region Conservation Authority, which laid out trails and re-created the Huron village, complete with palisade. So authentic is the habitation and the depiction of the lifestyles of its inhabitants that it has become a must-see for many school children from across Ontario

A 1.4-kilometre path leads to the lake from the gate, where interpretive signs explain its unusual origins and composition. A 7.2-kilometre trail leads further afield, through the dark woodlands, to a lookout point over the scenic Nassagaweya Canyon. The park is on the Guelph Line, a short distance south of Highway 401.

Crawford Lake is one of only two deep oxygen-deprived meromectic lakes in Ontario.

Rockwood's potholes.

Opposite: in addition to its geological pothole formations, the Rockwood Conservation Area is home to the photogenic stone ruins of an historic woollen mill.

136 POTHOLES OF PRIDE
Rockwood Conservation Area

MOST COMMUNITIES DON'T like to brag about their potholes, especially when they're 6 metres wide and 12 metres deep and number almost two hundred. Rockwood, Ontario, about 12 kilometres northeast of Guelph, is different. Residents not only boast of their potholes, but have created a park for them!

The reason for this pride is that the potholes are not a result of neglected roads, but are a fascinating creation of nature. Sedimentary rocks such as limestone or sandstone are among nature's softest. Easily eroded, they can be sculpted and washed by wind and water into a fairyland of shapes. Caves, natural bridges and rock pillars are but a few of the shapes that the rocks can assume.

Potholes are another form, occurring when boulders become trapped in the swirling eddies of fast-flowing rivers. As the boulders swirl around, they etch a hole in the bedrock beneath. Thousands of years must pass for the rocks to grind a hole even the size of a stew pot. Tens of thousands of years were required to form those at Rockwood.

This natural wonder is preserved in the Rockwood Conservation Area, on the western outskirts of the town. Trails lead from the parking lot up cliffs, past caves and finally to the potholes themselves. Here, the Eramosa River flows through a watery labyrinth of potholes, some of which have collapsed, while others have eroded through. Other potholes remain high and dry and lurk darkly beneath the forest vegetation. Looming over the lower parking lots are the stone walls of the former Harris woollen mill which opened in 1867 fabricating woollens and tweeds, as well as blankets and underwear. Today's stone walls date from 1884. The mill operated until 1925 when the family converted the property into a park.

The most interesting way to explore them is to rent a canoe and coast lazily through the watery maze. You'll see potholes as you've never seen them before.

137 FROM ON HIGH, THE BASILICA OF OUR LADY IMMACULATE, GUELPH

Look up from almost anywhere in downtown Guelph and you see the twin spires of the massive Basilica of Our Lady Immaculate. Many have deemed it Ontario's Notre Dame Cathedral. The term "basilica" refers to an ancient style of meeting hall used in ancient Rome as a court of law or for public assemblies. Subsequently adopted by early Christians, it is the name given to certain churches granted special privileges by the pope. In 2014, Pope Francis designated the church in Guelph as a Minor Basilica. The term Major Basilica applies only to the highest ranking Catholic churches.

A church on the site dates back to 1827 when Guelph's founder, John Galt, gifted the highest hill in the new settlement to his friend Bishop William MacDonnell, emphasizing in the deed "On this hill will rise a church to rival St. Peter's in Rome."

However, the first church on the hill was a simple wooden structure known as St. Bartholomew's and was finished in 1835. It was replaced in 1844 after it was destroyed by a fire. Based on the style of the Cologne Cathedral, construction of the present church was begun in 1877. Its architect was Irish-Canadian Joseph Connolly, who also designed St. Patrick's Cathedral in London, Ontario. However, his Guelph creation is considered to be his masterpiece.

The church was finished in 1888 and dedicated to Our Lady Immaculate. Its twin towers, added in 1926, soar more than 50 metres in the air.

The style is described as French Gothic Revival, consisting of a cruciform plan with side aisles and a prominent nave. It displays large rose windows; a steeply pitched roof with gables, dormers, pinnacles, pointed arches and tall, narrow window openings. The entrance is marked with a massive circular rose window set into a moulded pointed arch, with a row of lintel statuary within a blind arcade. The Gothic Revival interior includes tall, pointed-stain glass windows and rib vaulting and wood and stone carvings. Due to its excellent acoustics, masses in the vaulted Basilica reverberate with the sound of 2,950 pipes from an organ crafted in 1919 by the Casavant Freres of St. Hyacinth, Quebec.

Extensive restoration took place between 2007 and 2014 at a cost of $12 million.

Beside the church, the former convent is now home to the Guelph Museum, while across the lot, the three-storey stone former girls' school sits vacant and boarded-up, awaiting funding for its restoration.

The view from the front steps overlooks Macdonnell Street in downtown Guelph where the city has decreed that no structure shall rise higher than the church steeples.

Access to the large church parking lot is from Dublin Street, a block south of Paisley Street.

The Basilica of Our
Lady Immaculate has
been compared to the
Cathedral in Cologne.

138 TROLLEYS THROUGH THE TREES
Canada's Largest Streetcar Museum

FOR DECADES, THE main mode of urban transportation in Canada was the streetcar. Beginning in the 1870s the network of rails spread between towns and cities carrying passengers and freight across the countryside. Often known as "radials," because they radiated out from urban centres, the trolleys linked Toronto with Port Credit, Guelph, Lake Simcoe and Schomberg.

However, intense lobbying by the tire manufacturers, auto makers and oil companies soon ended most streetcar and interurban systems to make way for cars and buses. In several instances, auto makers bought out entire streetcar systems simply to shut them down.

In 1954, shortly after the city's first subway system began rumbling underground, the Toronto Transit Commission began sending its aging fleet of streetcars to the scrapyard. A group of local streetcar lovers fought to convince the TTC to save the last of the old streetcars, number 1326, from meeting that fate. To find a home for the vehicle, they purchased a property near the community of Rockwood and in 1972 opened the Halton County Railway Museum which today contains Canada's largest collection of vintage streetcars and interurban rolling stock.

Among the collection are the once familiar PCC streetcars which dominated Toronto's streets from the 1930s to the 1970s along with an open-sided tram, luxurious interurban coaches and an original "red rocket" from Toronto's first subway.

Visitors can board one of five interurban cars that date from 1912 to 1915 with polished wood interiors and separate smoking lounges, for a two kilometre journey along the original Toronto to Guelph route. The starting point is the Grand Trunk Railway station, which contains a museum and was relocated to the property from the nearby village of Rockwood.

In all, the museum houses more than 20 streetcars dating back to 1910 and an extensive collection of electric and gas-powered work equipment.

Many early vehicles from the TTC are included in the
collection of the Halton County Railway Museum.

⑬⑨ THE CHELTENHAM BADLANDS

Ontario's Painted Desert

MANY WESTWARD-BOUND ONTARIANS make Drumheller, Alberta, one of their must-sees. There, thousands of years of water and wind erosion have worn through layers of shale to create a landscape of barren hills and gullies punctuated by remnant pillars known as "hoodoos." While the desert-like terrain spurned farmers and ranchers, it did expose coal seams and a rich source of dinosaur bones.

But drylands are expected in the west. They are less so in lush, forested Ontario. Known as Medina shale, a deposit of red-and-green sediment appears throughout the Niagara Escarpment area, but nowhere is it so dramatically exposed as in a 37-hectare hillside north of the village of Cheltenham. Here, the shale has been sculpted into a dramatic landscape of smooth ridges and gullies, totally bereft of vegetation.

The age of the ancient seabed is estimated at 450 million years, not a period of dinosaur activity. And unlike in Alberta, the feature here is not entirely natural. Until the settlers arrived, the deposit lay beneath a forest and soil cover. But once the settlers cleared the land and began to graze their cattle, erosion of the hillside exposed the colourful layers. So hard was the exposed material that grasses and shrubs were unable to take hold. However, like those in Alberta, Ontario's badlands revealed an economic resource, the ingredients for brickmaking, that brought a boom to the area.

The deposit gave rise to a number of brickmaking villages in the area, such as Terra Cotta and the Cheltenham brickyards. When the brickmaking ceased, the villages dwindled. Terra Cotta remains a residential community, but the Cheltenham site now contains only the gaunt skeletal shells of the old kilns.

Located beside Old Baseline Road between Highway 10 and Mississauga Road, the ridges and gullies, with their colourful layers, have long been a local landmark — and a destination for many a geography class. The dramatic landscape has also attracted film location scouts seeking unusual topography for their sets. The site was acquired by the Ontario government in 1999 and transferred to the Ontario Heritage Foundation. It is managed by the Bruce Trail Association as part of its trail system. Today, fencing prevents foot traffic from further damaging the fragile landscape. There is a parking area a few paces to the east and a walkway that leads to the overlook where interpretive signage explains the evolution of this unusual feature.

An unexpected site on Ontario's otherwise green landscape
are these badlands near Cheltenham.

⑭⓪ BELFOUNTAIN PARK

The Stamp Man's Legacy

UNDER THE GAZE of a small cannon, the west branch of the Credit River plunges over a 10-metre waterfall and then tumbles down a rocky canyon. Beside the cannon are winding pathways lined with elaborate stonework, a chapel-like cave with the name Yellowstone, and a stone fountain with a bell on top.

This is the Belfountain Conservation Area. The creation of millionaire philanthropist Charles W. Mack, it is one of Ontario's most unusual parks. Better known as the industrialist who invented and then manufactured the cushion rubber stamp used by banks and post offices, Mack purchased this property on the rocky bank of the Credit River in 1908. Here, by the site of an early grist mill and quarry, he built a summer home for himself and his wife, and they named it Luck-e-nuf. He then hired master landscaper Sam Brock to create a park.

When finished, Brock had created a wonderland in stone. His park contained a dam for swimming, a lookout point and a cave that he had converted into a chapel-like room. He had slung a suspension bridge across the canyon and topped it all off with a stone fountain with a bell on top, to commemorate the name of the village.

Belfountain, which lines the canyon rim, began in 1825 as a pioneer settlement named McCurdy's Village. During the 1860s it became home to mining company executives who managed the stone quarries in the Credit Canyon below. By the time Mack showed up, the mines had closed, and the miners' villages of Brimstone and Forks of the Credit had become ghost towns.

But Mack's park was quite popular, for when he had finished it, he opened the grounds to the public. Visitors could come to picnic, hike or swim, provided that they obeyed Charles Mack's rules: no swimming on Sundays, and men were to wear swim tops and women skirts at all times.

After Mack's death in 1943, his park was sold and operated as a commercial business until 1955, when the Credit Valley Conservation Authority purchased the property. Additional acquisitions between 1961 and 1973 have given the grounds more space for picnicking and hiking trails.

Although Mack's modest cottage and cabin have been reduced to their foundations, most of Brock's handiwork remains in place. You can look into the Yellowstone cave, watch the waterfall from the lookout, cross the canyon on a bridge or simply sit by the fountain with the bell on top.

The park lies in the village of Belfountain on the Forks of the Credit Road.

Beautiful Belfountain Park was once a private estate.

141 NATURE REBORN
Orangeville's Tree Spirits

MANY RELIGIONS AFFIRM that following death, a person's spirit lives on, perhaps even reincarnated as another being. Few, however, would suggest that the same holds true for trees — that is, until they go to Orangeville.

Orangeville began life as a mill town around 1829 when John Corbit arrived and found a small millstream engulfed by towering pine trees and wide, shady maples. Orange Lawrence came on the scene in 1844 and opened the post office, naming the town after himself.

The community remained a small mill village until two railway lines converged on the site. As the main street grew into an avenue of stately brick stores and an elegant town hall, maple trees were planted along the streets in the residential sections of town. In the last few decades, Orangeville's growth has accelerated, turning it into a booming bedroom community for cities like Toronto and Mississauga.

Those stately maples, however, have not been so lucky. Pollution from passing trucks and simple old age have brought them to the end of their years. Most communities would cut such trees off at the base, yank out the roots and plant some newer, more exotic species that would be lucky to survive the salt of the winter. But not so in Orangeville.

The idea was Mayor Drew Brown's. While visiting Truro, Nova Scotia, Brown noticed that tree trunks were often carved into historical figures. He returned to his hometown and planted the notion that the town's doomed maples trees could enjoy, if not prolonged life, at least an "afterlife."

In 2003, the carvers began. The trees were cut down to 3 or 4 metres in height and seventeen renowned carvers, including Colin Partridge, Jim Menken, Walter vanderWindt and Peter Mogensen, began turning the lifeless trunks into eagles, dancers, fiddlers, bears, historic figures and tree spirits. Fifty-four carvings by eighteen carvers now line the streets of Orangeville.

Most line the north side of Broadway, the main street, west of downtown. Another cluster lines First Street north of Broadway. The remainder are scattered throughout the town. Much like the main street murals of Midland, Ontario and Chemainus, British Columbia, the dead trees of Orangeville have helped turn the town into one of Ontario's more unusual tourist attractions.

Add to that Orangeville's regular theatre productions, and the dead here have truly gained new life.

A Tree Spirit entitled "The Indian" was carved by Jeff Waters.

Ontario's miniature version of the Grand Canyon, Ouimet Canyon, is so deep and narrow that plants otherwise native to the Arctic thrive in its dark recesses. **See pages 324-325.**

The dizzying Barron Canyon is the most spectacular chasm in Ontario. **See pages 304-305.**

Northern Ontario & Cottage Country

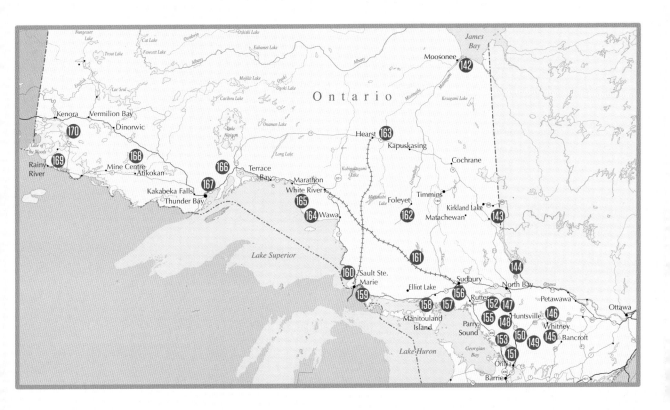

(142) A HOLY CHURCH

Moose Factory's Floating Church

LOCATED ON A desolate island in the Moose River, close to its mouth on James Bay, Moose Factory is claimed to be Ontario's oldest permanent settlement. The Company of Gentlemen Adventurers Trading into Hudson's Bay opened several posts across northern Canada. In 1673, they established Moose Fort, as the settlement was then called.

With the major European powers fighting for control of North America, ownership of Moose Factory alternated between the French and the English. By the time the Hudson's Bay Company and its rival, the North West Company, merged in 1821, the fighting had ended and Moose Fort became Moose Factory.

Between this time and the arrival in 1932 of the Temiskaming and Northern Ontario Railway at Moosonee on the mainland, the company added a number of new buildings to the trading post. The officers' dwelling was constructed in 1847; a building erected to house the fur trader's interpreter, a Cree of mixed ancestry named Joseph Turner, and the home belonging to the company carpenter, William McLeod, was added in 1889. One of the oldest buildings still standing is the company blacksmith shop, built around 1850. The shop operated until 1934.

And then there was St. James Anglican Church, fondly known as the "floating church." While it does not literally "float," the building was so prone to inundations from the river that special plugs were incorporated into the floorboards that could be removed in order to let the water come in. Otherwise the surging flood waters could seriously damage the church's foundations, or even lift it up and float it away.

Its first pastor, the Reverend John Horden, was the first to translate hymns, prayers and many passages from the Bible into the Cree syllables previously devised by John Evans.

The white frame church, with its slender spire, also contains a collection of attractive stained-glass windows. The nearby graveyard holds markers that date back to 1802.

While the Hudson's Bay Company moved away in 1989, the Ontario Heritage Foundation and the Moose Cree First Nation have worked to save many of the island's historic fur-trading buildings. The island is accessible by Cree freighter canoe from Moosonee, the Ontario Northland Railway's terminus for the popular Polar Bear Express tourist train.

Moose Factory's Anglican church was built with holes in the floor to prevent the frequent floodwaters from floating it away.

143 A CALENDAR OF BOULDERS
Ontario's Stonehenge

THE LARDER LAKE area of Ontario was one of the more significant spiritual centres for the early Indigenous Peoples who populated Ontario. Important early canoe routes made their way from the Ottawa River and Lake Temiskaming systems and mounted a height of land before making their way through the Abitibi and Moose River systems and on to James Bay.

Along the way, the most prominent feature is a looming cylindrical volcanic rock plug known as Mont Chaudron. Its physical dominance made it a place of worship for the Ojibwas and Crees who passed through the water system. Many chose the height of land on which to build their villages. The route was also used by early explorers and fur traders as well as by Chevalier Pierre de Troyes, who in 1686 led a surprise commando-style raid on the British Moose Fort on the Moose River.

But the most unusual of the route's features is an arrangement of eighteen massive boulders on the north shore of Larder Lake. How did such gigantic rocks end up in the same place and in a distinctive arrangement?

Recent investigations have revealed that the boulders are so configured that they line up with the sunrise and sunset at the times of the summer and winter solstices.

It is theorized, then, that the site represents a calendar used by Indigenous shamans about twelve hundred years ago. Its purpose would be similar to that of the stones used by the Druid worshippers at Stonehenge on the Salisbury Plain of England. Similar too would be the challenge in positioning boulders that, in some instances, are three times the height of the people who would have moved them. Such a focus would also be consistent with the use of Mount Cheminis as a place for spiritual worship.

The rocks are located near Pearl Beach on Larder Lake, east of the town of the same name. From Larder Lake, drive east on Highway 66 for six kilometres to an unmarked road to the south just before the Bob Lake/Tournene roadside picnic area. Take this road for 1.5 kilometres to a fork where you branch left. After 200 metres you will see the strange boulders.

Massive boulders near Larder Lake may have served a calendar-type purpose similar to that of the Stonehenge circle in England.

(144) WHITE BEAR FOREST
Temagami's Tall Pines

THE STATELY WHITE pine, Ontario's provincial tree, is threatened with extinction, thanks to the cutting plans devised by Ontario's Ministry of Natural Resources, along with the logging interests. The few remaining stands represent a mere 1 percent of the pine forest's original extent, and that makes them a rare heritage legacy. Many of those tall pines are to be found in the Temagami area of northeastern Ontario.

Situated about two hours' drive north of North Bay, the area contains a wilderness relic, with lakes and rivers surrounded by tall-pine forests. Of Temagami's tall-pine areas, the Lady Evelyn Smoothwater Park, accessible only by water, is perhaps the best known (although even it is now part of a ministry cutting plan).

A lesser-known tall-pine area, however, is easily accessible right within the limits of the village, and can be reached on foot. Known as the White Bear Forest, it takes its name from the last chief of a local tribe that used the area for hunting and trapping. In 1928, logging began on 500 square kilometres. But the company, run by the Gillies Brothers, decided to set aside the 800-hectare White Bear Forest as a reminder of what the ancient forests once looked like.

And it is here that the pines still loom large. The forest is the sixth largest old-growth white-pine forest still known, and, more remarkably, is the most accessible. Several kilometres of trail wind through the forest and can be accessed by car from the Caribou Mountain Ski Hill, or by boat from Northland Paradise Lodge on Snake Island Lake, which can also be reached by car. The trails range from one to two-and-a-half hours' hiking duration. While many ecological features dot the routes, from red-pine stands to beaver meadows, the highlight is the grove of soaring white pines on the north shore of Pleasant Lake (although they are found throughout the reserve). The forest also offers scenic lookouts and a preserved fire tower.

The village of Temagami, on Highway 11, contains a pair of small restaurants, a motel, access to several lodges, and a revitalized waterfront. The village's heritage centrepiece, however, is the historic Temiskaming & Northern Ontario (T&NO) railway station, restored by a local restoration trust. The Tudor-style stone station is one the most attractive in Northern Ontario. It continued to serve passengers travelling on the historic Northlander train until 2012, when the Ontario government cancelled the service.

The White Bear tall-pine forest at Temagami.

145 ONTARIO'S ALLIGATORS
Logging Boats of the Past

STEALTHILY AND SLOWLY, the hulking beasts made their way across the still lake waters. Once on land, they inched forward hauling their goods. These were Ontario's alligators.

To be clear, these were not of the animal variety, but rather wooden boats used by late nineteenth and early twentieth century loggers. As logging moved inland from the larger bodies of water, the companies needed some way of getting their boom boats between the smaller lakes. Also known as the steam-warping tug, the alligator was devised by Joe Ceborn West of Simcoe, Ontario. In 1889 he partnered with James Peachey and the two began manufacturing the odd vessels. By 1932 the company had made 230 alligators for the North American logging industry.

The square-shaped boats operated on water using a side paddle wheel and could travel at about 8 kilometres an hour, hauling a log boom behind it. However, if a head-wind arose against the square bow, forward movement would slow to a halt. To continue moving, the loggers rowed ahead of the boat with an anchor that they would drop. Using the anchor chain as a winch, the boat would then pull itself forward and the process repeated. The same means was used to drag the alligator across land, placing the anchor on the ground ahead and then winching forward on a crude road made of logs.

By the late 1930s the logging industry had changed, and trucks and rough logging roads replaced the all-water routes. The iconic alligators were largely stripped of their components, while others were left to rot.

Only two alligators remain intact in Ontario. One lies in the Logging Museum in Algonquin Park, along with other displays of Ontario's once dominant logging industry. The other, the *W.D. Stalker*, was restored in 1997 and is on display in the town of Simcoe, home of the alligator building industry.

Others lie in various states of ruin in at least two locations within Algonquin Park.

A restored alligator log hauling boat, more properly known as a steam warping tug, is part of the display at Algonquin Park's Logging Museum.

146 BARRON CANYON

Algonquin Park's Incredible Chasm

A T FIRST GLANCE it is hard to believe that Ontario has a canyon so deep and so precipitous. While the magnificent Ouimet Canyon in Northern Ontario is longer and wider and displays a collection of rare Arctic plants, the canyon on the Barron River in northeastern Algonquin Park is both narrower and considerably deeper.

Its origins are as unique as the canyon itself. After the rocks of the Canadian Shield were formed billions of years ago, they lay buried beneath the deposits of an ancient sea. Under the waters of that sea, the sandy deposits gradually hardened into limestone. When the entire area heaved upward, the limestone cap fragmented into fault lines that ran in a northwest to southeast direction.

Millions of centuries later, as the great ice sheets that covered Ontario retreated northward, the meltwaters drained along the fault lines. One channel became the outlet for an enormous post-glacial lake named Lake Algonquin. Some geologists estimate that the torrent equalled a thousand Niagaras, one of which gradually carved out the Barron Canyon. As the ice sheet continued its northerly retreat, the meltwaters found a lower outlet that became the Mattawa and Ottawa rivers.

Since then, erosion has continued its sculpting magic on the canyon. The harsh freeze-and-thaw action of the frigid Algonquin winters causes chunks of rock to fragment and cascade into the valley far below.

For a few decades the Barron River echoed to the shouts of loggers pushing their logs downstream to mills at Petawawa and Pembroke. After the last drive ended in 1936, the cleft became an awe-inspiring destination for canoeists and hikers. Birdwatchers observed such unlikely species as the swamp-loving yellow-bellied flycatcher and the common yellowthroat along the cliffs, as well as rare bald eagles.

Thanks to Algonquin's park planners, the canyon is easy to visit and photograph. From the parking area 11 kilometres west of the Sand Lake gate, a 1.5-kilometre loop trail leads to the lip of the precipice, a dizzying 100 metres above the river below. The trail is occasionally steep and the edge unfenced. From the top, breathtaking views extend far downstream to the east. Canoes can launch at a number of landings.

The portion of the river between the soaring walls is relatively placid, with only a few portages, and makes for a pleasant afternoon to view one of Ontario's more unusual and spectacular geological wonders.

The dizzying Barron River canyon is the most spectacular chasm in Ontario.

147 DYER'S DEDICATION

Muskoka's Wilderness Memorial

CALLING MUSKOKA A "wilderness" anymore may be a stretch. With lakeside condos and country homes, it is now more a form of low-density sprawl enhanced by lakes and woodlands. But as you negotiate your car along the narrow road that leads to the Dyer Memorial, north of Huntsville, and the trees on either side close in, you might be forgiven for thinking that you are indeed in the wilds.

That's what it was when Clifton G. Dyer and his wife, Betsy, began visiting the area. They spent their honeymoon canoeing in Algonquin Park in 1916 and fell in love with the land. In 1940 they built a cottage on the Big East River, near Huntsville, returning every year to that wilderness retreat until 1956, when Betsy died.

Dyer was devoted to his wife, and in the year after her death he built a moving tribute to her. On the highest point on his property, overlooking their beloved river, he erected a 14 metre stone cairn. He surrounded it with a 390-square-metre flagstone terrace, and around that created a 4-hectare botanical garden. On the top of the cairn, in a copper urn, he placed his wife's ashes to rest. Following his own death, in 1959, his ashes were placed next to hers.

In 2010, the Dyer estate donated the land to the Muskoka Conservancy. The Dyer Memorial Nature Reserve spans 155 acres and 1,800 feet of East River shoreline.

The memorial is open to the public. It is located near the hamlet of Williamsport, about 10 kilometres northeast of Huntsville. Small arrows point the way.

Although Clifton Dyer's cottage was sold long ago, the wilderness memorial to his wife will survive with his dedication to her: "An affectionate, loyal and understanding wife is life's greatest gift."

Dyer's wilderness memorial.

The historic *Portage Flyer* is ready to ride again.

148 THE RETURN OF MUSKOKA'S PORTAGE FLYER
The World's Shortest Railway

IT HAS COME back home. Following an absence of more than forty years, the famed *Portage Flyer* has returned to Muskoka. Once deemed the world's shortest commercial railway, the Huntsville and Lake of Bays Railway was a fixture on the landscape from 1904, when it began shuttling steamboat passengers between Peninsula Lake and Lake of Bays.

Although the Muskoka Lakes region had become a haven for tourists, roads and cars were many years in the future. Travellers would arrive by train and then transfer onto steamers for the trip to the many grand hotels that ringed the lakes. While vacationers could transfer easily from the Grand Trunk trains in Huntsville onto steamers bound for Fairy and Peninsula lakes, there remained a difficult height of land barring the route to the lovely Lake of Bays. A plan to connect Bracebridge to the lake by rail was scrapped when the steamboat company decided to link the lakes with a much shorter portage railway.

The narrow line had to climb more than 40 metres, doing so in just 3 kilometres. A pair of steam locomotives hauled two passenger coaches, which were converted from old Toronto streetcars. These were replaced in 1948 by newer engines. But the end of the era was in sight, and a decade later the Muskoka District had been infiltrated by new paved roads. Rather than taking steamers to lodges, city dwellers were packing their cars and driving to private cottages instead.

Steamers were floated into dry docks and scrapped; lodges were burned or demolished, and in 1959, the *Portage Flyer* made its last run. The equipment was sold and removed to Pinafore Park in St. Thomas, where it was a popular attraction. Finally, in 1984, the volunteer-run Huntsville and Lake of Bays Railway Society bought the old rolling stock and brought it back to Huntsville.

Finally, on June 1, 2000, the *Portage Flyer* once more puffed into service. The new route begins at the Muskoka Heritage Park in Huntsville, where a new two-storey station houses a waiting room, ticket office and historic photos, as well as community meeting rooms on the second floor. The trains now follow a 1.25-kilometre route along the banks of the Muskoka River to the shore of Fairy Lake, where the purser's cabin from the dock of a nearby hotel on Fairy Lake has become the Fairy Lake "station." To house the heritage rolling stock, the volunteers erected an engine shed and 500 metres of siding. The station is located on Brunel Street in Huntsville.

(149) ONTARIO'S LOG CHUTES
Vestiges of the Lumber Era

As LUMBER BARONS began to ravage the early pine forests of Ontario, they encountered a problem with moving the logs from dense forests to the mills. Ontario's Canadian Shield, a territory of rugged hills, small lakes and churning rivers, made such an operation a major challenge. While logs could be boomed across the larger lakes or hauled by alligator boat between them, the small rivers required something more. Canada's first chute was created in 1829 to guide the logs around the Chaudière Falls on the Ottawa River.

From those earliest times, chutes (or troughs) made from timber ran alongside the waterfalls and rapids, and provided passage for the logs to slip along quickly, much as slides in children's water parks do today. However, erosion and riverbank stabilization have removed nearly all evidence of this era; for the most part only replicas remain.

Algonquin Park's Logging Museum contains one such example, as does the High Falls in Pigeon River Provincial Park near Thunder Bay. Another lies in Crooked Slide Park along Old Barry's Bay Road, just northeast of Combermere (a quick 1.5 kilometres from Highway 62).

But the best example of an original chute is at the Hawk Lake Historic Log Chute site. Built in 1861, the 67-metre chute has been restored more than once due to flooding: in 1948, 1999, 2005 and again in 2017. The log chute itself is located on Big Hawk Lake Road. It is open spring, summer and fall, and free to enter. There are picnic facilities, walking trails and an interpretive centre. The Stanhope Heritage Museum, which contains more than 140 years of pioneering records and artifacts, is 11 kilometres south along North Shore Road about 1 kilometre east of Highway 35 and 5 kilometres north of Carnarvon.

A replica log chute forms part of a display in Crooked Slide Park near Barry's Bay.

Right: The long log chute near Carnarvon has been restored in the interpretive Hawk Lake Historic Log Chute Site.

Woodchester Villa, Bracebridge.

⑮⓪ EIGHT SIDES TO A HOUSE
Woodchester Villa

URING THE FIRST two generations of Ontario's European settlement, house styles were fairly uniform; from log cabins to Georgian mansions, the pattern was consistently boxy. But with affluence and stability, and with the increasing artistic curiosity of the Victorian age, there came more architectural experimentation. This brought one of the more unusual house styles ever seen in Ontario, and indeed in northeastern North America: the eight-sided house.

The origin of the design is credited to an amateur architect, American Orson Fowler, who featured it in his 1849 book, *A Home for All*. Its advantages, he argued, were that a greater floor-space-to-wall-space ratio made it cheaper to build. And with more external wall space for windows, it was brighter and therefore healthier.

Henry Bird apparently agreed. In 1882, he built one of Ontario's first octagonal houses in what was then a raw frontier town named Bracebridge. The owner of a large woollen mill, Bird built his home near the pioneer Muskoka Road, on a hill overlooking the town. The eight walls alternated between 5 metres and 4.5 metres wide, and were nearly a half-metre thick. The house remained in the Bird family for nearly a century, until it was sold to a local service club and shortly thereafter opened as a museum.

The style had many imitators, and by 1900 Ontario could boast more than one hundred octagonal houses. Today fewer than half remain, most in central or eastern Ontario, including in Lowville, Huttonville, Maple, Picton, Calabogie and Hawkesbury (which also claims an octagonal barn). Ontario's northernmost multi-sided building is a popular round barn near Sowerby, on the Trans-Canada Highway.

Woodchester Villa is located on King Street, close to the historic alignment of the Muskoka Road, although the steepness of the hill here closed the through route.

In 2009, a winter storm damaged the aging building so severely that the Town of Bracebridge had no choice but to close it to the public. In 2013, the town council approved nearly $1 million to repair the tourist attraction.

⑮ BOATS ON RAILS
The Big Chute Marine Railway

THE GROANING LIFT locks at Peterborough and Kirkfield are not the only unusual structures on the Trent-Severn Waterway. About 40 kilometres north of Barrie, County Road 17 leaves the village of Coldwater and takes you 20 kilometres along a winding road, past farms and through forests to the Big Chute Marine Railway.

By the turn of the century, urbanites, fed up with the noise and fumes of the industrial cities, were finding a tranquil escape at places like the mouth of the Severn River. By 1906 there was increasing pressure to open up still more of the Severn, and the federal government gave approval to a marine railway that would guide the boats over the steep falls known as the Big Chute (a temporary railway already existed for workers then constructing a hydro generator station at the same location).

In 1920 the marine railway was finished, but by 1922 it needed enlarging. The new car was 4 metres wide by 11 metres long. It operated by being lowered into the water at one end, where the boats could be floated over the carriage and secured. The carriage was then winched out of the water and pulled along rails to the height of land where the cables were manually switched for the descent into the water at the other end.

Following the Second World War, recreational boating experienced an unprecedented boom. By the 1970s the outdated marine railway had become such a bottleneck that considerable enlargement was necessary. In 1977 a new carriage, 13 metres wide and 36 metres long, began to rumble up and down the granite cliff. Unlike the old car, the new carriage uses a modern system of four winches operated by digital control and automatic cable transfer. The older historic car is still used to handle overflow.

Viewing is easy. Parks Canada has created an attractive park with hiking and picnicking facilities. Amid the benches you may see concrete steps. These once led to the large houses that were home to the original workers in the hydroelectric plant. But it's the sight of a luxury yacht creaking up a cliff on a railway car that you won't easily forget.

The site can now also be reached by following Muskoka Road 34 east from Highway 400 at Exit 162, just north of Port Severn.

A more modern carriage now carries boats up the steep
incline at the Big Chute on the Trent-Severn Canal.

(152) THE ALMAGUIN HIGHLANDS' FIELD OF SCREAMS

The Unique Midlothian Ridge Sculpture Garden

VISITORS TRAVELLING THE Midlothian Road west of Burk's Falls will surely do a double take when they sense that they are being watched by the Screaming Heads of the Midlothian Ridge sculpture garden. Inspired by his concern for the environment, Peter Camani has constructed a display of 84 screaming heads and misshapen trees to reflect the Earth's reaction to the havoc being wreaked upon it.

Made from concrete over steel frames the giants measure 6 metres high. Their massive mouths are wide open in a silent scream (vaguely reminiscent of Edvard Munch's famous work, "The Scream").

Beside a lagoon, heads and hands appear to be emerging from the ground. In another corner of the farm, twenty large screaming heads take the form of an eye when viewed from above. In the open fields visitors may make out the "Four Horsemen of the Apocalypse" and some dragons' claws emerging from the ground. Other sculptures resemble misshapen trees.

Around the sculptor's home, which resembles a castle, various fowl enjoy a free-range life style, including a rare white peacock. In addition to the heads, Camani has planted 22,000 trees and dug lagoons throughout the property.

There is no admission charge to visit the grounds, and visitors may wander at will. The paths are cleared and easy to walk and they all eventually lead to sculpture after sculpture. Being a private outdoor art exhibit, there are no facilities such as refreshments or washrooms. And Camani's castle home is off limits.

To reach the property, follow Highway 520 west from Burk's Falls (a town with a picturesque covered bridge over a foaming waterfall beside an historic main street), and then turn onto Midlothian Road. The Screaming Heads will begin to appear through the trees after about 5 kilometres.

Left and right: The Screaming Heads sculpture garden.

(153) STARRY, STARRY NIGHT

The Torrance Barrens Dark-Sky Preserve

MOST OF ONTARIO's urban dwellers are fortunate if, when they gaze into the nighttime sky, they are able to make out more than a handful of stars or planets through Ontario's urban haze. This is what makes Muskoka's Dark-Sky Preserve located within the unusual Torrance Barrens so special.

The barrens are the roots of an ancient mountain chain eroded over time by wind and water, and finally sculpted by glaciers into bare smooth hummocks. So sparse is the soil cover that vegetation consists of little more than stunted scattered oaks and clumps of shrubs. Rough trails wind past small ponds and swamps where rare animal species, like the five-lined skink or the southern bog lemming, might lurk along with the occasional Massasauga Rattlesnake.

Its uninviting terrain discouraged settlement and the location remains remote from towns or even villages. With no nearby light sources and the surrounding land either protected or utterly undeveloped, the visibility of the night sky is unlike any other location in southern Ontario. Distant galaxies, the Milky Way and brilliant dancing northern lights glow right overhead. In 1997, the Ontario government designated the 2,000-hectare barrens as a conservation reserve and two years later as a dark-sky preserve prohibiting most new light sources.

Remarkably, the location is quite accessible. The Torrance Barrens Conservation Area lies along Southwood Road 8.3 kilometres from the community of Torrance, which is 21 kilometres from Gravenhurst via Muskoka Road 169. After winding through overgrown farmlands and forested gullies, the road suddenly mounts a ridge to the abrupt starkness of the desert-like rock barrens. A parking area is available at the Ministry of Natural Resources sign.

A view of the night sky from the Torrance Barrens Preserve.

The Wawa Goose is one of the Trans-Canada Highway's most iconic northern roadside sights.

Left: White River's Winnie the Pooh roadside icon marks the birthplace of the real-life bear that inspired A.A. Milne to create his popular children's' stories.

⑮ Ontario's Roadside Icons

From Cheese to Chairs

ROADSIDE ICONS ARE meant to depict the character of the communities which built them. While roadside icons, odd and meaningful, lurk along Ontario's roadsides everywhere, the roads of the North seem to offer the majority.

The largest Muskoka chair sits in the Sawdust City Brewing Company parking lot in Gravenhurst. Beside the Trans-Canada Highway in Kenora, "Husky the Muskie," remains the best known roadside fish. The Wawa Goose has greeted motorists since Trans-Canada Highway opened.

While the Big Nickel near the Inco plant in Sudbury is another well-known icon, giant coins can also be found in Virginiatown (a gold coin), Campbellford (a Toonie) and Echo Bay (a Loonie).

A wooden carving of the legendary lumberjack, Big Joe Mufferaw, is appropriate for the historic logging community of Mattawa while the fictional image of Winnie the Pooh stands roadside in White River.

Jumbo the elephant in St. Thomas pays tribute to the sad demise of that popular circus attraction by an oncoming freight train. Wiarton Willie makes his appearance each Groundhog Day, although his image is on display year-round in the town. The First Nations community of Zhiibaahaasing on Manitoulin Island proudly proclaims its heritage with a large dreamcatcher, drum and peace pipe.

Terry Fox, at 22, became a Canadian legend and a hero. In 1980 the one-legged athlete limped along Canada's highways doing a punishing marathon each day to raise money for cancer research, the disease which had cost him his leg. His Marathon of Hope ended after 143 days just east of Thunder Bay when his cancer proved too much for him to continue. He died the following year. One of Ontario's most moving roadside icons, one depicting Terry Fox, lies on the Trans-Canada Highway, 10 kilometres east of Thunder Bay, and marks the location where the recurring cancer forced him to end his journey.

Many icons reflect a local sense of humour. The Flying Saucer in Moonbeam wants to attract visitors from other planets. In Nolalu a giant mosquito resting atop a Studebaker is testimony to the region's notorious pests.

The strangest of Ontario's roadside icons is a huge beast, known as "Koilos," with a tentacle for a head created by sculptor Michael Christian. During its sojourn in Bala, locals took to calling it the "Bala Bog Monster" in reference to the area's cranberry bogs. Today it resides at Muskoka Farms and Winery. In 1893, Perth became known around the world for the 8-ton cheese it sent to the World's Fair in Chicago. A replica now sits by the Tay Basin in downtown Perth.

The grey arches of a one-time railway roundhouse peer from the woods at the site of the once bustling port of Depot Harbour.

(155) DEPOT HARBOUR

A Georgian Bay Ghost Port

URING ITS HEYDAY, Depot Harbour was a busy railway terminus and Great Lakes port, and with sixteen hundred residents, it threatened to eclipse places like Midland and Owen Sound. But today the wind blows across cracked sidewalks and overgrown foundations, as Georgian Bay's waves now lap against silent shores.

It all began in the 1890s, when lumber baron John Rudolphus Booth forged a rail link across the middle of Ontario. His Ottawa, Arnprior and Parry Sound Railway would not only access his rich pine forests but also give Canada's western grain growers their most direct route to the ice-free Atlantic Ocean ports.

A dispute over the location of the terminus on Georgian Bay led Booth to seek a site where he could build his own town. On Parry Island, beside the Great Lake's largest natural harbour, Booth built the town of Depot Harbour. The town contained three churches, a school, railway yards and a roundhouse, two large grain elevators and more than one hundred dwellings.

For three decades the place prospered. Then, in 1928, the Canadian National Railway, which had by then assembled a collection of bankrupt rail lines, amalgamated its facilities at a location south of Parry Sound.

Five years later, an ice floe damaged a trestle in Algonquin Park and CN closed the route.

The lifeline of Depot Harbour was severed, a calamity from which it never recovered. In 1945, the port facilities, which were then storing the volatile cordite for a nearby munitions factory, erupted in a midnight fireball that lit up the streets of Parry Sound, 10 kilometres away. Depot Harbour's story was over. The houses were sold off for $25 each and residents moved away.

By the 1960s only the Catholic church, the shell of the roundhouse and a single dwelling remained standing. Today, the roundhouse alone survives. Beyond it, hidden by a forest now a half century old, lie the foundations, the old sidewalks, the remains of the company vault and the massive wharf, all now silent. Although the ruins become more and more obscured as the years pass, it remains Ontario's most extensive ghost town. In 1996, the townsite reverted to the ownership of the Wasauksing First Nation and has become the site of the community's annual pow wow.

To reach Depot Harbour, follow the Rose Point Road from Parry Sound across the railway bridge to a T intersection. The ghost town is down a side trail, about 5 kilometres to the west.

156 A GREEN SUDBURY

A Moonscape Revitalized

COULD THE BARREN moonscape once described as one of the world's worst environmental disasters ever be green again? So barren was the soil of Sudbury that American astronauts practised their moonwalks on the tormented terrain.

A century ago Sudbury was green. Pine forest covered the granite rocks. In 1883, the Canadian Pacific Railway blasted these rocks to make way for the national dream of a rail line to the Pacific, and the discovery of the world's largest deposit of copper and nickel in those rock cuts turned the little railway junction into a major mining town. But nickel refining is also one of the most polluting industries.

An obsolete process called "roasting" caused the damage. Crushed ore was laid on vast beds of burning cordwood. The roasting beds burned for months, sending billowing clouds of sulphur-laden smoke across the landscape. The smoke killed everything it touched. The refinery stacks were even worse, spewing tiny particles of nickel and copper oxide, which seeped into and poisoned the ground.

Trees were killed in all directions. The ground was barren. Nothing grew in the poisoned terrain.

Then, in 1969, when Inco constructed a superstack to spread the fumes further afield, local residents decided to make Sudbury green again. Although the first efforts at reforestation on the infertile ground were dismal failures, a few years later a Laurentian University biology professor Keith Winterhalder began to experiment with lime. By laying down a layer of lime first, the poisons were neutralized. A variety of grasses were then planted. Once the grass took hold, the trees followed.

Schoolchildren, youth and miners all clambered over the hillsides and tailings, planting trees by the thousands. The efforts have won several national and international awards, including the Lieutenant Governor's Conservation Award, the United States Chevron Conservation Award and the United Nations Local Government Honours Award, presented at the Earth Summit in Rio de Janeiro.

In 1997, the regional municipality unveiled a plaque beside its premier landmark, the Big Nickel, announcing the planting of the three millionth tree. Since that date, a further 9.7 million trees have been planted on more than 3,400 hectares. Ironically, looming on the hill next to the plaque are the now-cleaned-up Inco stacks, and in between, a young forest of saplings that could only have been imagined a few years earlier.

Nine million trees have been replanted on what was once a barren, polluted moonscape.

157 THE WHITE CRESTS OF KILLARNEY
Ontario's Rocky Mountains

D
RIVING WEST ON Highway 637, just south of Sudbury, you soon see the domes of white, gleaming above the low, green forest. Your first thoughts are that freak weather has preserved a mountain of snow into the summer season. But as you drive closer you realize that these are the legendary La Cloche Mountains of Killarney, and the "snow" is quartzite rock of pure white.

About two billion years ago an ancient sea laid down a bed of sand that was unusually rich in silica. As the shifting bedrock hurled the seabed into a giant mountain range, the layers of silica were compressed into masses of white quartzite, forming a mountain range

loftier than today's Rockies. Eons of rain, wind and grinding glaciers eroded the peaks into the round, white knobs that today provide the spectacular backdrop for the northern shores of Georgian Bay and Lake Huron. The white wall of mountains stretches in a thin line for about 60 kilometres and soars in places to heights of 500 metres.

The early French explorers gave the mountains their word for "bell," because they reported that certain rocks, when struck, echoed like a bell.

The area's early history has little to do with the scenery. Following the days when Killarney was a stopover for Indigenous

The pure white quartzite rocks of the Killarney mountains resemble a hillside of snow.

and French-Canadian fur traders, logging companies began to strip the pine from the mountainsides. The village of Killarney, now dependent upon tourism for its survival, originated as a fur-trading post and fishing village.

But it was the scenery that attracted the area's earliest tourists. Among them were a pair of young painters named Franklin Carmichael and A.Y. Jackson, whose works *Summer Storm*, *Bay of Islands* and *Nellie Lake* are among the most prized Group of Seven works. Their works in part inspired the Ontario government to create the much-visited Killarney Provincial Park, with its campsites, canoe routes and hiking trails, one of which is 100 kilometres long.

The park is 70 kilometres west of Highway 69 along Highway 637.

You can also travel by boat to Killarney and explore the mountain-lined fjords. Or you can approach the mountains on Highway 6 south of Espanola to a soaring pass over the Tower Mountain summit near Willisville. But regardless of how you get there, the La Cloche Mountains of Killarney remain one of the most unusual alpine destinations east of the Rockies.

158 THE LITTLE CURRENT RAILWAY SWING BRIDGE

Cars Only

ONE OF ONTARIO'S more interesting anomalies is that the only road access to the world's largest freshwater island is via a railway bridge.

Since the end of the last ice age, Manitoulin Island was considered a sacred place for its Indigenous populations. Europeans began to drive those inhabitants from their land in the 1860s, and within a few years most of that land was in the hands of the settlers.

For several decades the "Haweaters," as the Manitoulin pioneers called themselves (for their dependence on the local hawberry),

depended on water crossings to link them with the mainland. Then in 1893, the Algoma Eastern Railway began building a track from Sudbury to the island with the idea that its line would eventually link up with a line to Tobermory on the tip of the Bruce Peninsula. But, as with many a railway dream, the plan fell short, terminating instead at the island port of Little Current.

To span the gap between the mainland and the island, a long bridge was needed — one that would also allow the passage of the busy steamship traffic of the North Channel.

The only vehicular access to the world's largest freshwater island, Manitoulin, is via a century-old railway swing bridge.

In 1913, the bridge opened to train traffic. At 225 metres long it contains a 112-metre span, which swings open and allow ships to pass. Until 1946 it served rail only, with all other traffic using a nearby ferry. In those days it remained open until a train arrived. Since 1946, however, when vehicles began to share it, the bridge has remained in the closed position, opening during the ice-free season for 15 minutes out of every hour to allow boat traffic through.

Finally, in the 1980s, train service was cut back and the bridge planked in. Today the entire rail line has been abandoned. Although cars may also use the ferry *Chi-Cheemaun* between Tobermory and South Baymouth, it is the old railway swing bridge that remains the iconic symbol of the island, while hawberry jelly has become a popular souvenir gift item.

The bridge forms part of Highway 6 south of Espanola.

159 A History in Ruins

Fort St. Joseph

Tourists travel to distant lands in cramped airplanes and stuffy tour buses in order to see famous ruins. In Europe and Latin America, these piles of stone and rubble bring in millions of tourist dollars. In Ontario, ruins and historic foundations are usually just an excuse to build a new condo tower. That is what makes the ruins of Fort St. Joseph unusual: they remain as ruins.

Throughout most of Canada and the United States, forts are often less than authentic restorations, even replications (such as Fort George and Fort Erie). Kingston's popular Fort Henry, part of a UNESCO World Heritage Site, was never a ruin to begin with and never even saw combat.

Fort St. Joseph, on the other hand, pre-dates Fort Henry and was a vital outpost during the War of 1812, playing a key role in that conflict.

After being forced to cede Fort Michilimackinac to the Americans following their revolutionary war in 1786, the British needed more defences on the vital St. Mary's River that linked Lake Superior with Lake Huron, so Fort St. Joseph was built in 1796.

In 1812, as the new conflict was beginning, the British troops set forth from the fort to recapture Fort Michilimackinac in the Straits of Mackinac, which connect Lake Michigan with Lake Huron. While Fort St. Joseph lay vacant, a small contingent of Americans burned it to the ground. Having won the war, the British no longer needed a fort at that location and moved their base to Penetanguishene.

Today the ruins are a National Historic Site. A video in the visitor's centre introduces tourists to the history of the site, while a self-guiding tour leads to the foundations of such original structures as the bake house, block house, kitchen and stores building. By the water are the remnants of the wharf and the location of the civilian village that serviced the soldiers.

The fort lies on St. Joseph Island, a tranquil rural oasis located southeast of Sault Ste. Marie and is accessible by Highway 17 (Trans-Canada Highway).

The ruins of Fort St. Joseph represent a true 1812 heritage ruin on the north shore of Lake Huron.

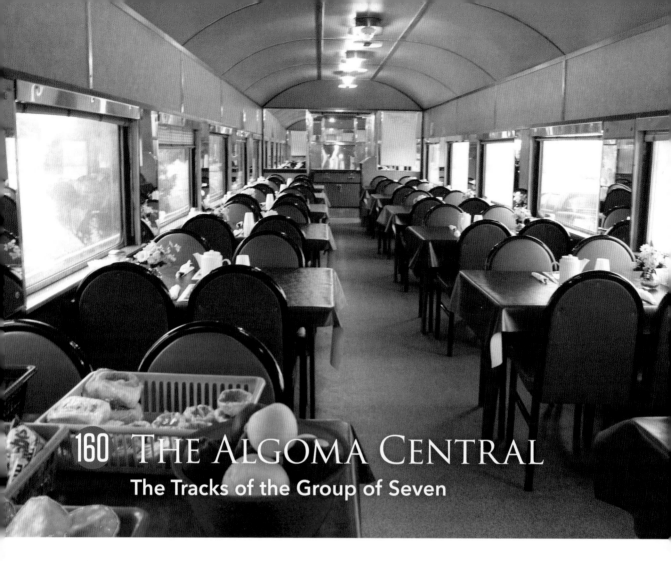

160 THE ALGOMA CENTRAL
The Tracks of the Group of Seven

AMONG ONTARIO'S MOST iconic train experiences is the popular Agawa Canyon Tour Train. The Algoma Central Railway began in 1899 when Frances Clergue, owner of vast iron deposits near today's Wawa, established the line to haul ore from the mines, as well as the rich harvest of timber.

En route, the trains passed through a narrow defile known as the Agawa Canyon in the heart of some of Ontario's most spectacular mountain scenery. The beauty of that scenery soon became popular with a growing tourist industry. In the 1920s, the artist's collective known as the Group of Seven would travel the train into the Algoma area to paint its gloomy peaks and brilliant fall colours. Winter wasn't a barrier either, as their snowy images became among their more popular.

Thanks in part to those paintings and promotion by the Algoma Central, the route has become popular around the world and one that remains vital to the tourism economy of Sault Ste. Marie. Today, a modern and comfortable station has replaced the historic red stone station, which still stands. Dining car service includes breakfast, hot and cold lunches or picnic box lunches, while snack

Above: The Agawa Canyon tour train prepares to depart Sault Ste. Marie. Pictured on the facing page is the interior of the dining car on the Agawa tour train.

bars are conveniently located throughout the train. Travellers may listen to a GPS-triggered commentary available in five languages. Video screens connected to the front of the engine show the engineer's perspective of the mountains, valleys and soaring bridges, such as the mighty Bellevue and the Montreal River trestles.

The layover in the Agawa Canyon allows time to hike the trails or climb to a lookout high above the canyon.

Since the tracks reached their northern terminus at Hearst, a local train had followed the historic route to access hunt camps, tourist resorts, canoe routes and trap lines. Sadly, the federal government withdrew funding of this local train in 2015. To fill the gap, a consortium initiated by the Missanabie Cree First Nation is working to restore the essential service subsequently known as the Musk-wa Oo-ta-ban, or Bear Train.

Right: The ghost town of Biscotasing is one of many on the route of VIA Rail's 'ghost town' train.

VIA's "Ghost Town Train" awaits its return trip at the CPR station in White River.

161 ONTARIO'S GHOST TOWN TRAIN

THE FIRST LINE through Ontario's North Country was the Canadian Pacific. By the 1880s, its rails led through North Bay and Sudbury, steaming through the great pine forests. Along its route countless sawmills and villages for the workers grew up at trackside. By the 1930s, most of the timber supply was depleted, and the mills closed or burned. Those communities fortunate enough to attract other industries managed to struggle on. Most, however, simply died.

These chrome coaches were formerly known as *The Superior*. It is one of five wilderness routes operated by VIA Rail across the country. Operating three times a week, the journey takes about 8 hours to travel between Sudbury and White River (home of Winnie the Pooh). Along the way, the train may stop up to twenty-five times for local inhabitants, lodge guests, anglers, canoeists, or to drop off needed supplies to wilderness operators. Light snacks are available on board.

After rumbling through Sudbury's suburbs, and mining towns of Onaping and Levack, It pauses at the grand old station in Cartier. It then hurtles through the ghost towns of Benny, Sheahan, and Metagama, unless stopping upon request.

Perhaps the most prominent ghost town on the route is Biscotasing. Looming high above the station shelter is the weathered ruin of the Roman Catholic church.

Next up is a vast meadow that, until the late 1970s, was the site of the Korpela and Maki mills that gave the place its name — Kormak. Stops may also happen at remote settlements like Missanabie or Sultan or the isolated railway junction of Franz.

After stopping for a break in the divisional town of Chapleau, the train once more enters the woods, where it quickly comes to the ghost town of Nicholson. Nicholson's railway tie mill burned in the 1930s, but much of the town remained intact until a fire in the mid-1970s destroyed a large part of the main street. Today the ruins can still be seen in the woods.

The train then rushes past — the remains of the mill town of Dalton Station. After stopping at the former mining town of Missanabie, it continues on to the one-time gold-mining town of Lochalsh.

The train ride ends at White River where a First World War army captain named Harry Colbourne purchased a bear cub which later became the inspiration for Winnie the Pooh, another divisional town, returning to Sudbury the following day. With history and wilderness scenery lining the route and the stunning fall colours or snowy forests, the train ride is popular with rail excursion companies as well.

(162) THE WHITE SPIRIT MOOSE OF FOLEYET

Protecting an Endangered Species

IT WAS IN the 1970s when Jane Armstrong noticed an animal unlike any she had seen before. It was a moose all right, but it was white.

Since that time, other white moose have been seen, primarily in the Foleyet area of northeastern Ontario. The animals are protected by the Ontario government's Ministry of Natural Resources, although their numbers are estimated at only a half dozen. Despite their scarcity, local tour operators can take visitors to the vicinity of the animals' population.

These ghostly creatures are not albinos, but rather display a recessive gene in their genetic makeup, which spawns moose individuals that are not only white, but light brown as well. This type is known as the Armstrong-White Moose strain, after their discoverer.

Most sightings have occurred along Highway 101 between Timmins and Foleyet. In addition to trains, cars and predators, non-local hunters who prize a white moose trophy threaten the "spirit" moose. Local groups have been urging the Ontario government to strengthen their regulations by removing the white moose from the hunting roster entirely.

The government, however, has other ways of protecting our animal species. Among the deadliest road accidents in northern Ontario are those involving vehicles and moose. While deer and elk can also inflict serious damage and injury, collisions with a monster moose are the deadliest. This is why Ontario's Ministries of Transportation and Natural Resources opened the province's first wildlife bridge over a newly built stretch of Highway 69 south of Sudbury.

As highway construction inched northward from Parry Sound in 2012, the need to avoid potentially deadly wildlife crashes became increasingly evident. The crossing is located a short distance from the turnoff to the idyllic Georgian Bay port of Killarney, where there is a large moose and elk population. Six kilometres of fencing along the roadway guides the animals to the overpass. A series of underpasses also help the animal population to avoid crossing the busy road.

To enhance the aesthetic appeal of the new structure, several carvings of moose and elk decorate the sides of the new bridge. While in the area, drop into the Ministry of Natural Resource's new French River Visitor's Centre on the French River. It tells the story of the river, including its geology and its role in the early days of the fur trade. A pedestrian and snowmobile bridge crosses the deep gorge of the river as well.

Ontario's first wildlife bridge is located on Highway 69 just south of Sudbury.

Right: A rare white moose is an unusual member of the moose family.

This Northern Ontario monument recalls a tragic labour dispute.

(163) MONUMENT TO MURDER

Massacre at Reesor Siding

UNLIKE THE MORE popular Trans-Canada Highway, which follows the spectacular shore of Lake Superior, there is another "trans-Canada highway." Numbered as Highway 11, it passes through northeastern Ontario, offering landscapes that are much less dramatic. Much of it traverses the northern Clay Belt, where sleepy railway towns appear at regular intervals throughout the flat farmlands. It comes as a surprise then to see above an overgrown field a monument to a murder.

In January of 1963, more than one thousand members of the Lumber and Sawmill Workers Union working in eight bush camps staged a wildcat strike to protest the slow progress of contract talks with the Spruce Falls pulp mill in Kapuskasing. But they weren't the only suppliers of logs. Local farmers also hauled logs from their own lots as independent contractors, and they had no affiliation with the union. Suspicious of unions, they refused to support the strike and continued to pile their logs at nearby Reesor Siding for shipment to the mill.

Tensions ran high. The company refused to negotiate until the workers returned to the camps. The workers refused to return until the company began to negotiate. Calls for the provincial government to appoint a conciliator went unheeded. The government then made the situation worse by granting permits to the independent farmers to continue to supply logs. Frustrated by the lack of progress, and angered by the farmers' antipathy, the strikers began to vandalize the log piles at the siding.

On the night of February 11, four hundred strikers marched on the siding to once again unpile the logs. Alerted by the police, the farmers, now armed, huddled in a cabin waiting for them. Shots rang out in the cold night air and three strikers fell dead. Another eight lay wounded.

Twenty of the farmers were brought to trial, charged with "non-capital" murder. Without proof of who fired the guns, they were acquitted. Meanwhile, more than two hundred strikers were convicted of participating in a riot and fined. To commemorate the tragic deaths of the union strikers, the United Brotherhood of Carpenters and Joiners has erected a large monument, which rises incongruously above the flat landscape of the deserted siding and speaks for itself. In a fitting act of irony, the workers now own the mill.

The monument looms above a field on Highway 11, 50 kilometres west of Kapuskasing.

Pictographs on Lake Superior depict early Indigenous omens and myths.

(164) STORIES ON THE ROCK
The Agawa Pictographs

A SHEER GRANITE WALL assailed by the crashing waves of Lake Superior would be the last place one would look to find Indigenous stories, but here in Lake Superior Provincial Park are some of the best preserved pictographs anywhere in Canada.

Pictographs are quite different from petroglyphs, such as those found near Stoney Lake, which are etchings. Pictographs are paintings. Made of mixtures of red ochre and animal fat, the images are surprisingly durable. Those on the Agawa rock wall may date back more than three centuries.

Here, on the sheer 30-metre rock face, nearly three dozen images portray what is said to be a victory battle by a party of Ojibwa over invading Iroquois. Following the devastating raids by the Iroquois against the Hurons in the mid-seventeenth century, groups of Ojibwa warriors retaliated, driving many of the invaders back across the Great Lakes and into their home territory of upper New York State.

Rediscovered in 1958, the images appear in four panels (three of which are accessible), the main one depicting a pair of large snakes and a great lynx guarding a canoe of Ojibwa fighters. According to Indigenous lore, the lynx is the protector of the Ojibwa. Other panels portray other animals, including an eagle, a beaver and a heron, purported to represent different clans. The presence of a horse suggests that the drawings were done post-contact with Europeans.

A 500-metre trail, open May to September only, leads down through a narrow defile in the rock to the site. Because access is only via a narrow ledge along the lake, visits should not be attempted in stormy weather. An unusual sight along the trail itself is a huge boulder wedged solidly between narrow canyon walls high above the trail. The park straddles Highway 17, south of Wawa.

Above: Visiting the exposed Agawa pictographs on Lake Superior is off-limits during rough weather on the lake.

These unexplained excavations are found throughout Ontario.

(165) THOSE PERPLEXING PUKASKWA PITS

Pukaskwa National Park

SOME OF ONTARIO's most unusual places predate recorded history. Early inhabitants left behind mounds, pits and paintings, features that filled crucial roles in their lives, but left question marks for a modern generation. While today's archaeologists may understand the paintings and the petroglyphs, no one has yet unravelled the mystery of the pukaskwa pits.

Found primarily around the shores of Lake Superior, pukaskwa pits (pronounced puk-a-saw) are manmade excavations dug into boulder beaches, which formed when the lake waters were about 30 metres higher than they are today. The conical pits average 1.3 metres across and 0.2 metres deep, with excavated stones piled protectively around the rim. Although clearly manmade, the lack of other evidence of human occupation, such as burial mounds, dumps or habitation areas, heightens their mystery. Archaeologists have found only bits of pottery, flints and caribou bones, suggesting that the use of the pits was likely short-lived.

One theory suggests that they were vision pits. Young men of each tribe isolated themselves until the spirit of the animal that guided their lives visited them. Others speculate that the pits were shelters from the storm-tossed waters of the lake during the peak of the fur trade. Their location, close to the water but away from the waves, makes them excellent shelters for canoeists. Huddled inside, one is protected from the cold winds, while soaking up the sun. Some of the larger pits appear to have had hearths and possibly protective coverings.

The greatest concentration of pukaskwa pits is found along the northeastern shore of Lake Superior, where more than 250 are protected in Pukaskwa National Park. Because they can be easily altered, or even destroyed by accident or carelessness, their exact locations are not published. Pukaskwa Park epitomizes Northern Ontario. Mountain peaks soar 640 metres high, wild rivers plunge through steep canyons, dense forests cloak the steep hillsides and waves thunder against a rocky shore where cliffs loom high above the grey waters.

The park is accessed from Highway 17 by following Highway 627 through Heron Bay. Here you find the Friends of Pukaskwa store. From the campground and visitor centre, hikes vary from a 30-minute walk to a 60-kilometre hiking trail along the coast to Hattie Bay. A well-travelled canoe route follows the shore, with campsites at several locations. And although the locations of the mystery pits are not given, those who hike or canoe the shoreline of the park will quickly find a few of these mysterious holes and ponder their origin.

⑯⑥ GRAND CANYON NORTH
Ouimet Canyon

IT'S LITTLE WONDER that Group of Seven painters A. Y. Jackson, Franklin Carmichael and Lawren Harris fell in love with Superior country. Nearly every bend in its rivers and nearly every bay in its lakes displays a panorama of mountain scenery that is as unexpected as it is awesome. And when, at the end of a trail through a pine forest near Nipigon, Ontario, the land drops away, unannounced, at your feet, to reveal a sudden and magnificent canyon, you understand how scenery can be called "unexpected."

As a tourist attraction, Ouimet Canyon Provincial Park is relatively unknown. No motels have sprung up to accommodate the hoards, no gift shops line the roads. Most Trans-Canada Highway travellers simply ignore the simple brown sign that points the way. But as a visual spectacle, Ouimet Canyon is breathtaking and unique.

The craggy crevice, 150 metres wide and 100 metres deep, twists several kilometres north from the lip of the grand plateau into which it has been cut. So little sunshine penetrates the deep gully that winter ice can linger into summer, and only hardy Arctic species of mosses, lichens and liverworts can survive.

The canyon traces its origins back to the last great ice age, when glaciers 2 kilometres thick crept southward, scouring and gouging everything in their path. Here at Ouimet Canyon, a tongue of ice crept down what was an eroded diabase sill. That diabase was formed a billion years ago when magma rose to the surface, creating the pillar-like formations that line the valley walls. Some of those pillars, owing to erosion, are free-standing.

Eleven kilometres to the east, the privately operated Eagle Canyon Adventures offers visitors the chance to brave Canada's longest suspension bridge and a formidable zip line across a geologically similar canyon.

From the viewing areas, the panorama encompasses not only the defile itself but also its rugged gates at the rim of the plateau, the forested lands beyond and, along the far horizon, the grey waters of Lake Superior.

As you gaze at the results of nature's remarkable strength, as the northern stillness rings in your ears and as the sharp, pine-scented air stings your nostrils, you will understand why the Group of Seven kept coming back. Access to the two canyons is from the Trans-Canada Highway, about 60 kilometres east of Thunder Bay.

Ontario's miniature version of the Grand Canyon, Ouimet Canyon, is so deep and narrow that plants otherwise native to the Arctic thrive in its dark recesses.

⟨167⟩ A Touch of Asia

The Thunder Bay Pagoda

FOR MANY DECADES, it was the first thing visitors to Port Arthur would see. As they disembarked from a CP steamship, or a train at the CPR station, visitors would make this unusual tourist information centre their first stop. Situated by the harbour and the tracks, and on the walk to the Prince Arthur Hotel, Port Arthur's "publicity pagoda" was built in 1909. Given Port Arthur's harsh climate of long, bitterly cold winters and uncompromising terrain, civic leaders and the business community desperately needed something to enhance their town's appeal. After all, the new Prince Arthur Hotel was slated to open in 1910, and the town was anxious for a visual icon to counter rival Fort William, by then a major transportation hub.

And so the town leaders hired a local architect named H. Russell Halton to create what has become Ontario's most unusual tourist pavilion. Octagonal in shape, the brick and stone pavilion is topped with a Hindu-style chatri roof, with Tuscan-like columns supporting a veranda around it. The local culture is represented by a bas-relief beaver and maple leaf carvings above the French-door entrance. At the time, the pavilion was known as the "publicity pagoda" — notion being to create an "east-west" concept to make all visitors feel welcome.

By the mid-1980s, rail passenger service had dwindled and ultimately ended altogether. The CPR station was demolished and the pagoda moved inland to accommodate new roadways along the waterfront. Although it survived a period during the 1970s with a polka-dotted roof, in 1986 the office closed and the pagoda appeared doomed. In an effort to save the structure, the federal government declared it a national historic site. Fortunately, in 1988, the city, which in 1970 had become Thunder Bay with the amalgamation of Port Arthur and Fort William, received a Heritage grant and restoration began.

Today, the remarkable pagoda still stands — the Prince Arthur Hotel on one side and the stunning Canadian Northern railway station, with its twin pyramid roofs, on the other. It is considered Canada's oldest information office. Happily, the polka dots are now gone.

As it has for more than a century, Thunder Bay's unusual pagoda-style information booth welcomes visitors to what was downtown Port Arthur.

The log White Otter Castle was built by one man alone in the bush.

⑯⑧ THE LOG CASTLE ON WHITE OTTER LAKE

A One-Man Mansion

THOSE THINGS THAT are the hardest to reach often offer the richest rewards. So is the case with the strange log castle on White Otter Lake, some 64 kilometres north of Atikokan, in northwestern Ontario. Accessible only by boat, float plane or four-wheel drive, this three-storey mansion was constructed entirely of red pine logs by a wiry little man only 5 foot 7 inches, with no help and no machinery.

In 1887, James McOuat arrived from Scotland to carve out a farm in the wilderness of northwestern Ontario. A decade of inconsistent crops followed. Then came the cry "gold!" The northwestern Ontario gold rush was on, and McOuat joined the stampede into the bush. But he fared no better at prospecting than he had at farming. Determined to show his worth to society and, it is said, to attract the love of a lady, McOuat decided to build a castle. He chose a sand beach on the northwest arm of White Otter Lake. Here, facing west, he could enjoy his favourite image, the spectacular northwestern sunset.

He carefully chose the finest logs, hand winched them through the bush, squared them on three sides and carefully dovetailed the ends to make an airtight fit. By using skids, holes and pegs, McOuat patiently and painstakingly inched the logs up the walls, until finally his tower stood four storeys high and measured more than 3 metres square at the base. The main house was three storeys high and 7 metres square, while a further two-storey addition at the back served as his living quarters.

Contrary to later legend, McOuat was neither a hermit nor an eccentric. Rather, he enjoyed company and travelled frequently to the busy railway town of Ignace, the nearest supply point, and often showed off photographs of his home.

The irony was that his castle was never his own, for he had squatted on Crown land. For three years he carried on a futile effort to acquire the title, but the Department of Lands and Forests repeatedly denied his requests. His dispute abruptly ended in 1918 when he become entangled in his fishing nets only metres away from his castle and drowned. He was sixty years old.

For seven decades his castle has stood empty, damaged by water but generally free from vandals. In 1955 the department added concrete foundations, new roofing and better bracing. It was later more fully restored by the Friends of White Otter.

You can reach White Otter Castle from a number of fishing camps on the lake, or by boat from Clearwater Lake on Highway 622. And as you watch the sun set over the quiet, northern lake, you will understand why Jimmy McOuat called it home.

⑯⑨ A STEEPLE WITHOUT A CHURCH

Emo's Unusual Norlund Chapel

MANY CHURCHES HAVE lost their steeples, sometimes to fire, sometimes to old age. But the Norlund Chapel in Emo, Ontario, is a steeple that has lost its church.

Emo is located in the far northwestern reaches of Ontario. Here, the surprising land is flat and the soil is black and almost treeless. Geologically, this part of Ontario is an extension of the prairie landscape. To reach this rich land, the first settlers travelled along the wide Rainy River by steamer. Along the way villages grew up around the many little steamer landings. In 1904, the railway arrived, eliminating the role of many of the steamer villages.

Midway between the railway towns of Fort Frances and Rainy River, Emo got a station and became a busy town. But its origins as a steamer stop remain visible, with a main street that developed along the riverfront. As it grew, Emo attracted businesses, schools and churches. In 1935, St. Patrick's Roman Catholic Church was built on the outskirts of the village. Its 12-metre-high wooden steeple was topped with a 2-metre-high wrought-iron cross fashioned by a local blacksmith.

In 1971, lightning struck and destroyed the church. Incredibly, the steeple survived, nearly unscathed. To celebrate the miracle, Elmer Norlund and Ed Sletmoen designed a chapel around the steeple. Its diminutive size, just 2 metres by 3, is barely enough to allow eight people to fill the building. Now nondenominational, it is open to worshippers of all faiths. Emo's Norlund Chapel-in-a-steeple is one of the world's smallest churches, and can be found on the north side of Highway 11/71 at the village limits.

Norlund Church in Emo – a steeple without a church.

North America's longest single-span wooden bridge extends over the Sioux Narrows.

170 OVER THE SIOUX NARROWS

North America's Longest Wooden Bridge

IOUX NARROWS IS an unlikely place to find North America's biggest anything. A tiny tourist town of fewer than four hundred, Sioux Narrows straddles Highway 71 about 80 kilometres southeast of Kenora, Ontario. It also straddles the Sioux Narrows, an intriguingly named channel of water along the eastern shore of the Lake of the Woods. Although the territory traditionally belonged to the Cree, the Lake of the Woods was subjected to frequent raids by the Sioux tribes, who lived to the south. Key defensive locations such as Sioux Narrows were often named to celebrate decisive victories over the intruders. According to legend, an entire flotilla of invading Sioux warriors was wiped out as they passed beneath the soaring cliffs by the narrows.

In the early years of the twentieth century, the gold mines and the lumber camps in the area attracted Europeans, who stayed and became settlers. With no railway nearby, the homesteaders relied on the lake steamers and a dirt trail to the south for transportation. In 1936, the Depression-era road-building program brought highway links to both the north and the south. Only the Sioux Narrows on the Lake of the Woods stood in the way of a through route.

Using creosoted Douglas fir from British Columbia, the highway engineers bridged the chasm, and in so doing gave Sioux Narrows its unusual claim to fame — the longest single-span wooden bridge in North America. The bridge's total length is more than 110 metres, with its main span, the Howe Truss, covering 64 metres. It was situated high enough above the water to allow early steamships to pass beneath.

By 2003, the bridge had deteriorated to the point where large vehicles could no longer use it and by 2004 it was closed to through traffic. On July 1, 2008, a new bridge opened to traffic that incorporated timbers from the original structure and retaining the truss style.

INDEX

Answer to the Bean Cryptogram

Starting with the letter "I," read in a zig-zag counter-clockwise direction and the following dedication appears:

"In memoriam Henrietta, 1st wife of S. Bean. M.D. who died 27th Sep 1865 aged 23 years 2 months and 17 days & Susanna his second wife who died 27th April 1867 aged 26 years 3 months and 15 days.

"2 better wives 1 man never had. They were gifts from God and are now in Heaven. May God help me S.B. to meet them there."